MCNROE COLLEGE LIBRARY

3 7340 01026536 8

D0733315

Bilingual Education in Elementary and Secondary School Communities

Toward Understanding and Caring

Christian J. Faltis
Sarah J. Hudelson
Arizona State University

Allyn and Bacon
Boston • London • Toronto • Sydney • Tokyo • Singapore

LC
3731
.F345
1998

Senior Editor: Virginia Lanigan
Editorial Assistant: Kris Lamarre
Marketing Manager: Kathy Hunter
Editorial Production Service: Chestnut Hill Enterprises, Inc.
Manufacturing Buyer: Suzanne Lareau
Cover Administrator: Suzanne Harbison

Copyright © 1998 by Allyn & Bacon
A Viacom Company
160 Gould St.
Needham Heights, MA 02194

Internet: www.abacon.com
America Online: keyword: College Online

All rights reserved. No part of the material protected by this copyright notice may
be reproduced or utilized in any form or by any means, electronic or mechanical,
including photocopying, recording, or by any information storage and retrieval
system, without written permission from the copyright holder.

Library of Congress Cataloging-in-Publication Data

Faltis, Christian,
    Bilingual education in elementary and secondary school communities
 : toward understanding and caring / by Christian J. Faltis and Sarah
J. Hudelson.
        p.   cm.
    Includes bibliographical references.
    ISBN 0-205-17120-6
    1. Education, Bilingual—United States.   2. Education, Elementary—
United States.   3. Education, Secondary—United States.
I. Hudelson, Sarah.   II. Title.
LC3731.F345   1998
370.117′5′0973—dc21   97-28098
                                                                   CIP

Printed in the United States of America

10 9 8 7 6 5 4 3 2 1   02 01 00 99 98 97

Contents

Preface

There is little doubt that the number of immigrant and minority students who are entering school with a language other than English is growing and will continue to do so in substantial proportions well into the second millennium. To succeed in school, many of these students will require teachers who have the ability and desire (1) to teach literacy and content in the students' native language; (2) to integrate language and content teaching in English as a second language; (3) to make schooling culturally relevant; and (4) to take a stance against antibilingual forces in society and education, especially those who believe that the best way to teach all non-English speaking children and adolescents is by submersing them in English-only classrooms.

We intend that this book be an introduction to bilingual education for education majors who are studying to become classroom teachers. We believe that classroom teachers of non-English speaking students should speak the same language as their students. We define bilingual education as teaching students in their native languages to develop socioacademic literacy and ways of talking about the various content areas of interest in school and society, while they *are integrated into* the same content areas in English as they progress through school. In our view, this is the best way to ensure that these students will grow into thoughtful, curious, knowledgeable, and responsible bilingual, biliterate adults. However, in schools with students who speak diverse languages, but with no one predominant language, or in schools where there are just a few students who speak the same non-English language, other approaches for serving these learners may be more feasible than teaching language and content through the native language.

In our experience, there is a great need for teachers who can teach in languages such as Spanish, Arabic, Russian, Chinese, and American Indian languages because children and adolescents who speak these languages tend to live in particular communities and either attend neighborhood schools or are bussed to schools with students who are speakers of the same native language. In Arizona, for example, bilingual programs are available in Navajo, Spanish, and Yaqui because there are large numbers of students who speak these languages at home. Likewise, there are numerous Spanish–English bilingual schools in El Paso and Houston, Texas, as well as in New York and Chicago, where Spanish is the first language of thousands of school-aged children. In the Los Angeles area, there are bilingual programs offered in Cantonese, Hmong, Korean, Mandarin, Spanish, and Vietnamese. When refugees from Haiti began relocating to Cambridge, Massachusetts, the school district organized and implemented a Haitian Creole bilingual program.

We believe strongly that schools in which there are large numbers of students who are speakers of the same non-English language should provide teachers who know—and can advocate for—students. It is important for teachers to be able to interact with students about academic and social matters in the language of their community. This enables students to become literate and knowledgeable in a language they understand and can use to exchange ideas. Moreover, when students become literate and knowledgeable in their native language, the opportunities for them to succeed socially and academically in English-language classroom settings increase. Literacy and the ability to solve problems generalizes across languages. This book is about preparing teachers to teach and learn in school communities that work toward understanding and caring for children and adolescents who are becoming bilingual.

There are four features in this book that you will not find in other books about bilingual education. First, the book is written for education students who are interested in becoming bilingual teachers. You are the audience that we have in mind, not other academics or researchers. We have tried hard to write a book that is reader friendly to education students, based on our combined experience as teacher-educators in the field of bilingual education over the past twenty years.

The second feature that distinguishes this book from others is that we lay out our philosophical and theoretical stance about language and learning and show you how it operates in actual classroom settings. As you will see in Chapters 4, 5, and 6, we present a set of principles that, for us, form the foundation of how children and adolescents acquire literacy, and find ways of integrating literacy and knowledge.

The third feature is that we illustrate what actually happens in certain bilingual classrooms and schools through detailed vignettes of social interaction involving children, adolescents, and their teachers. Vignettes are short scenes that describe events and people in them so that the reader can visualize what happens during the incidents. We relate the vignettes to our principles for learning and language learning.

Finally, the fourth feature presents information and vignettes about secondary students and schools. As we point out, virtually all that has been written about bilingual education focuses on elementary-level bilingual education. In recent years, the number of students entering middle and high schools in need of bilingual education has increased dramatically; as a result, the need for well-prepared teachers is great. In short, this book makes the case that bilingual education based on a set of principles about language learning can meet the needs of many children and adolescent students who come to school speaking a language other than English.

To the Teacher

This book is organized to give your students a brief introduction to early and modern-day forms of bilingual education before introducing them to the theoretical principles we believe are at work in many bilingual classes and schools. We realize that many, perhaps even a majority, of bilingual education programs and classrooms, regardless of school level or language, are culturally insensitive and often provide minimal support for students' native languages. Instead of reinforcing the status quo in bilingual education, we are convinced that teacher-education students can be better prepared for bilingual education when they learn about what actually happens in classrooms that support native languages (including literacy) as well as the students' cultures. After presenting a discussion of bilingual education in elementary and secondary schools, we introduce readers to our theoretical position on language and learning. Here, you might want to discuss your own theoretical concerns about language, literacy, and learning to help students begin to construct their own understandings of the role theory plays in teaching and learning. We suggest spending ample time discussing Chapter 4 because the theoretical principles presented are brought up again and again in the ensuing chapters in vignettes of classroom collaboration and social interaction.

In the next two chapters, we use detailed vignettes of bilingual classrooms at the elementary (Chapter 5) and secondary (Chapter 6) levels to invite readers to envision what goes on in various bilingual contexts. In addition we want students to see the theoretical principles we put forth in Chapter 4 in action. Because we have provided multiple examples of bilingual classrooms, you should feel free to select from the vignettes according to your own needs and course time constraints. All but two of the vignettes we use come from Spanish–English bilingual classrooms. There are two reasons for this: (1) both of us are highly proficient Spanish speakers, and (2) our work in bilingual education has mainly involved Spanish-speaking classroom settings and communities. If you are working with other language groups, you may want to include your own vignettes or have students work together to produce their own. In either case, we recommend that students discuss and write about which principles are at work.

The final chapter presents a discussion of caring for bilingual education within a framework of compassion and caring in general. The goal of this last chapter is to consider why teachers and others should care about what happens in bilingual classrooms and schools. Our hope is that students will use this chapter as a springboard for a critical discussion of bilingual education as they have learned about it by taking your class and by reading this book.

To the Student

In choosing teaching as a profession, you are entering one of the most challenging and crucial fields of your generation. Many of the children and adolescents who will learn in your classrooms will be children of families who speak languages other than English. By preparing to become bilingual teachers, you will be responsible for learning not only how to teach in a language other than English, but also to teach in ways that enable children and adolescents to become literate, curious, knowledgeable, and caring individuals. An important goal of this book is to help you create classroom environments in which students collaborate, wonder, and talk about things that matter to them and to society. In this book, we present bilingual education in ways that represent the theoretical stance we hold about language and learning. You will read and discuss theory, but not in isolation. Once you have made yourselves familiar with the theoretical principles we lay out, you will have a series of interactive scenes that relate these principles to what actually happens in the bilingual classrooms we have studied and observed. We hope that by reading and discussing these vignettes you will be prepared to enter bilingual classrooms on your own and to work toward teaching and learning in ways that reflect the principles illustrated in the vignettes. Finally, we want you to care about bilingual education and the children and adolescents it invites into bilingualism, biliteracy, responsibility, and ways of communicating about knowledge. We end, therefore, with a short chapter on compassion and caring and ask you to consider bilingual education from these perspectives. Our hope is that, by the time you complete this final chapter, you will have a clearer and more compassionate understanding of why you want to become a bilingual teacher, an understanding that is based on both theory and on what happens in some bilingual classrooms.

Acknowledgments

The authors wish to acknowledge the following reviewers whose instructive comments helped us in finalizing this book: Bernadine Bolden, University of North Florida and Francisco Rios, California State University, San Marcos.

1

Why Bilingual Education?

We begin with this apparently simple question for a couple of reasons. First, we assume that you are new to the field of bilingual education, as this book is written for readers who are interested in becoming bilingual teachers. A major part of becoming a bilingual teacher involves understanding and caring for bilingual education based on principles about teaching and learning. Teachers need to be able to make decisions about what goes on in the classroom and in school, decisions about what it means to "be schooled," including decisions about ways to interrupt social injustice. In this book, we share our philosophical stance about bilingual education, and invite you to share the principles that we consider essential for developing the kinds of bilingual classrooms and schools we support. We illustrate these principles in Chapters 5 and 6. We are well aware, as you should be, too, that there are many bilingual classrooms, programs, and schools that hurt rather than help children and adolescents who are becoming bilingual. The literature on bilingual education is rife with examples of teachers and schools that disparage non-English languages and denigrate the children and adolescents who use them (for examples of what happens in these kinds of programs and classrooms, see Minicucci & Olsen, 1991; Moraes, 1996; Skutnabb–Kangas, 1988; Wong Fillmore, 1991).

In this book, we are interested in sharing with you what can happen in classrooms and schools that are working well for bilingual children and adolescents. By "working well" we mean that students are invited into the discourse of schooling by teachers who understand that: (1) Learning comes from being involved in socially shared interaction that has direct relevance to students' everyday lives and challenges them to think about what they read, write, and say; (2) Learning happens best in a language that students understand and use to construct meaning about what matters in school and society; and (3) Becoming bilingual requires students to participate socially in English. We elaborate these central ideas in Chapter 4.

A first step to becoming a bilingual teacher like those we highlight in later chapters is to gain a basic understanding of how and why bilingual education came into being, its social history. Answers to "how" questions hinge critically on the sense we make of the "why" of bilingual education, because how bilingual education developed relates strongly to the social and political climates in which bilingual education was and continues to be formed. By examining the social and political climates of the times, we can begin to appreciate why bilingual education, "a seemingly simple label," is such "a complex phenomenon" (Cazden & Snow, 1990, p. 9).

In starting out with a brief social history of bilingual education, we hope to raise questions about what bilingual education can be and about the role of schools in constructing bilingual education that benefits students and their communities. One of the goals of this chapter, therefore, is for you to talk with peers and others about the events and social contexts that lead to the development of bilingual education in its multiple forms. Such dialogue will help you begin to construct your philosophical stance on bilingual education. With each ensuing chapter, we invite you to become more familiar with bilingual education program types, bilingual methodology, second language and literacy participation, and other key issues connected with bilingual education. By the end of this book, we intend for you not only to have developed a relatively strong philosophical stance toward bilingual education, but also the ability to recognize teaching and learning environments that support the ideals and principles we offer in this book. In other words, as a result of reading and discussing the contents of this book, you should be able to make some important decisions about various approaches to curriculum, about teaching and learning activities for students who are native speakers of languages other than English, and about social and educational issues worth fighting for, generally and specifically, within bilingual education.

Part of the answer to how and why bilingual education came about depends on the rationales that people have constructed about why schools and society need bilingual education. Therefore, to fully understand and appreciate the development of bilingual education, it is important to examine the various ways that people have struggled and worked to support the value of and need for bilingual education. And, we will try to do this with a critical perspective; that is, we will examine the rationales that have developed for bilingual education by connecting what is said about bilingual education to issues of power.

Early Forms of Bilingual Education

When the original thirteen colonies won their independence from England in 1776 and became the United States, a distinguishing feature of the new nation and the lands that it would eventually take over was multilingualism (Kloss, 1977). At that time, more than 150 languages belonging to some fifteen language families were spoken by American Indian groups. The settlers who moved throughout the new nation also brought with them their native languages, adding to the existing linguistic diversity. Tragically, however, the addition of new European languages came with a price: the slow, but eventual demise of American Indian languages. Only some twenty American Indian languages are actively used in the present (Crawford, 1995).

As the colonists and subsequent European immigrants moved westward, there was an effort to maintain and even promote the use of non-English languages (Heath, 1981). Dutch, French, German, Russian, Spanish, and Swedish were used along with English in the newly founded communities (Brisk, 1981). By the eighteenth century, many of these communities had established their own schools and taught bilingually or exclusively in languages other than English. For example, German was the language of most private and some public schools in the states of Pennsylvania, Maryland, Virginia, and the Carolinas well into the nineteenth century (Leibowitz, 1971). In 1847, the legislature of the state of Wisconsin passed a resolution to enable German, Norwegian, Dutch, and Swiss to be used for instruction within their respective communities. Similarly, the state of New Mexico passed a law in 1884 requiring each county to set up a school district for teaching literacy in either Spanish or English, based on the particular district's needs (Casanova & Arias, 1993).

As the nation moved into the industrial age, and a campaign for a common school system began to build momentum, educators began to compete with private schools by offering school programs for non-English speaking immigrant children in their primary languages (Heath, 1981). These early bilingual programs offered instruction in the students' native language, and later added English as a second language instruction.

In the late nineteenth century, the Bureau of Indian Affairs initiated a campaign to "civilize" Indians by sending children of diverse language and tribal groups to boarding schools, located in isolated sites throughout the nation. (This practice continued well into the late twentieth century.) Several American Indian groups resisted these efforts and attempted to set up their own bilingual schools as a way to stop the eradication of their languages and cultures (Spring, 1994). However, the Bureau stepped in to close the schools, and insisted that children be sent off to boarding schools to learn English and Western culture.

Early forms of (European-based) bilingual education lasted into the early twentieth century when the general population of the United States began to change significantly. From the mid-1800s through the 1920s, the number of immigrants from Eastern and Southern European countries, as well as from China, increased dramatically. Moreover, with the conquest of northern Mexico, the United States appropriated a vast new territory, along with the Mexican peoples and myriad American Indian groups who lived there. In 1876, The United States also purchased Alaska from Russia. In addition, as part of the spoils of the Spanish–American War of 1898, the United States annexed the Philippines, Puerto Rico, and several Pacific Islands. (The Philippines gained independence from the United States in 1946.) Increases in the number of non-Western European immigrants, coupled with the "foreign element" associated with Alaskan natives, new Mexican peoples, and others who spoke languages different from the "original few," led to calls by political and intellectual leaders for restrictions on immigration. Lawmakers also began submitting legislation to ensure that new Americans spoke English to be eligible for U. S. citizenship. An outcome of this movement was a new definition of "being American": giving up old ways and learning to speak and be literate in English.

In 1882, the federal government instituted the Chinese Exclusion Act to limit the number of immigrant workers from China. Fourteen years later, congress passed the Nationality Act of 1906, which required (male) immigrants to pass an English proficiency test in order to become naturalized citizens (Leibowitz, 1971). The emphasis on becoming an American through assimilation had a devastating effect on bilingual education. Using non-English languages for any kind of classroom instruction was significantly curtailed nationwide. However, the final blow came when the United States entered World War I in 1917. While there was already widespread sentiment among established immigrants of Western European origin that using a language other than English was "un-American," once the United States entered the war against Germany, all languages other than English were formally banned from use in public schools (Crawford, 1992). This fear of languages other than English resurfaced strongly again as a result of World War II. A general mistrust of non-English languages remained relatively intact until the 1960s when Chicano and American Indian groups, who had been working hard at local levels, began demanding radically new types of schools for their children at the national level (San Miguel, 1978). And, the first Cuban exiles from the newly formed Communist Cuba arrived in Florida.

The Reemergence of Bilingual Education

The Role of Chicano and Latino Activists

Educators and political activists who saw a moral, ethical, and educational need for teaching children in a language they understood began flexing their political muscle in the 1960s. Chicano activists, in particular, called for Chicano-oriented curricula, and schoolbooks that more realistically reflected the contributions of Mexicans and Mexican Americans to U.S. society (Valdez & Steiner, 1972). Many activists also believed strongly in the value of teaching children in the language they could understand and relate to best (Donato, 1997).

Prior to the 1970s, school districts serving large numbers of non-English speaking children gave little thought to implementing bilingual education as a way to prepare these children for English-only schooling. Virtually all children who were speakers of a language other than English were immersed in English-only classrooms, left on their own devices to "sink or swim." Under these conditions, the majority of these children sank, with many leaving before finishing high school. Not only did these children not develop literacy abilities in their native language, but they also suffered academically in classes taught entirely in English. La Raza Unida and other post-World War II Latino groups (GI Forum, League of United Latin American Citizens) responded to these abhorrent conditions in several ways. Some began lobbying for specific kinds of instructional programs for Spanish-speaking children, including bilingual education and the teaching of Chicano Mexican culture in schools (Donato, 1997). Others worked more locally and were involved in school "blowouts," in which high school students staged sit-ins to demand Chicano studies programs on their campuses (Valdez & Steiner, 1972). Chicano educators also called for increasing the number of ethnic minority teachers and teacher education faculty at universities. In California, Mexican American educators, such as Ernesto Galarza, set up curriculum laboratories to develop culturally appropriate school materials and to provide workshops for schools with large bilingual populations (R. A. DeVillar, personal communication).

The 1960s was also a time when Chicano and other Latino writers began publishing their works in Spanish and English. Many of these bilingual writers were actively opposed to the ways that schools treated Latino and language minority children in general (Valdez & Steiner, 1972). Most writers supported efforts to teach Spanish-speaking children in Spanish in order to maintain their mother tongue as they became bilingual.

The Cuban Refugees Arrive in Florida

As efforts to reintroduce bilingual schooling mounted in California and the Southwestern states of Texas, Arizona, and New Mexico, an unrelated event occurred in southern Florida that may have cleared the pathway for the acceptability of bilingual education by the government and its constituents. The children of upper-class, educated Cubans who fled the island of Cuba (recently taken over by Fidel Castro and his group of freedom fighters), settled in southern Florida and immediately placed their children in the Dade County public school system. These new immigrants were welcomed as anticommunist refugees, but what were schools to do with several hundred Spanish-speaking children who needed to be integrated into the school system?

The answer decided by the schools, under pressure from parents, was to provide instruction in Spanish throughout the primary grades while the children learned enough English to participate more fully in all-English classes. However, since neither the school nor the parents wished for their children to be separated from English-speaking children, the schools offered a two-way model of bilingual education. The model operated as follows: Beginning at grade one, each group of children spent half of the day learning in the native language and half of the day in the second language setting. In the primary grades, English- and Spanish-speaking children were mixed for art, music, and physical education classes. In the intermediate grades, the children spent more time in ethnically mixed classes, in which instruction was conducted using the two languages, for example, half the grading period spent studying a particular subject using Spanish and half the grading period studying using English. The aims of the program were that all children would become bilingual and biliterate, that all children would achieve academically on a par with their monolingual peers, and that children would be able to operate biculturally as well as bilingually. These aims were borne out in the program evaluations conducted (Mackey & Beebe, 1977).

The most well-known school to have this kind of bilingual program was the Coral Way School, which received national recognition from researchers who pointed to the success of both the Cuban and the American children who attended the school (Mackey & Beebe, 1977). News of the Coral Way bilingual program quickly spread to other elementary and secondary schools in the county, and by the late 1960s several cities in the Southwest began to import a version of the Coral Way program (Malakoff & Hakuta, 1990). However, the new version left out the two-way aspect of bilingual education, and instead focused on using the non-English language as a transition to English.

The War on Poverty

Interestingly, the federal government seized on the success of the Coral Way program to push for bilingual education as part of President Lyndon B. Johnson's War on Poverty. This campaign focused on the role of schooling in wiping out poverty, based on the idea that poor people were grossly undereducated. Providing educational services and programs to the children of the poor would enable these children to lift themselves out of poverty and eventually become part of the mainstream middle class. Many of the poor school children who were failing in school were speakers of languages other than English, primarily Spanish speakers of Mexican origin. In 1966, citing the success of bilingual programs with the children of wealthy, educated Cuban refugees, Texas Senator Ralph Yarborough spearheaded a move to provide federal monies for school districts to set up bilingual education programs for children of low-income Mexican immigrants. In this manner, bilingual education, at the federal level, became a new weapon in the War on Poverty. Unfortunately, the kind of bilingual education advocated by Chicano and Native American activists—prolonged native language instruction and a culturally relevant curriculum—was not considered in the government's version of bilingual education.

The argument put forth by mainstream, government-promoted social scientists supporting bilingual education for poor non-English-speaking children was a straightforward one: Teaching children in a language they understand enables schools to meet the educational needs of poor children who are disadvantaged because of their inability to speak English. The basis of this argument is what is often referred to as the *Language Mismatch Hypothesis*. This hypothesis predicts that children who enter school speaking a non-English language are more likely to fail than children who speak English (Faltis, 1997), placing them at an educational disadvantage compared with their English-speaking counterparts. The hypothesis also predicts that the greater the match is between the home language and the school language, the greater the chances are that the children will succeed in school. Accordingly, this hypothesis placed the blame for school failure on the child's lack of school-language proficiency, which in turn strongly related to being poor.

There were a number of other events occurring throughout the latter half of the 1960s that provided ammunition for the federal government to address poverty among non-English speaking children. One of the most important was that the federal government earmarked substantial amounts of federal aid money for social and educational programs. One such program was the Elementary and Secondary Education Act (ESEA) of 1965. This legislation set aside millions of dollars for federal intervention in schooling efforts targeted for poor, low-achieving students.

The ESEA is still in existence today, providing funds for numerous special instructional programs, each designed to address a specific population and/or innovative program approach. For example, Title I provides monies to fund programs that aim to increase the reading and mathematics achievement of underachieving students. The purpose of Title III is to promote innovative approaches to education. Title IV sets aside monies for special programs for American Indian students. Title IX addresses the issue of equal educational opportunity through heritage studies programs (Andersson & Boyer, 1978).

Mainstream educators also got involved in supporting bilingual education for Mexican and Mexican American children. In 1966, the National Education Association issued a report called *The Invisible Minority*. The report specifically recommended native language and bilingual instruction for preschool and the primary grades, and the promotion of Mexican culture in school.

A Growing Non-English Speaking Population

At the same time that certain ethnic groups were calling for recognition in schools and separate programs to promote their own histories, perspectives, needs, and values, the number of Spanish-speaking children in schools was increasing greatly. The 1960 census data indicated that the Spanish-surnamed population had increased by more than 50 percent, from 2.3 million in 1950 to nearly 3.5 million in 1960. The data also indicated that Spanish-speaking children as a group were faring poorly in school compared to other ethnic minority groups and compared to white students in general. *The Invisible Minority* (NEA, 1966) reported that Spanish-speakers comprised more than one-sixth of the school-aged population in the Southwest.

Bilingualism as an Asset

On another front, educators concerned with providing bilingual instruction to non-English proficient students were encouraged by research coming out of Canada by Peal and Lambert (1962), who found a positive relationship between being highly bilingual and higher levels of intelligence. Prior to the 1960s, bilingualism was reported in the research literature as being either detrimental to or unrelated to intelligence. Early research in the 1920s showed that bilingual immigrants scored significantly lower on intelligence tests (given in English) than English-speaking monolingual citizens. This research concluded that being bilingual caused mental confusion, and probably lower intelligence (Saer, 1923). Several decades later, researchers (Pinter & Arsenian, 1937; Jones, 1959) found that bilinguals scored no better or worse than monolinguals, and concluded that bilingualism did not necessarily cause any sort of intellectual disadvantage. Nor, however, did these studies conclude that bilingualism provided any measurable advantage in intellectual abilities. In 1962, Peal and Lambert investigated the question again, using a more appropriate research design and this time found that bilingualism resulted in a source of intellectual advantage. In their study, highly bilingual ten-year-olds performed significantly better than matched monolingual English-speaking peers on fifteen of eighteen activities associated with intelligence. They concluded that bilingualism facilitated greater mental flexibility, more abstract thinking ability, superior concept formation, and the transfer of knowledge between the bilingual's two languages.

In summary, several factors, individually and in combination, promoted the reemergence of bilingual education as a viable program as the 1960s came to a close:

1. long-standing and increased pressure from Chicano and other minority political groups to improve education for their children;
2. the availability of federal monies coupled with a desire to combat poverty through education;
3. the success of bilingual education for Cuban refugees in Florida;
4. the growing numbers of Spanish-speaking children of immigrants; and
5. the finding that high bilingualism brings with it intellectual advantages.

Title VII: The Bilingual Education Act of 1968

In January 1967, Texas Senator Ralph Yarborough introduced a four-page bill for consideration as an amendment to the Elementary and Secondary Education Act of 1965. Its purpose was to provide federal assistance to local education agencies for setting up bilingual programs for poor, native Spanish-speaking children for whom English was a foreign language. The bill began as follows:

In the Southwest part of the United States—bordered by my state of Texas on the east, California on the west, and reaching to Colorado in the north— there exists, as in the rest of the country, a folklore that we have achieved equality of economic opportunity, that everyone has an equal chance to succeed. The reality lurking under this belief is that for a group of 3,465,000 persons, 12 percent of the Southwestern states, equality of economic opportunity awaits within the future. It is a myth, and not a reality, today for the Mexican-Americans of the Southwest. . . . I believe that the time has come when we can no longer ignore the fact that 12 percent of the people of the Southwestern United States do not have equal access with the rest of the population to economic advancement. The time has come when we must do

something about the poor schooling, low health standards, job discrimina-
tion, and the many other artificial barriers that stand in the way of the
advancement of the Mexican American people. . . . The most prominent area
for progress is in the field of education. Here Mexican Americans have been
the victims of the cruelest form of discrimination. Little children, many of
whom enter school knowing no English and speaking only Spanish, are de-
nied the use of their language. Spanish is forbidden to them, and they are re-
quired to struggle along as best they can in English, a language understood
dimly by most and not at all by many. . . . The time for action is upon us
(Crawford, 1992, pp. 323–324).

The bill went on to argue for native language instruction along with English as a second language teaching. As you might imagine, the timing for the
introduction of the bill was grand. Not only was bilingual education gaining
recognition as a potential solution to poverty, miseducation, and undereduc-
cation, Chicano and other minority activists and political leaders were pushing for its arrival as well. By the summer of 1967, however, the bill was near
death. A number of senators insisted that the Senator expand assistance for
bilingual education to *all* low-income, non-English-speaking groups in the
United States, not just Spanish speakers in the Southwest. In order to save the
bill and move it through the Senate, Senator Yarborough compromised, adjusting the language of the bill to be maximally inclusive. Fellow Texan President Johnson signed the bill, making it a law on January 2, 1968. The bill was
officially registered as Title VII of the ESEA of 1965, but it has since become
more commonly known as the Bilingual Education Act (BEA) of 1968.

On that otherwise ordinary day, bilingual education became a federal
educational policy for the first time in the history of the United States. Here
is what Title VII did: It authorized federal monies to be set aside for funding
to: (1) develop special instructional materials for use in bilingual education
programs, (2) provide in-service training for teachers, teacher assistants, and
counselors working in bilingual programs, and (3) establish, maintain, and
implement special programs for children who are adding English as a second language (Andersson & Boyer, 1978, p. 224). You should know that the
BEA did not specifically mandate or define bilingual education. It was assumed that bilingual education meant some form of native language instruction along with English as a second language. Accordingly, during the
first years of implementation, grants were awarded only to schools that:
(1) developed and operated dual language programs for low-income, non-
English-speaking students, (2) made efforts to attract and improve the skills
of bilingual teachers, and (3) established communication between the school
and community being served.

Bilingual Education as a Civil Rights Issue

Although bilingual education became a federal reality, many school districts with large numbers of non-English proficient students dragged their feet in providing any kind of special programs for these students. Doing nothing meant that these students neither participated in nor benefited from instruction provided only in English. Fortunately, teachers and community activists complained to the Office of Civil Rights (OCR). In 1970, investigators from the OCR checked out the complaints and found what they considered to be discrimination on the basis of national origin (35 *Federal Register*, 11595, 1970). The Office sent a formal memorandum to school districts having large numbers of students for whom English was a second language (Malakoff & Hakuta, 1990). The memorandum pointed out the conditions of Title VI of the Civil Rights Act of 1964 in relation to these students, noting that a team of investigators had encountered "a number of practices which have the effect of denying equality of educational opportunity to Spanish-surnamed pupils" (35 *Federal Register*, 11595, 1970). The memorandum also specified that the school district must take affirmative steps to rectify English language deficiencies in cases where "the inability to speak and understand English excludes national origin minority children from effective participation in the educational program" (35 *Federal Register*, 11595, 1970). The memorandum did not stipulate what the "affirmative steps" should be nor did it mention teaching students literacy and subject matter content in their native language (Malakoff & Hakuta, 1990).

This memorandum was important for several reasons. First, it set the stage for a series of major battles over the legal obligation of school districts receiving federal funds to comply with Title VI guidelines. Second, it reinforced the purpose of bilingual education, reaffirming the transitional/remediational characteristic given to it by the BEA of 1968. That is, non-English-speaking students are both language deficient and educationally disadvantaged, and, thus, are bound to fail in school unless and until they learn English (The Mismatch Prediction). From this perspective, the children are the problem, and the schools have the potential solution: Teach them English. Third, by not specifying how school districts might best meet the need of non-English-speaking children (to learn English), the memorandum left open the possibility that merely providing students with some form of English as a second language instruction would suffice for compliance.

On the one hand, then, the OCR memorandum was momentous because it alerted schools that discrimination against children who speak a language other than English would not be tolerated. On the other, *the action* recommended in the memorandum left something to be desired. In effect, the memorandum defined the problem in terms of students who lack English speaking and understanding abilities rather than in terms of schools that lack native language instruction programs and teachers equipped to accommodate bilingual learners. This perspective of where the problem resides not only placed much of the blame on the students, it also made not speaking English the focus of the problem. Hence, the recommended action did little to change the nature of teaching and learning for children who did not speak English.

At this point, you may be asking yourself questions like these: "Wait a minute, don't these children need to learn English?" "Isn't this a legitimate problem?" "What's wrong with helping these students learn English? Won't that help them do better in school and to function in the United States?" These are reasonable questions to consider at this point.

Learning English is of paramount importance, no doubt about that. But you could also ask several other questions, such as: "Why is not speaking English a problem?" "Why did the OCR have to ask schools to make the necessary changes to accommodate non-English-speaking children?" "Why didn't the OCR specify native language instruction as a way to ensure that students participated in and benefited from school?" "What about reading and writing?" These questions look at the problem of educating non-English children from a different angle. Bluntly speaking, these questions stem from a perspective in which the children aren't the problem; one in which speaking a language other than English is not the problem; and in which being unable to read or write in English is not necessarily the problem. From this perspective, the problem is located primarily in the school and in the way that teachers are prepared to work in school communities. Accordingly, the problem then and now is that many teachers do little or nothing to enable children to participate in school so that they both understand what is going on, and are invited to participate in and benefit from learning activities regardless of their English abilities.

Lau v. Nichols: *The Legal Battle Begins*

Every once in a while, when a group of minority parents sees that a school is doing little or nothing in the way of enabling their children to progress normally, while majority children are, that group fights for their children's right to equal education as guaranteed by the equal rights amendment, Title VI. In 1970, a group of Chinese parents in San Francisco filed a class action suit against the school district on behalf of their children. The parents, led by the Lau family, claimed that their Chinese-speaking children were being denied equal educational opportunity. Here is the basis of their suit against the school district and its administrator, Nichols: The school district had identified 2,856 non-English-speaking children but provided ESL instruction to less than half of them. The school district did not dispute the number of students in need of special instruction nor that it had attempted to serve the needs of this population. At the heart of the claim was that Chinese children who didn't speak English were not receiving an equal education in an English-only main-stream classroom because they couldn't participate in or benefit from in-struction given in a language they didn't speak or understand. Therefore, the parents argued that the school district had a legal obligation to provide spe-cial instructional programs so that their children received opportunities to learn that were equal to those afforded to English-speaking children.

Guess who won the suit at the federal district court level? Superinten-dent Nichols and the school district. The court ruled in favor of the school district, finding that because the non-English-speaking children were receiv-ing the same curriculum in the same classrooms as English-speaking children they were being treated no differently and thus were not being discrimi-nated against by the school district. Moreover, the court concluded that the school district was under no obligation to provide special services to non-English-speaking students. Instead, the court encouraged the school district to address the students' needs as an educational rather than a legal obliga-tion (August & García, 1988). The parents appealed the ruling to the Ninth Circuit District Court of Appeals, which on January 8, 1973, upheld the lower court's decision.

But the parents did not give up the fight. They appealed their case all the way to the Supreme Court. In the meantime, another group of parents, this time, Mexican American parents, sued the Portales, New Mexico Municipal School District. The case was almost identical to the *Lau v. Nichols* case except that it involved non-English-speaking children of Mexican origin. In *Serna v. Portales Municipal Schools,* however, the court found in 1972 that the non-English-speaking children were being treated *differently* when they received the same curriculum and instruction as their native English-speaking peers and thus were being discriminated against (Malakoff & Hakuta, 1990). In re-sponse to the ruling, the school district submitted a nonbilingual plan as a remedy to the problem, but the court rejected it, based on expert testimony that endorsed a native language approach to bilingual education. The school district appealed the ruling to the Tenth Circuit Court of Appeals, which in 1974 ruled in favor of the parents. The Court of Appeals found that the stu-dents' Title VI rights had been violated and, consequently, they had a right to bilingual education.

In that same year, the Supreme Court presented its decision on the *Lau v. Nichols* case. The Supreme Court justices relied heavily on Title VI of the Civil Rights Act of 1965, the Office of Civil Rights memorandum issued in 1970, and the finding of the *Serna v. Portales Municipal Schools* case. In the ruling, the justices pointed out that the guidelines presented in the 1970 OCR memo-randum "clearly indicate that affirmative efforts to give special training for non-English speaking pupils are required by Title VI as a condition of federal aid to public schools" (414 U.S. 569). In other words, schools that receive federal monies are obligated to abide by the rules that govern the distribution of those monies, namely, Title VI. The justices also proclaimed what the parents in *Lau* had argued from the beginning: that students with limited knowledge of English who are submersed in mainstream classes to compete with native English-speaking students are "effectively foreclosed from any meaningful education" (414 U.S. 566).

The *Lau* decision meant that school districts and schools attended by numbers of non-English-speaking learners could not ignore the special educational needs of these students. Some educational treatment/services, geared specifically to the situations of these students, needed to be provided. *Lau v. Nichols* did not mandate any particular remedy, such as bilingual or English as a second language instruction, it merely said that schools had to do something. The Court recommended that school districts take into account the number and language backgrounds of the students involved when making decisions concerning an appropriate remedy. In this manner, a remedy could differ from school to school.

Following the *Lau* decision, Congress legislated the Supreme Court ruling in the Equal Educational Opportunity Act (EEOA) of 1974. The EEOA extended the *Lau* decision to all public schools, not just those receiving federal funds. Accordingly, as of 1974, a school district with non-English-speaking students in any of its schools is required to "take appropriate action to overcome language barriers that impede equal participation by its students in its instructional programs" (20 U.S.C. Sec. 1703[f]). This particular section of the Act was significant because it addressed the issue of "discriminatory effect" versus "discriminatory intent" (Malakoff & Hakuta, 1990). The idea here was that schools could be in violation of Title VI of the Civil Rights Act if non-English-speaking students were not receiving some sort of special instructional remedy even if no substantial intent to discriminate was found. Schools could no longer claim ignorance or other excuses for not providing special services to non-English-speaking learners. Not providing special services was tantamount to discrimination on the basis of national origin, whether schools had intended to discriminate or not.

Then and Now

It is important to understand that, just because much of the legal and social support for bilingual education took place in the early 1970s, this doesn't mean that the underlying rationales and need for bilingual education are any different today. While it is true that the legal and social *contexts* that supported bilingual education have changed over time, several facts have not, namely: (1) Children learn best in a language they understand and use for communication; (2) Schools have a social, moral, and legal responsibility to educate all children regardless of their English proficiency; and (3) Schools that do nothing to assist the learning of non-English-speaking students are discriminating against these students, and thus are in violation of Title VI of the Civil Rights Act of 1965. Perhaps the only fact that has changed dramatically since the 1970s is that the number of school-aged non-English-speaking children (ages 5–17) has more than doubled, and will reach 3.5 million by the year 2000 (Palla, Natriello, & McDill, 1989). In 1990, the Hispanic population reached 20.8 million, an increase of more than 12 million people since the 1970s (U. S. Bureau of Census, 1991).

Despite the legal protection of *Lau v. Nichols* and the EEOA of 1974, as well as the increase of non-English-speaking children in our schools, there are many in society who remain opposed to bilingual education. The U. S. government under the Reagan and Bush administrations used disinformation tactics to disparage the need for and effectiveness of bilingual education (Cummins, 1991). For example, President Reagan proclaimed in 1981:

> *It is absolutely wrong and against American concepts to have a bilingual education program that is now openly, admittedly dedicated to preserving students' native language and never getting them adequate in English so they can go out into the job market and participate* (Democrat-Chronicle, *Rochester, March 3, 1981, p. 2A, cited in Cummins, 1991, p. 187).*

Reagan's "argument" is that bilingual education is basically unAmerican. His administration also set out to "prove" that bilingual education didn't work by setting up a study by Keith Baker and Adriana de Kanter (1981) to review the research evidence on bilingual education. Not surprisingly, these two government-sponsored academics found that transitional bilingual education programs were no more effective than English-only programs in promoting academic development among students who were becoming bilingual. We present a more thorough analysis of the effectiveness research in the next chapter. The point here is that there are plenty of people out there (your neighbors, friends, family members, and political servants) who have been disinformed about the need for and effectiveness of bilingual education. One group that has been especially unfriendly to bilingual education is *U. S. English,* a politically conservative group of some 240,000 members dedicated to making English the official language of the United States, and to disallowing the use of non-English languages for instruction, as is the case in most bilingual education programs (see Crawford, 1992). Another is *English First* of Springfield, Virginia, with its 100,000 members across the United States. This group has contributed ideological and financial support for national and local legislation to make English official, and to restrict the use of languages other than English in government and public schools (McGroarty, 1992).

These disinformation and antibilingual movements have had substantial impact on the quality and extent of bilingual education students receive in schools. For example, a study conducted by the National Education Association (Rodríguez, 1990) found that in the 1989 academic year, bilingual education programs served only an estimated 5.6 percent of the students who would have benefited from instruction in their native language. The rest were presumably served by special English instruction (English as a second language) or provided no help at all; that is, submersed in English-only settings. Assuming that Rodriguez's figures are accurate, the number of students served by bilingual education programs has decreased considerably from 1980, when Stein (1986) estimated that bilingual programs served approximately 10 percent of all becoming bilingual students. The National Association for Bilingual Education newsletter reported in 1994 that one-fourth of all students eligible for bilingual education in the state of California were neither receiving any sort of native language nor English as a second language support (*NABE News,* December, 1994). These findings are disturbing to us. Not only are students who need bilingual education services not receiving them, but the services are becoming scarcer rather than greater as we move into the twenty-first century.

Why do you think so many schools in areas where there are sizable numbers of non-English-speaking students have been reluctant to implement bilingual education programs, have chosen to provide ESL instruction, or have done nothing at all for these students? The answer to this question is complex. Part of the answer is historical; part of it has to do with the philosophy of cultural assimilation versus cultural pluralism and the goals of schooling; and part has to do with beliefs that people hold about the fastest and best way to make non-English-speaking students learn English. In this section, we would like to deal primarily with the part that has to do with beliefs about how to learn English as a second language. (See DeVillar, 1994 for an excellent discussion on the philosophy part, and Crawford, 1992 on the historical part.) These beliefs are in no small way connected to the beliefs that people hold about the goals of schooling.

Therefore, we ask you to continue learning about the social, moral, and legal rationales for bilingual education beyond the ones we briefly provide in this chapter so that you not only keep building your philosophical stance in a proactive manner, but possess the knowledge to present sound counterarguments to the disinformed as well.

Let's move on, then, to another perspective on the need for bilingual education and why it enables students who are becoming bilingual to participate more fully in school. This final perspective grew out the need to establish an educational rationale for teaching students in their native language before introducing them to schooling in English

Popular Beliefs about Learning English Quickly

Jim Cummins, a respected educator and educational psychologist interested in bilingual education, has pointed out that people who view the assimilation of immigrant students as an essential function of schools also tend to believe in what he characterized as the "more equals more" notion of what students need in order to learn English and succeed in school (Cummins, 1981). According to this belief, the more experience and practice with a language learners have, the more they will learn it. Now, if we plug English into this

FIGURE 1.1   Separate Underlying Proficiency

Artwork by Jon Faltis. Adapted from drawing in C. Faltis (1997). *Joinfostering: Adapting Teaching for the Multilingual Classroom.* Upper Saddle River, NJ: Merrill/Prentice-Hall, p.148.

statement, it becomes: The more time learners spend in English, the more English they will learn. This belief derives from a conceptualization of bilingualism that represents the two languages as separate, independent compartments. Cummins (1981) calls this way of viewing bilingualism the *Separate Underlying Proficiency (SUP) Model* because people who hold this view assume that the two languages operate independently with no transfer between them. In other words, what happens in one language has no bearing on what happens in the other. Accordingly, providing students with schoolwork and literacy in their native language would be a waste of time and effort, because the way to develop English is to provide as much exposure to English as possible, preferably by submersing learners in all-English settings.

Although the SUP model may appeal to common sense, the two languages of a bilingual are highly interdependent in cognitive functions (Cummins, 1981; Krashen, 1996), with the possible exception of certain kinds of separate memory storage of vocabulary in adult bilinguals (Kolers, 1963; Paivio, 1986). The attention paid communicatively (in both oral and written language) to one language significantly affects what happens in the other. This is especially important in the context of classroom learning. Consider this well-established finding with respect to the interdependence of literacy: Children who learn to read and write in their native language can readily transfer these abilities to the second language (Edelsky, 1982; Faltis, 1986; Hudelson & Serna, 1994; Krashen, 1996). The principle holds for mathematics, science, and other academic concepts as well (Henderson & Landesman, 1992; Minicucci, 1996). According to Cummins (1981), the explanation for this is that the language through which a bilingual student learns academic abilities operates through a single underlying cognitive system. Cummins's perspective is that the two languages of a bilingual are noticeably separate only at the surface level. Below the surface the two languages function through a single operating system that is responsible for cognitive processing of language. This operating system connects the two languages of a bilingual so that what an individual knows and is able to do academically through one language readily applies to situations carried out in the other language. Cummins refers to this view of bilingualism as the *Common Underlying Proficiency (CUP) Model* (see Figure 1.2).

The CUP model of bilingualism doesn't appeal to common sense as easily as the SUP model. The CUP model took educational psychologists interested in bilingualism many years of research and writing to construct (see Cummins, 1980 for a discussion of its origins in psychology and language learning). We argue in this book that the CUP model is certainly a better representation of reality than the SUP model, but we don't agree with the idea that bilingualism is totally cognitive, as the CUP suggests. We posit instead that a bilingual's proficiency in two languages is as much a matter of socially

FIGURE 1.2 Common Underlying Proficiency

Artwork by Jon Faltis. Adapted from drawing in C. Faltis (1997). *Joinfostering: Adapting Teaching for the Multilingual Classroom* Upper Saddle River, NJ: Merrill/Prentice-Hall, p.148.

shared interaction as it is a matter of underlying cognitive processes presumed to drive the two languages. We present a fuller version of this argument in Chapter 4. Suffice to say at this point that while part of an individual's proficiency in two languages stems from cognitive factors, we propose that language abilities are largely social and that they rely on shared interaction about topics that matter.

A Counterintuitive Proposition

One of the aspects of the CUP model that we do appreciate, however, is that it provides a strong rationale for bilingual education, especially the need for students to learn in a language they find meaningful and can use for learning. Assuming the two languages of a bilingual are connected, what students learn well in one language does not need to be relearned in the second language (Krashen, 1996).

Furthermore, teaching students first in their primary language ultimately leads to greater English proficiency. Cummins (1981) calls this counterintuitive idea the "less equals more" rationale for bilingual education. The idea is that non-English-speaking students will learn more English when they are first allowed to participate fully and meaningfully in school learning activities. The way to accomplish this is through a language they understand and use for oral and written communication. Less English early on leads to more English later on, because as students become bilingual they draw on a socially shared knowledge base that is comparable to that of their English-speaking peers. When students learn and become schooled in their primary language, they don't lose out on literacy development, language arts, math, science, social studies, health, art, music, classroom rules, and classroom life in general. English as a second language proficiency is strengthened because students are very much a part of classroom activities. Learning English comes naturally and easily for students when they feel they are a part of the classroom community (Hudelson & Serna, 1994).

Bilingual Education as a Human Rights Issue

The final reason we offer for providing bilingual education has to do with the right of people to maintain and develop their mother tongue, the language they learned first, identify with, and use to communicate across time and space (Hernández–Chávez, 1978; Skutnabb–Kangas, 1988). Bilingual education can enable children to realize their linguistic human rights, which, as Skutnabb–Kangas (1994) defines them, are:

> *that all people can identify positively with their mother tongue and have that identification accepted and respected by others whether their mother tongue is a minority language or a majority language. It means* the right to learn the mother tongue, orally and in writing, including at least basic education through the medium of the mother tongue, and use it in many official contexts *(emphasis added). It also means the right to learn at least one of the official languages in the country of residence (p. 625).*

We view these linguistic human rights as essential to the fundamental rights of school children, such as the right to communicate with adults with the same mother tongue, and the right to participate in and benefit from the educational services provided through public education.

One of the implications of these linguistic human rights is that children need to have access to teachers who teach and communicate in their primary language. And so we come full circle: Bilingual education offers a way to fulfill the linguistic human rights of children to have teachers who speak their language and who can teach them so that they understand and benefit from education.

Concluding Remarks

One of the goals of this book is to invite you, the reader, into bilingual education, its social past and its present condition. In this chapter, we have laid out some of the reasons why bilingual education is needed in the United States. We are not concerned that you recall in detail all of the reasons, but rather that you understand that there are good reasons for supporting bilingual education, and that part of engaging in bilingual education entails learning the ways of talking about its social history, especially why it came about.

All of the reasons we have presented in this chapter were constructed by individuals who think and feel that providing students instruction in their native language and English is necessary. Our hope is that you come to share this understanding and knowledge. One way to accomplish this is by talking about bilingual education to your friends, colleagues, and family members. In this manner, you can gain practice in the discourse of bilingual education. It is important to exchange ideas and use your developing knowledge about bilingual education. This will facilitate your entry into the world of teaching in general and into the world of bilingual education in particular.

Here are some key points to consider as you prepare for the next chapters:

- Bilingual education has a social history that is tied to the civil rights movement and the efforts of Chicano and other minority activists and political leaders;
- There is legal support for bilingual education;
- Students learn best in a language they understand and with which they identify;
- What students learn in their native language transfers to their second language;
- It is a linguistic human right to be able to communicate with and be taught by adults who speak your mother tongue;
- Learning about bilingual education is a matter of joining in its social history and current knowledge base through multiple discussions in which you use your own and others' discourse about bilingual education.

In the next chapter, we introduce and discuss the various kinds of bilingual programs at both the elementary and secondary levels of teaching and learning. Chapter 2 shows how bilingual education programs tend to reflect the interaction between early policy decisions and the social and historical contexts of school.

References

Andersson, T., & Boyer, M. (1978). *Bilingual schooling in the United States,* 2nd ed. Austin, TX: National Education Laboratory Publishers.

August, D., & García, E. (1988). *Language minority education in the United States.* Springfield, IL: Charles C. Thomas.

Baker, K., & de Kanter, A. (1981). *Effectiveness of bilingual education: A review of the literature.* Washington, DC: Office of Planning, Budget and Evaluation, U. S. Department of Education.

Brisk, M. E. (1981). Language policies in American education. *Journal of Education, 163*(1), 3–15.

Casanova, U., & Arias, M. B. (1993). Contextualizing bilingual education. In M. B. Arias & U. Casanova (Eds.), *Bilingual education: Politics, practice, research* (pp. 1–35). Chicago, IL: University of Chicago Press.

Cazden, C., & Snow, C. (1990). Preface. *The Annals of the American Academy of Political and Social Science, 508,* 9–11.

Crawford, J. (1995). Endangered Native American languages: What is to be done, and why? *Bilingual Research Journal, 19*(3 & 4), 17–38.

Crawford, J. (1992) *Hold your tongue: Bilingualism and the politics of "English only."* Reading, MA: Addison-Wesley.

Cummins, J. (1991). The politics of paranoia: Reflections of the bilingual education debate. In O. García (Ed.), *Bilingual education: Focusschrift in honor of Joshua A. Fishman* (pp. 183–199). Philadelphia, PA: John Benjamins.

Cummins, J. (1981). The role of primary language development in promoting educational success for language minority students. In California State Department of Education, *Schooling and language minority students: A theoretical framework* (pp. 3–49). Los Angeles, CA: California State Department of Education.

Cummins, J. (1980). The construct of language proficiency in bilingual education. In J. Alatis (Ed.), *Georgetown University round table on languages and linguistics 1980* (pp. 81–101). Washington, DC: Georgetown University Press.

DeVillar, R. (1994). The rhetoric and practice of cultural diversity in U. S. schools: Socialization, resocialization, and quality schooling. In R. A. DeVillar, C. Faltis, & J. Cummins (Eds.), *Cultural diversity in schools: From rhetoric to practice* (pp. 25–56). Albany, NY: SUNY Press.

Donato, R. (1997). *The other struggle for equal schools: Mexican Americans during the civil rights era.* Albany, NY: SUNY Press.

Edelsky, C. (1982). Writing in a bilingual program: The relation of L_1 and L_2 texts. *TESOL Quarterly, 16*(2), 211–228.

Faltis, C. (1997). *Joinfostering: Adapting teaching for the multilingual classroom.* New Jersey: Merrill.

Faltis, C. (1986). Initial cross-lingual reading transfer in bilingual second grade class-rooms. In E. García & B. Flores (Eds.), *Language and literacy research in bilingual education* (pp. 145–157). Tempe, AZ: Arizona State University Press.

Heath, S. B. (1981). English in our language heritage. In C. A. Ferguson & S. B. Heath (Eds.), *Language in the U.S.A* (pp. 6–20). Cambridge: Cambridge University Press.

Henderson, R., & Landesman, E. (1992). *Mathematics and middle school students of Mexican descent: The effects of thematically integrated instruction.* Santa Cruz, CA: The National Center for Research on Cultural Diversity and Language Learning.

Hernández–Chávez, E. (1978). Language maintenance, bilingual education, and philosophies of bilingualism in the United States. In J. Alatis (Ed.), *International dimensions of bilingual education* (pp. 500–527). Washington, DC: Georgetown University Press.

Hudelson, S., & Serna, I. (1994). Beginning literacy in English in a whole-language bilingual program. In A. Flurkey & R. Meyer (Eds.), *Under the whole language umbrella: Many cultures, many voices* (pp. 278–294). Urbana, IL: National Council of Teachers of English.

Jones, W. R. (1959). *Bilingualism and intelligence.* Cardiff, England: University of Wales.

Kloss, H. (1997). *The American bilingual tradition.* Rowley, MA: Newburg House.

Kolers, P. (1963). Interlingual word association. *Journal of Verbal Learning and Verbal Behavior,* 2, 191–200.

Krashen, S. (1996). *Under attack: The case against bilingual education.* Culver City, CA: Language Education Associates.

Leibowitz, A. H. (1971). *Educational policy and political acceptance: The imposition of English as the language of instruction in American schools.* Washington, DC: Center for Applied Linguistics.

Mackey, W. F., & Beebe, L. V. (1977). *Bilingual schools for a bicultural community: Miami's adaptation to the Cuban refugees.* Rowley, MA: Newbury House.

Malakoff, M., & Hakuta, K. (1990). History of language minority education in the United States. In A. M. Padilla, H. H. Fairchild, & C. M. Valadez (Eds.), *Bilingual education: Issues and strategies* (pp. 27–44). Newbury Park, CA: SAGE.

McGroarty, M. (1992). The social context of bilingual education. *Educational Researcher,* 21(2), 7–9.

Minicucci, C. (1996). *Learning science and English: How school reform advances scientific learning for limited English proficient middle school students.* Santa Cruz: CA: National Center for Research on Cultural Diversity and Language Learning.

Minicucci, C., & Olsen, L. (1991). *An exploratory study of secondary LEP programs,* vol. 5. Berkeley, CA: BW Associates.

Moraes, M. (1996). *Bilingual education: A dialogue with the Bakhtin circle.* Albany, NY: SUNY Press.

NABE News (December, 1994.) California students shortchanged. 18, no. 12, pp. 2, 18.

National Education Association (NEA). (1966). *The invisible minority.* Washington, DC: National Education Association.

Paivio, A. (1986). *Mental representations: A dual coding approach.* Oxford: Oxford University Press.

Palla, A., Natriello, G., & McDill, E. (1989). The changing nature of the disadvantaged target population: Current dimensions and future trends. *Educational Research, 18,* 16–22.

Peal, E., & Lambert, W., (1962). The relationship of bilingualism to intelligence. *Psychological Monographs, 76*(27), 1–23.

Pinter, R., & Arsenian, S. (1937). The relation of bilingualism to verbal intelligence and school adjustment. *Journal of Educational Research, 31,* 255–263.

Rodríguez, R. (1990, July). Escasez de maestros bilingües en una etapa crítica [A paucity of bilingual teachers in a critical period]. Los Angeles, CA: *La Opinión,* 5.

Saer, D. J. (1923). The effects of bilingualism on intelligence. *British Journal of Psychology, 14,* 25–38.

San Miguel, G. (Summer/Fall, 1978). Inside the public schools: A history of the Chicano educational experience. *Atisbos: Journal of Chicano Research,* 86–101.

Skutnabb–Kangas, T. (1994). Linguistic human rights and minority education. *TESOL Quarterly, 28*(3), 625–628.

Skutnabb–Kangas, T. (1988). Multilingualism and education of minority children. In T. Skutnabb–Kangas & J. Cummins (Eds.), *Minority education: From shame to struggle* (pp. 19–44). Clevedon, England: Multilingual Matters.

Spring, J. (1994). *Deculturalization and the struggle for equality.* New York: McGraw-Hill.

Stein, B. (1986). *Sink or swim: The politics of bilingual education.* New York: Praeger.

U. S. Bureau of the Census. (1991). *The Hispanic population of the United States: March 1990.* Washington, DC: U. S. Government Printing Office.

Valdez, L., & Steiner, S. (Eds.) (1972). *Aztlán: An anthology of Mexican American literature.* New York: Vintage Books.

Wong Fillmore, L. (1991). When learning a second language means losing the first. *Early Childhood Research Quarterly, 6,* 323–346.

2

What Does Bilingual Education Look Like?

In Chapter 1 we looked at some of the historical, social, and political factors that influenced educators and policy-makers as they struggled with how to provide more effective educational experiences for nonnative English-speaking students in our schools. We examined some of the legislation and court decisions that supported the use of languages other than English in classrooms and that contributed to the rebirth of bilingual education. We saw that there has been continued opposition to and propaganda against bilingual education, which has meant that many programs have operated in a climate of misunderstanding and open hostility. Nevertheless, many program planners have worked diligently to offer quality learning opportunities to non-English-speaking students. In this chapter we examine the variety of approaches that have been utilized in both elementary and secondary school settings.

As you will remember, the *Lau vs. Nichols* Supreme Court decision made it clear that school districts could not ignore the special educational needs of non-English-speaking students by assuming that children placed in English language classrooms would eventually pick up enough English to learn school content. *Lau vs. Nichols* did not mandate what kinds of programs should be established, but it did specify that programs had to be carried out. Given this flexibility from the Court, given legislative flexibility at federal and state levels, and given the political realities in many communities where the promotion of languages other than English has been deemed to be unAmerican (Crawford, 1992a; Daniels, 1990), schools have utilized a variety of instructional approaches to assist English language learners to achieve to their full potential.

Most programs, responding to local, state, or federal funding requirements, utilize some sort of formal language dominance and/or proficiency instrument to determine both children's eligibility for and entrance into a bilingual program and their exit from it. Often these instruments (for example, the IDEA Proficiency Test, the Bilingual Syntax Measure, the Language Assessment Scales) rank children's language abilities (in English and often in the native language as well) on a scale from 0 or 1 to 5, and children need to achieve a specific proficiency in order to exit from the program (see Faltis, 1997, for a review of these tests). In our view, there are several significant problems with and limitations to the kind of proficiency testing that is usually done.

1. Many of the tests examine only children's ability to understand and speak English, yet to achieve academic success in English language classrooms, strong reading and writing abilities are essential. Frequently children are exited from programs when they can carry on basic conversations in English, but they are not able to cope successfully with English language content instruction and are not literate in English.

2. The tests assume that children will perform in English when called on to do so. We know that there are significant cultural differences with regard to how children respond to requests to answer questions to which the answer is already known (as in "Tell me what this is" in reference to a picture that both the examiner and child can see). Mainstream, middle-class children, for example, are much more willing to respond to known answer questions than are children from other backgrounds. There are also significant differences in how children from different cultures respond to questions posed by an unfamiliar adult (Au, 1993; Labov, 1970; Heath, 1983). Yet the language proficiency tests, which do not take possible cultural differences in response into account, are based on this kind of performance.

If a child chooses, for example, not to label certain items or not to create a narration from a sequence of pictures, the child may be labelled "not proficient." The reality may be that the child has chosen not to talk because the test asks the child to use language in ways that violate the norms of the child's home and community. The tests assume that if children know the language forms, they will use them. Children may know the forms but be unfamiliar with how to use the forms in particular settings (such as testing).

3. Often the tests require specific answers for the child to receive credit. If the child responds using other words, she may not receive credit for doing so and again be mislabelled. For example, the IDEA test uses a picture of a man in a white coat holding a pair of scissors and asks the child looking at the picture: Who cuts your hair? The only acceptable answer is "a barber." However, in a bilingual school with which we are familiar many children answer my uncle, my father, my mother, because in their families hair is cut in the home, not at a shop. Others have been heard to make comments with regard to the picture such as: "Is that a dentist?" "That looks like a doctor," but they receive no credit for such responses.

4. Given the ways that the tests are scored, some children may be labelled as not proficient either in English or their native language. In our experience with the IDEA Proficiency Test (which claims to measure children's native and second language proficiency), for example, numbers of children who have taken the test several times simply refuse to "play the game" and give no answer at all or respond with noncredited answers. These children often end up labelled as "semilingual," that is, having limited proficiency in both the native language and English and are even considered by some to have "no language." As we will see in Chapter 4, a social interactionist perspective on language acquisition makes it clear that even very young children are able to communicate effectively within the homes and families in which they have been nurtured (Lindfors, 1987). We reject the suggestion that large numbers of non-English-speaking children are deficient or semilingual in their native language as well as English.

5. The tests are based on monolingual norms of reference. Many children who are placed in bilingual classrooms have grown up in homes and communities in which two languages are heard and used. The proficiency they acquire in the two languages and the ways in which they use their two languages may be qualitatively and quantitatively different from that of monolingual speakers of each language. Accordingly, comparisons made between a bilingual child's language abilities in two languages with monolinguals' use of each language may be inappropriate (Grosjean, 1982).

In later chapters, when we describe specific classrooms, we will provide examples of learners' authentic use of spoken and written language. We argue that the language generated in classroom activities provides educators with much richer and more valuable information about children's language abilities than the kinds of instruments currently in use.

We hope that we have made it clear that the focus of transitional bilingual education, as mandated in the original Bilingual Education Act (see Chapter 1), is to prepare non-English-speaking children to learn only through English, so that assimilation into the mainstream will occur. Generally, there is no real concern for valuing and promoting non-English languages and cultures. In some programs a superficial nod to other cultures may be given, but it most often appears, if at all, in the form of tangible aspects of culture such as foods (tacos in the cafeteria, goldfoiled covered chocolates for Chinese New Year) and holidays (folkloric dancers for Cinco de Mayo). While there is nothing intrinsically wrong with this inclusion, there is little concern demonstrated for what we consider more important aspects of culture, for example, cultural influences on learning and ways that teachers might adjust their teaching to take such differences into account.

Even the term that the federal government has coined to label learners in transitional bilingual programs, *Limited English Proficient* (LEP), is, in our view, a term that promotes a view of the learner as deficient in some way and contributes to the notion that transitional bilingual education is compensatory education (Crawford, 1989). The term *Limited English Proficient* contributes to the tendency of educators to see learners in terms of a supposed deficiency (they don't speak English) and to conceive of the bilingual education program as helping students to compensate for this deficiency. We prefer to work from the stance of the strengths and abilities learners bring with them to school, and we applaud the work of colleagues and organizations that have proposed other, more positive labels. Casanova (1991) uses the acronym SOL (Speakers of Other Languages); Hamayan has substituted PEP (Potentially English Proficient) for LEP; Rigg and Allen (1989) suggest that we refer to learners as REAL students (Readers and Writers of English as Another Language). In a recent document, the National Board for Professional Teaching Standards (1996) utilizes ELL (English Language Learners). TESOL (Teaching of English to Speakers of Other Languages), an international organization, uses the term ESOL learners, English speakers of other languages (TESOL, 1996). Kachru and Nelson (1996) argue that English as a *second* language may also be considered pejorative. Their reasoning is twofold: First, in the United States, there is tremendous emphasis on being first; being second is not as good as being first. Second, from a world perspective, there are many *native* speakers of English from countries such as India, Ghana, Liberia, Malta, and Zimbabwe, and certain islands who use a variety of English for multiple purposes, yet their English is often referred to (disparagingly from their point of view) as a second language. Given our distaste for the term *LEP* and its possible implications, we will not use it in this volume. Rather, we will refer to the learners with terms such as *second language learners, ESL* (English as a second language) *students,* or *bilingual* or *becoming bilingual learners.* When we do refer to ESL students, we mean students who come from countries where English is not used widely as a native language by large numbers of the general population.

Maintenance/Late Exit Bilingual Education

In contrast to transitional bilingual education, maintenance bilingual education has as a major goal the development of proficiency in both the learners' native language and in English, and the utilization of both languages in the learning of significant content. In this model, which is often termed *late exit bilingual education,* languages other than English are valued for their own sakes, and children are encouraged to continue both learning the native language (for example, attaining high levels of native language literacy) and learning through the native language, as well as learning English and learning through English (Baker, 1988). Thus, maintenance programs reflect and encourage linguistic pluralism. Sometimes the non-English language receives a more prominent place in the curriculum than English because the minority language, which generally has lower prestige outside the school setting, needs to be supported more strongly (Appel & Muysken, 1987).

In the elementary school setting, maintenance bilingual programs advocate that children begin their literacy and content learning experiences in the native language. So, for example, Spanish-speaking children, in their early schooling experiences, use Spanish to develop mathematics concepts, to study content in science, and to read and write about topics that matter. However, unlike transitional programs, maintenance classes encourage children to continue to use the native language to learn, even when they have developed considerable proficiency in English. This means, for example, that teachers would encourage children to continue to read and write in Spanish even after they are able to read and write in English. It could also mean that learners might use both English and Spanish to carry out science or social studies projects or to engage in mathematics learning. Figure 2.2 depicts the amount of use of languages other than English in maintenance bilingual classrooms.

Ideally, maintenance bilingual education acknowledges, values, and seeks to promote the linguistic and cultural identity and vitality of non-English-speaking children and communities. It does so through such classroom practices as utilizing stories and literature from the culture, promoting the inclusion of cultural forms and traditions, and including themes for study that are relevant to students and families. But as with transitional bilingual education, the focus is exclusively on the non-English-speaking or minority language (Baker, 1988) learners.

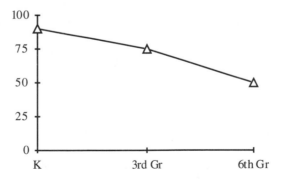

FIGURE 2.2   Typical Use of Languages Other Than English in U. S. Maintenance Bilingual Programs

Enrichment/Two-Way Bilingual Education

The terms *enrichment bilingual education, bilingual immersion, two-way immersion, two-way maintenance bilingual education, dual language programs,* and *developmental bilingual education* are all used to label elementary school bilingual education programs that are designed for both English language learners and native speakers of English (Christian, 1994). The basic goals of enrichment bilingual education are that the speakers of each language will: (1) learn the language of the others as well as their own language (develop a high degree of proficiency in both their native and second languages); (2) achieve academically through and in both languages; and (3) come to appreciate each others' languages and cultures (Lindholm, 1994). Thus, if monolingual Navajo speakers and monolingual English speakers are in an enrichment bilingual education program, all the children will become speakers of both languages, become literate both in Navajo and English, and use both languages to study school content, developing high levels of proficiency as they use both languages for academic purposes (Commins, 1994; Holland, 1997). The non-English, minority language is thus elevated in status, and its influence extended beyond the minority community. The non-English language, in this case, Navajo, is recognized as being of value for English speakers (Hornberger, 1991).

In two-way programs, language minority and language majority children are integrated in classes in which a significant amount of daily instruction is carried out only in English and where a language other than English is also used exclusively for a significant part of the school day (Lindholm, 1994). This means that all learners spend a significant amount of time immersed in their second language and that all learners are acquiring the curriculum through two languages (Collier, 1995b). This design is based on the successful Canadian immersion programs, in which English-speaking children were immersed in French for their first years of schooling. The English-speaking children learned literacy and content initially through their second language and gradually added on English, their native language (Genesee, 1987). The success of these programs in Canada led to replications of the immersion model in the United States, with French, Spanish, and German being the immersion languages (Cohen, 1975; Campbell, 1984). In these Canadian and U. S. contexts, immersion education resulted both in high fluency in the second language as well as English language achievement equal to or above that of native English speakers schooled exclusively in English (Cohen, 1975; Genesee, 1987; Lambert & Tucker, 1972).

A two-way approach was also the design of one of the first bilingual education programs of the 1960s, the Coral Way Bilingual Elementary School in Miami, Florida (see Chapter 1; Mackey & Beebe, 1977).

There are currently some 200 two-way programs in U. S. schools, most of them Spanish–English (other languages served include Cantonese, French, Japanese, Korean, Navajo, Portuguese, and Russian). Typically these programs have adopted one of two models for language development. In the "fifty/fifty" model, learners receive instruction for equal amounts of time in each language. In the "ninety/ten" model, about 90 percent of instruction is in the minority language in the primary grades, with the time distribution moving to about equal time by fourth grade. Figure 2.3 shows the quantitative contrast in the use of languages other than English in the two models of two-way bilingual education.

Individual programs decide what will be taught in the two languages. Some allocate the two languages by content (e.g., teaching social studies and math in one language and science and the arts in the other). Some utilize time divisions (half a day or a day in one language, half a day or a day in the other). Others employ team-teaching, one teacher using only one language, and the other using the other language. Whatever specific decisions are made, all of the children receive their instruction together, with teachers using a variety of instructional strategies that make instruction more comprehensible. Most of the programs also emphasize hands-on, experiential learning, thematic approaches, and collaborative work among children, so that the native speakers of both language groups assist their peers in the learning of content through the second language (Christian, 1996; ERIC Digest, 1994; Holland, 1997). While the student populations of the early two-way programs, such as Coral Way Elementary, tended to be upper-middle-class children, the learners served in the current programs represent significant socioeconomic and cultural diversity (Christian, 1996; Collier, 1995a; Holland, 1997). Two-way bilingual education is no longer only for the elite.

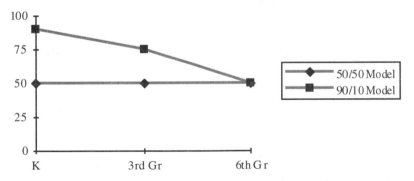

FIGURE 2.3 Typical Use of Languages Other Than English in U. S. Enrichment Bilingual Programs

The Transitional Philosophy in Nonbilingual Settings

While dual language instruction of some kind is a reality in many schools, it is *not* the only approach that may be used to meet the educational needs of elementary school non-English-speaking learners. In many places, children are being schooled exclusively or almost exclusively through English. The reasons for this are many. In some schools the English language learners come from many different native languages, and educators fluent in these languages are not available. Instructional materials are more readily available in some languages than others. In some settings, community pressures (including pressure from non-English-speaking parents who believe that their children should learn only in English) preclude bilingual education. At local, state, and national levels the rhetoric from groups such as U. S. English proclaiming that bi- or multilingualism is divisive and antiAmerican has effects on decisions about instruction (Crawford, 1992a, 1992b). The common sense belief that using the native language for instruction retards English language development also influences educational policy-makers.

A particularly noteworthy example of this influence occurred in 1984 when the Title VII legislation came up for reauthorization and changes in the legislation could be made. Conservative influences at that time, including the reality of a Republican president and Secretary of the Department of Education, resulted in a provision for "special alternative instructional programs" being written into the Title VII legislation. What distinguished these programs from others was that they made no use of the native language; they were English-only programs. For the first time, then, school districts could receive bilingual education funding for programs that were not bilingual.

Because the *Lau vs. Nichols* decision directs that some specialized instruction be implemented but does not specify bilingual instruction, special English language instruction is an instructional option. That is the basis for the English as a Second Language (ESL), or English for Speakers of Other Languages (ESOL), or Teaching of English to Speakers of Other Languages (TESOL) approaches that many schools use. We maintain that this approach falls clearly within the transitional philosophy in that the emphasis is on English language competence and achievement only.

There are several ways that English-only programs are organized in elementary schools. A common delivery model is that which is termed *ESL pullout* or *ESL resource*. In pullout and resource settings alike, second language learners are assigned to mainstream English medium classrooms. There they generally receive the same instructional program as do the English speakers. In addition, they receive regularly scheduled ESL instruction from an ESL teacher, usually for blocks of time that range from fifteen minutes to an hour or more. Students are "pulled out" of their regular classroom to receive special ESL language instruction, hence the designation *pullout.* Often second language learners are grouped for this special instruction according to second language proficiency. In this manner, for example, the ESL teacher may work with a group of English beginners together followed by a group of more advanced learners, in contrast to bringing together learners from a multiplicity of language abilities.

Ideally, the ESL teacher has a special credential and has received specialized training in teaching a second language to children. Ideally, too, the ESL teacher has coordinated instruction with classroom teachers, so that there is a relationship between what the children are doing in ESL and what they are doing in the mainstream classroom. Sometimes, for example, the ESL teacher will examine content taught in the mainstream setting and organize an ESL curriculum that provides learners with experiences that are directly connected to this content, experiences that often highlight the language aspects of the content. However, we know from experience that the reality often falls short of the ideal. Too often the ESL teacher and the mainstream teacher do not communicate in any depth about learner needs, and there is little or no instructional connection between the two settings. Neither knows what the other is doing. Often, too, ESL teachers may not be accorded status as professionals, and their expertise and function may be questioned.

To help counteract this lack of communication and coordination, some schools have moved away from a pullout delivery of services and have instead sent ESL teachers into mainstream classrooms to work alongside the classroom teachers for regularly scheduled periods of time. Some districts refer to this as the push-in model. In this model second language teachers have been able to offer special assistance to the second language learners, lower the student–teacher ratio, make it more possible to break up the class into small groups, and provide some expertise in adapting instruction to teach second language learners more effectively.

A major challenge with this model is the recognition of the ESL teacher as an equal of the mainstream educator, not an instructional aide. The ESL professional must be able to provide input into the substance and delivery of content and not serve simply as another body in the classroom to assist children. Another challenge is the differences that may exist between the teaching philosophies of the classroom teacher and the second language educator. The classroom teacher, for example, may view appropriate instruction in writing as focusing on grammar or spelling lessons, while the ESL teacher may believe that children learning a second language need experiences with writing that focus on the creation of original texts, even though those texts are not written in entirely conventional English. In order for these individuals to collaborate effectively, they must try to work out their differences.

Another alternative to the pullout ESL program in elementary school settings has been what some districts call *self-contained ESL* classrooms. This calls for a teacher, who is credentialed in both elementary education and ESL, to serve in a regular classroom teacher capacity, but be assigned a class populated exclusively by ESL learners or a class with significant numbers of second language learners (in one school district in our area, for example, the program design calls for approximately equal numbers of native English speakers and second language students in the designated ESL classrooms). The ESL teacher *is* the classroom teacher, and as such assumes all-day responsibility for the ESL children's content and language learning. Ideally, the students who are becoming bilingual represent a variety of English language proficiency levels, and there are native English speakers in the class, so that peers as well as the teacher can facilitate language learning. In the self-contained classroom the teacher knows the children well, as individuals, as language learners, and as learners in general. This enables the teacher to plan and implement instruction that will best facilitate all learners' linguistic, academic, social, and personal development. However, in classes populated only or heavily by nonnative speakers, the issue of linguistic and social segregation is a real one: How do second language learners learn to use English and to associate with native speakers if they do not come into social contact with them? This reality must always be kept in mind (see Faltis, 1993a, for a discussion of the benefits and detriments of linguistic and social segregation).

From the perspective of language learning, currently accepted views of effective language learning environments assert that children learn both oral and written language most effectively when they are using language to examine content that is of interest to them, rather than when they are studying the language as an entity, or for its own sake (Collier, 1995b; Faltis & Hudelson, 1994; Cantoni-Harvey, 1987; Hudelson, 1989; Rigg & Allen, 1989). In high quality self-contained ESL classrooms this is what occurs. As children, for example, use oral and written language to investigate topics of interest in curricular areas such as social studies and science, as they read and respond to literature, as they work to explain how they arrived at certain answers to problems presented in mathematics, they learn more English and they learn how to use English to accomplish their academic as well as their social purposes. The teacher works to set up the environment to facilitate this learning, engaging in what has been referred to as *language sensitive content teaching* (Faltis, 1997).

A variation on the self-contained elementary school ESL classroom just described is what has been labelled *structured immersion* (cited in the previously mentioned 1984 Title VII reauthorization legislation as an alternative instructional program eligible for funding). Ostensibly based on the above-mentioned Canadian immersion programs designed for English-speaking learners (Ramírez, 1985), this program makes exclusive use of English as the medium of instruction. Non-English-speaking children, all speakers of the same primary native language, receive instruction in English language literacy and engage in content area study in English from the beginning of their schooling experiences. The teachers in structured immersion have specialized training in second language methodology, with an emphasis on teaching English through the content areas. In many structured immersion classrooms, the teachers speak, or at least understand, the native language of the learners and allow them to use the native language during instructional activities. Generally the teachers respond to native language comments in English, although a teacher may use the native language with an individual learner to clarify instruction. However, the agenda clearly is English acquisition and use, not the use and maintenance of other languages. In contrast, the goal of the Canadian model, and of two-way programs in the U.S., is bilingualism, biliteracy, and the use of the two languages for academic purposes (Hornberger, 1991; Ramírez, 1992).

A Role for the Student's Native Language

One of the questions we hear asked frequently about ESL teaching is whether teachers should allow learners to use their native language in the ESL setting. We often hear comments such as: "If you let them use their native language, they'll become lazy and never want to use English." "The native language is just a crutch." "The only way they'll learn English is if they're forced to use it." Twenty-five to thirty years ago most professionals probably would have urged teachers not to allow students to use their native language(s) when they were supposed to be learning English. More recently, however, this position has changed. Numbers of ESL educators, and organizations such as TESOL and NCTE (National Council of Teachers of English), now recognize that the learners' native language may be a resource for learning both content and English, a way for learners to negotiate their learning (NCTE, 1996; TESOL, 1996). There is also a much greater acknowledgement that students may learn more in school (including more English) if they believe that their home and community languages and cultures are acknowledged and valued. Hence, there have been calls for teachers to allow and even encourage the use of learners' native languages in ESL settings in schools (Auerbach, 1993; Faltis & Hudelson, 1994; González, 1994; Lucas & Katz, 1994).

If you are not bilingual, you may be thinking: How can I encourage the use of another language when I am monolingual in English? Or you may have been in classrooms in which the children come from multiple language backgrounds and you may be saying: I don't know all those languages. How can I let the children use their home languages if I don't know them? These are important questions, and we believe that a general answer to them may be stated in terms of our belief that learning is fundamentally social, that learners learn from each other, as well as from the teacher, which means that child–child collaborations may take place in the children's native languages (as well as in English) even if the adults do not speak those languages. Our belief is supported by Pease–Alvarez and Winsler (1994), who conducted a case study of an elementary classroom teacher who didn't speak Spanish, but had a class full of monolingual and bilingual Spanish-speaking children. The teacher wanted to do everything possible to promote the use of Spanish and to provide the children with a positive classroom environment. Pease-Alvarez and Winsler describe in some detail the multiple ways that this teacher valued the learners' native language and culture despite the fact that he didn't speak their language.

The are many ways for monolingual English teachers to demonstrate their commitment to valuing students' languages and cultural experiences. They may, for example, make literature and other learning resources available in more than one language, allow children to write in more than one language and share their writing with others who know that same language, pair up children who share the same home language but have differing abilities in English so that they can help each other to produce a final product in English, invite bilingual adults into the classroom to share their stories and life experiences in their own languages, ask children and/or adults to create classroom and school signs in multiple languages, utilize adult and peer volunteer tutors proficient in the learner's home languages, and explain to parents the importance of continuing native language development at home (Collier, 1995b; Freeman & Freeman, 1993, 1994). We favor making use of children's native languages in ESL settings, because we believe in acknowledging and valuing these language abilities, for their own sake, as well as for promoting learning and literacy in two languages.

Figure 2.4 summarizes the approaches to bilingual education in elementary school settings that we have described in the previous sections.

Varieties of Bilingual Education Approaches in Secondary School Settings

Secondary Transitional and Maintenance Programs

Bilingual education approaches in middle schools and high schools are either transitional or maintenance. To our knowledge, enrichment bilingual education is not an option used at the secondary level. Transitional bilingual education at the secondary level typically means that non-English-speaking learners are provided with variable coverage of subject matter content in their native language, plus English as a second language classes designed to provide students with basic oral and written communication skills. In the transitional approach, native language coursework is available only to new students while they learn enough English to participate in regular subject

MODEL	Enrichment	Maintenance	Transitional	ESL
EDUCATIONAL GOAL	linguistic pluralism, academic achievement in L_1 and L_2, appreciation of L_1 and L_2	linguistic pluralism, academic achievement in L_1 and L_2, appreciation of L_1 and L_2	learner achievement in English in three years or less	English language competence and achievement only
LEARNER SERVED	nonnative and native English speakers	nonnative English speakers	nonnative English speakers	nonnative English speakers
LANGUAGE OF INSTRUCTION	L_1 and L_2	L_1 and English, with continued use of L_1 throughout program	L_1 and English, with use of L_1 only until learner is functional in L_2 classroom	English
PROGRAM DURATION	through grade 6 (can be extended)	through grade 6 (can be extended)	typically through grade 3	typically three years or less
DELIVERY SYSTEM	self-contained classroom	self-contained classroom	self-contained classroom	ESL pullout/ ESL resource/ self-contained classroom
SERVED BY	bilingual teacher/ monolingual teacher for each language	bilingual teacher/ monolingual teacher for each language	bilingual teacher/ instructional assistant/resource teacher	ESL teacher/ regular classroom teacher

FIGURE 2.4 U. S. Elementary Bilingual and ESL Programs

matter classes. In contrast, the maintenance approach enables students to continue taking coursework in their native language all through their secondary school experience.

The complexity of the bilingual program students receive depends on several contextual factors: (1) students' prior schooling experiences; (2) their native language literacy abilities; (3) their age and level of entry; and (4) the number of students of the same language background (Lucas, 1993). It is easier to provide a quality bilingual program to students who have had parallel schooling experiences in their native countries, who have good native language literacy abilities, and who all speak the same native language than it is to provide quality bilingual instruction to students who enter school with limited formal schooling, limited academic and literacy abilities, and who speak a variety of native languages other than English.

Transitional Philosophy in Nonbilingual Settings

The transitional philosophy is especially prevalent in secondary schools where there are students who speak a number of non-English languages. There is a sense of urgency to get these students into mainstream English classrooms as quickly as possible. And there are two reasons for thinking this way. First, as mentioned earlier, there is a tremendous shortage of secondary level content area teachers with the ability to teach subject matter content in a non-English language. Secondary level subject matter courses require highly sophisticated vocabularies and ways of talking. Few secondary teachers in the United States have had the opportunity to study in depth their content area specialties in a non-English language.

Second, there is the matter of time. It takes time for students to acquire English, to gain the abilities needed to participate in oral and written exchanges with fellow native English students and their teachers. Students who enter secondary school knowing little or no English may need up to seven years to develop high levels of oral and written English proficiency (Collier, 1995a). How quickly they are able to learn depends on their native language schooling experiences and literacy abilities, the support they receive in the U. S. school, and the number of same-language speakers in the U. S. school. Generally speaking, students with parallel schooling in their native language who attend U. S. schools that are sensitive to their needs, and who do not have lots of opportunities to use their native language with peers, learn English faster than students with limited native language schooling experiences, who attend unsupportive schools, and who are segregated into classes in which there are only students who speak the same language.

In secondary schools in which a transitional philosophy predominates, English learners typically have two avenues for becoming bilingual: (1) ESL classes, and (2) sheltered content classes.

ESL Classes

English-as-a-second language (ESL) classes are most often organized into proficiency levels—Level I, II, III, IV, and transitional English. In theory, the levels correspond to oral and written English abilities, with Level I being for true beginners, and Level IV for students who can functionally interact orally and in writing with most native English speakers about familiar and unfamiliar topics. Levels II and III are intermediate levels designed to strengthen vocabulary and sentence structure abilities. Typically, students in Levels II and III can talk and write about familiar topics in the here and now. They can create with language in the sense that they no longer rely on memorized phrases or sayings, and can make themselves understood to people who are used to interacting with ESL learners. They still make lots of speaking and writing errors, but they can communicate effectively, nonetheless.

In reality, things are not so neat. It is not uncommon for students with intermediate proficiency in English to be placed in Level I ESL classes, or for students with low English proficiency to be assigned to Level III classes. One reason for this is that many secondary schools do not have sophisticated assessment and diagnosis procedures to accurately place students according to both their oral and written English proficiency levels. ESL students enter secondary school with a wide range of language and schooling experiences, and while many may have functional oral English abilities, it is likely that their literacy abilities in their native language and English are much lower than their oral abilities (Faltis & Arias, 1993). Another reason is that there simply may not be enough room for students at certain levels, so the students are placed in classes where there is room.

The highest level of ESL classes are often called transitional English classes. These classes are basically content-based ESL classes in which language teaching principles are integrated with content learning (Crandell, 1987). Transitional English teachers use and adapt exisiting content and materials, and present these using traditional ESL methodology—namely, vocabulary development exercises and sentence-based oral and written activities to practice language in the context of subject matter content. For example, a transitional English class may be organized around social studies and literature. Students would study social studies topics and read pieces of literature, and then do lots of activities to practice the language and vocabulary associated with the topics and readings.

The goal of these classes is to offer English language learners access to the kinds of mainstream content that they will be asked to cope with in regular classes. However, the focus of assessment in these classes is on English language skills and functions, not content knowledge (Salinas, 1992). The reality is that, although transitional English teachers have secondary certification and many have an ESL endorsement, they are not necessarily certified in the content area they teach to English learners. Their expertise is as language teachers rather than teachers of content. And even that expertise may be limited. Few states have full secondary certification for English as a second language because ESL is not considered to be a subject matter content area. Rather, ESL is offered as an endorsement to be added on after initial certification.

Sheltered Content Classes

The second way that students who enter secondary school with a language other than English become bilingual is through sheltered content classes. Sheltered content classes are subject matter content courses designed specifically for ESL students *with intermediate or above* level oral and written proficiency in English.

Sheltered content teaching began in California in the mid-1980s. Educator and second language theorist Stephen Krashen developed sheltered content teaching as a way to provide English learners with comprehensible content area instruction (Krashen, 1985). Krashen wanted English learners to be "sheltered" from the potential learning problems they might experience from having to compete with native English speakers in a mixed language classroom, thus "native speakers of the language of instruction are excluded" (Krashen, 1985).

Since its inception, sheltered content teaching has included three features that distinguish it from regular content area classes and from traditional ESL classes, including content-based ESL:

1. COMPREHENSIBLE LANGUAGE. Sheltered content teachers make an effort to make the language used to present and explain information comprehensible to all students. Students typically use the same textbooks and materials as regular mainstream classes, although recently some major textbook companies are publishing textbooks for sheltered U. S. History, Basic Math, and General Science.

2. FOCUS ON ACADEMIC CONTENT. Language is not the focus of teaching; rather, the goal is to facilitate the understanding of academic subject matter concepts, principles, and vocabulary. Classroom tasks and assesssment of them emphasize subject matter understanding, not the correct use of English. The content is not watered down, although the language of the text is adjusted to be more active and hands-on, and teacher talk tends to be language-sensitive. Sheltered content classes carry full academic credit toward graduation.

3. SEGREGATION. Only English learners with intermediate level spoken and written English and above should be assigned to sheltered content classes. The students may or may not be from the same primary native language

background. However, students in sheltered classes usually have opportunities to interact socially with monolingual and bilingual native English speakers as they progress in language and content learning.

Sheltered content teachers are normally certified to teach in their content areas of specialization and usually have some academic preparation in teaching English as a second language (Salinas, 1992). This better assures that students will receive content comparable to that taught to native speakers of English, but with adaptations in presentation.

Sheltered content classes work best when students enroll in them while they are still taking at least one class taught in their native language, and are enrolled in one or more mainstream courses taught exclusively in English, such as Physical Education, Music, Art, Woodshop, and other nontext-driven courses. Figures 2.5 and 2.6 show where and when students might take sheltered content classes within a fully developed bilingual program and within a program in which native language courses are not possible, respectively.

It is important to comment here that most high schools offer one or two levels of ESL classes and sheltered teaching for only a relatively small number of content classes. For example, Minicucci and Olsen (1992) found that more than half of the thirteen California high schools they studied had "major gaps in their offerings or offer[ed] no content classes at all" (p. 8). Five of the thirteen schools offered a smattering of sheltered and ESL classes, but no primary language content classes; three offered some primary language content classes and a range of ESL classes, but not sheltered content classes, and two had no special programs whatsoever. They located only one high school that offered a full curriculum in the students' primary language (Spanish) and

Year 1	ESL Content-Based Instruction	Language L_1	Math L_1	Science L_1	Social Studies L_1
Year 2	ESL	Language L_1	Math-Sheltered	Science-Sheltered	Social Studies L_1
Year 3	Sheltered Literature	Language L_1	Math-English	Science-English	Social Studies Sheltered
Year 4	Language L_1	ENGLISH Content Area Classes			

FIGURE 2.5   Secondary School Bilingual Programs with Native Language Plus Sheltered Content Courses

Year 1	Newcomer Class + Content-Based ESL (+ Community L_1)					
Year 2	ESL		Sheltered Instruction (Science and Math) (+ L_1)			
Year 3	Sheltered Literature and Social Studies		English (+ L_1)			
Year 4		English	Content	Area	Classes	(+ L_1)

FIGURE 2.6   Secondary School Bilingual Programs with ESL and Sheltered Content Courses Only

some ESL classes, but no sheltered content classes. Finally, all except two high schools segregated non-English-speaking students for part of the day, and continued this practice as long as the students remained in a special instructional program.

Does Bilingual Education Work?

By now, you may be asking these kinds of questions: Why are there so many approaches to teaching students who are nonnative speakers of English? Is one approach better than the other? Does bilingual education really work? Don't learners learn English more slowly if you teach them through their native language? These questions come up again and again in debates about bilingual education, and we would like to focus on the issue of whether bilingual education works in this section of Chapter 2.

Effectiveness Issues

A continuing controversy in the field of bilingual education has been that of the effectiveness of bilingual education. Since the passage of the Bilingual Education Act in 1968, numerous federally funded evaluation projects have been conducted to examine whether non-English-speaking learners educated bilingually achieved *in English* as well as or better than non-English-speaking learners educated solely through the medium of English. No attention has been paid to the evaluation of learners' native language abilities (Pease–Alvarez & Hakuta, 1992). Notice that what is implicit in this examination is that achievement in the non-English language is insignificant, a typical transitional philosophy position.

Many influential educators, politicians, and policy-makers have insisted that the best and fastest way for children to learn English was to be educated exclusively through English. The research, which compares the bilingual with nonbilingual ESL approach, however, does not support this claim unilaterally. Some investigators have not found dual language instruction to be any more effective than English-only instruction in terms of the acquisition of English by second language learners (AIR, 1975; Baker & deKanter, 1983; Rossell & Baker, 1996). Others, sometimes reanalyzing the same data, have concluded that bilingual education programs are at least as effective as English-only programs and sometimes more effective (General Accounting Office, 1987; Willig, 1981; 1985). Respected bilingual education advocate and researcher Lily Wong Fillmore accounts for these different findings this way: "Bilingual education done well gives excellent results; bilingual education done badly gives poor results, just as one would expect" (Crawford, 1992b, p. 367).

The most recent large-scale study of bilingual education, funded by Title VII, was carried out by David Ramírez and his associates (Ramírez, Yuen, Ramsay, & Pasta, 1991; Ramírez, 1992). To study the relative effectiveness of bilingual instruction, these researchers compared the English language, English reading, and mathematics achievement (as measured by standardized tests) of English language learners enrolled in three different educational programs: early exit, transitional bilingual education programs; late exit, transitional bilingual programs (which also have been labelled as maintenance because children continue to have opportunities to develop literacy in the native language after third grade); and structured immersion (no use of the native language) programs. Initially, the researchers measured student achievement at the end of each school year, from kindergarten through third grade. When the three groups were compared to each other, no significant differences were found in terms of achievement. Regardless of instructional program, children achieved in English more or less equally well.

In response to the argument that the most effective way to learn English is to learn exclusively through English, these researchers found that substantial use of the native language did *not* impede children's acquisition of English. Bilingual education proponents have used these results to argue for bilingual education, noting that if learners can become biliterate without adverse effects on English achievement, they should be encouraged to do so.

Subsequently, Ramírez and his colleagues collected English language, reading, and mathematics achievement data from the fourth, fifth, and sixth graders who were students in the late exit bilingual classes. When they compared these learners' rates of growth to native English-speaking children on whom the tests had been normed, they found that English language, English reading, and mathematics growth was *greater* for the late exit program children than for the norming population. These findings not only support the earlier conclusion that time spent in the native language does not take away from English, but they are in accord with the position taken by many in bilingual education that high levels of proficiency and literacy in the native language contribute to second language proficiency, and that native language learning and ability is applied to the second language (Carlisle, 1994; Collier, 1995a; Cummins, 1981; Edelsky, 1982; Hudelson, 1987; Krashen, 1996). These findings, then, suggest that more rather than less native language support results in higher achievement in English (Collier, 1995b).

There have been neither large- nor small-scale effectiveness studies conducted at the secondary level. What is available in this regard is a handful of case studies of successful secondary bilingual programs. One example is the Spanish Dual Literacy program at Liberty High School in New York City (Marsh, 1995). Liberty High is a ninth-grade newcomer program open to recent immigrant arrrivals. Newcomer programs are designed to provide "temporary stopovers . . . for recently arrived immigrant students" (Friedlander, 1991, p. 2). Ideally, newcomer programs provide a safe haven for students. The curriculum emphasizes academic as well as nonacademic support systems, such as counseling, health, and information about U. S. school systems (Constantino & Lavadenz, 1993).

The Spanish Dual Literacy program at Liberty High is a special school within a school. Many of the students in the program are from the Dominican Republic and have not had many experiences with literacy in Spanish. The program offers them Spanish literacy classes, plus other content area classes in Spanish. For students who are communicatively fluent in English and literate in Spanish, there are sheltered content classes in social studies, math, and science, and various levels of ESL. Marsh (1995) reports that students who exit from the program enter the regular program at Liberty High well-prepared for the literacy and academic demands of their classes.

Three other case studies of secondary bilingual programs are the bilingual enrichment program at a middle school in Philadelphia, Pennsylvania (Hornberger & Micheau, 1993); a middle school bilingual program in Paradise Valley, Arizona (Faltis, 1994); and the high school Literacy Program for Recent Immigrants in South Texas (Hewlett–Gómez & Solís, 1995). All three studies describe and analyze the design and approaches used to teach bilingually and through sheltered content classes to promote native language literacy and content learning. Although none offers comparative data with nonbilingual programs, all three report successes that mirror those found in well-functioning elementary bilingual programs.

How Long Does It Take to Become Academically Proficient in English?

In a similar vein to the work done by Ramírez and his colleagues (1991), Virginia Collier and Wayne Thomas have carried out a series of longitudinal research projects with school districts across the country. Their aim has been to examine the question of how long (how many years) it takes second language learners enrolled in different kinds of educational programs to compete academically (in English) with native English-speaking students. In order to answer this question, Collier and Thomas (Collier & Thomas, 1989; Collier, 1995a, 1995b; Thomas & Collier, 1995; Olsen & Leone, 1994) have collaborated with five school districts representing different regions of the United States. All of these districts have substantial numbers of second language learners; all have well-established programs for these learners; all have experienced teachers. Using school district records covering a period of eight to twelve years, Collier and Thomas have analyzed ESL student performance in English from kindergarten through twelfth grade according to type of bilingual or ESL program in which the learners were enrolled: ESL-only; ESL taught through content areas; early exit bilingual with traditional ESL; early exit bilingual with ESL taught through content areas; late exit bilingual; and two-way bilingual in which English speakers and language minority students received academic subject matter taught through two languages.

These researchers found that, for second language learners schooled in the United States from kindergarten on, the most effective program in terms of academic achievement is a two-way developmental bilingual program. English as a second language learners in well-designed two-way programs were most likely to attain grade level achievement each year in the native language and achieve in English as well as English speakers *if they had received four to seven years of bilingual schooling*. Following the developmental bilingual model in terms of effectiveness were: maintenance bilingual education, transitional bilingual education with content ESL, transitional bilingual education with traditional ESL, and ESL only (Thomas & Collier, 1995). *However, in the transitional and ESL models, the nonnative English speakers never achieved as well as native English speakers did on standardized tests.*

Collier's and Thomas's findings support their previous research that suggests that it takes from five to seven years for second language learners who have received at least two to three years of schooling in their L_1 to compete with native speakers. Their work also demonstrates that it takes students with no L_1 schooling (either in their home countries or in the United States) seven to ten years to be able to compete with their native English-speaking peers, findings also confirmed by previous research (Collier, 1987; Collier & Thomas, 1989). Their work, then, also supports bilingual education, and specifically bilingual education that acknowledges, as Ramírez and his colleagues found, that *native language support for extended periods of time is beneficial to learners' academic growth.* As Collier (1992) has noted, "the greater the amount of L_1 instructional support for language-minority students, combined with balanced L_2 support, the higher they are able to achieve academically in L_2 in each succeeding academic year" (p. 205). The greatest hope for the long-term achievement of second language learners is quality, long-lasting bilingual education.

Bilingual Education and Native Language Maintenance

We have just considered the effectiveness of bilingual education in terms of bilingual learners' academic achievement in English. But, you may be asking, what about the native languages that children bring to school with them? A major concern of many people is that bilingual education, particularly transitional bilingual education, which places little or no value on the native language, may actually promote subtractive bilingualism, a phenomenon that results when non-English-speaking children choose not to use the native language and shift to more or exclusive use of English (Commins & Miramontes, 1989; Lambert, 1974; Appel & Muysken, 1987). On the one hand, the native language may be used for instruction, but on the other hand the message that children receive is that it is English achievement that counts. So rather than adding on English to what they already use, many ESL learners substitute English for the native language and subtract the native tongue from their linguistic repertoires.

In thinking about the phenomenon of subtractive bilingualism, it is important to keep in mind that schools exist within larger societies. In the United States, many would argue that English, while not the official language of the country (since the United States has no official language policy), enjoys a certain status over other languages used in this country. Joshua Fishman (1976) has described this status in terms of what he calls *markedness* and *unmarkedness.* In most contexts in the United States, English is the language we expect to hear and see—it is the expected, unmarked language. Other languages, those we are surprised to hear and see, are marked languages. According to Fishman, an unmarked language has a status that a marked language lacks.

The Power of English

Using different terms, Sheila Shannon (1995) has argued that English enjoys what she terms *hegemony* over other languages. By hegemony she means the unequal status of languages vis-à-vis each other. One language is believed to be superior, desirable, and necessary, while the other(s) is/are considered inferior, undesirable, and unnecessary. In the United States, English is the dominant language, the language of politics and government, the language of most social and economic opportunity. While other languages are used in this country, they do not share this status and are, in fact, overwhelmed and dominated by English. Thus societal pressure to use English is great. We agree with Shannon that the agenda of transitional bilingual education is consistent with the hegemony of English in this country.

It should not be surprising, then, that numbers of studies have demonstrated that non-English-speaking children in many bilingual education programs choose to use English, rather than the native language, early on in their schooling experiences. In an extensive examination of a bilingual school, for example, Escamilla found significant discrepancies between the status accorded to Spanish and English, so that the message transmitted to children was that Spanish was useful only as a bridge to English (Escamilla,1994). In a single transitional bilingual education classroom setting, Griego–Jones (1994) found that Spanish-speaking kindergarten children she interviewed expressed a preference for using English even though they were more fluent in Spanish. In another classroom study, Spanish-speaking first graders in a bilingual program with a stated goal of bilingualism for all children consistently tried to communicate with their English-speaking peers in less than fluent English rather than their fluent Spanish. Conversely the English-speaking children did not try to use the Spanish they supposedly were learning, but instead expected the Spanish speakers to use English (Edelsky & Hudelson, 1980, 1982).

In a maintenance bilingual program that utilized children's literature in Spanish and English, Hudelson (1992) found that the Spanish speakers began to choose to read books in English long before their teachers began formal literacy instruction in English and, by third grade, many expressed preferences for English books. There is even evidence that preschool non-English-speaking children in ostensibly bilingual preschool and Head Start programs may begin to choose English over the native language before they enter the public schools (Wong Fillmore, 1991). Thus the predominant bilingual education model that places value exclusively on achievement in English may have negative effects on children's use and retention of languages other than English (Escamilla, 1994). Speakers of languages other than English often feel the need to shift into using English in order to achieve acceptance and status in school (Commins, 1989; Commins & Miramontes, 1989). Preference for English over Spanish has even been documented among children enrolled in two-way bilingual programs, although this happens more noticeably among older (fourth graders and above) rather than younger children (Lambert & Cazabon, 1994; Holland, 1997).

And what about the native English speakers enrolled in some (but certainly not all) bilingual classes? The hegemony of English has effects on their second language learning as well. In most transitional and maintenance bilingual programs, English speakers do not achieve second language proficiency, especially in comparison to the non-English-speaking children's achievement of proficiency in English. The predominance of English in most communities (and even in bilingual schools) virtually assures that English speakers do not learn the non-English language of bilingual programs (Edelsky, 1991). In well-designed two-way programs, there is evidence of significant second language learning by the English speakers, (Cazabon, Lambert, & Hall, 1993; Holland, 1997; Lindholm, 1994; Lambert & Cazabon, 1994), especially because students have multiple opportunities to use the target language with native-speaking peers as they engage in academic learning (Genesee, 1994), but these programs, as noted earlier, do not predominate (there are fewer than 200 nationally).

Resisting English Hegemony

We do not want to suggest that *all* bilingual classrooms contribute, intentionally or otherwise, to the devaluing of languages other than English. Many teachers *are* concerned to promote learners' home languages, and we have several documented examples of teachers who actively resist the hegemony of English and work deliberately to build the status of the nonEnglish language in the bilingual classroom (Constantino & Faltis, 1997). For example, in one multiage (grades 1, 2, and 3) primary Spanish–English class, with almost equal numbers of native English and Spanish speakers, the bilingual teacher, Ms. G., works to promote the use of both languages for learning. She makes Spanish as visible as English in the classroom in the form of wall charts, content area semantic webs, labels, directions, the calendar, alphabet trains, songs, rhymes, chants, and so on. The class collection of Spanish language children's literature is equal in quality and quantity to the English language collection. Ms. G. reads aloud to the whole class every day in both Spanish and English, providing paraphrasing in the other language as necessary. She also teams with the teacher next door to split their classes for language-specific read alouds, providing a time for children from both language groups to listen to and discuss a story read in one language exclusively. Ms. G. often reads aloud poetry in Spanish without translating, in order for all the children to enjoy the rhythm and sounds of Spanish.

Ms. G. uses both languages for all aspects of the school day and allows the children to work in the language or languages they choose. Both languages are used constantly. In class meetings Ms. G. calls attention to children's use of their second language, celebrating especially attempts of English speakers to use Spanish. Ms. G. speaks frequently about the importance and value of being bilingual and encourages the children to do so as well. Bilingual children frequently serve as translators for children who are not bilingual, and they are able to lead activities such as class meetings because they can use both languages. Finally, children are not allowed to make fun of the ways others speak or of attempts to experiment with a new language. This kind of behavior is discussed and sanctioned at class meetings (Turner, 1994).

In a fourth grade classroom populated by English- and Spanish-speaking children, the bilingual teacher, Ms. Andrade, has decided that she wants to emphasize the value of both languages, and the importance of utilizing one's native language as a learning tool. She accomplishes this in a variety of ways. In whole group discussions Ms. Andrade elicits comments from the children in Spanish as well as in English, even when the lesson is being conducted basically in English. The Spanish-speaking children receive encouragement to write in their native language as well as English, and the English speakers receive encouragement to experiment with writing in Spanish. When children share their writing with the class, the teacher asks the English speakers, with the help of a bilingual buddy, to try to translate or paraphrase from English into Spanish.

The classroom is organized into groups, each group consisting of English speakers, Spanish speakers, bilinguals, boys and girls, and children of varying abilities. Ms. Andrade creates these heterogeneous clusters in order to put the language groups in constant contact with each other, promote children assisting each other, and challenge the children to learn each other's language. The children use both languages for their learning. The bilingual children frequently use both languages to make sure that everyone in the group understands the task to be accomplished and contributes to the final product (Reyes, Laliberty, & Orbansky, 1993).

A third example of resisting the hegemony of English comes from another fourth grade teacher who teaches a class of English speakers, Spanish speakers, and bilingual learners. This teacher, Ms. D., believes strongly that bilingual teachers have to monitor themselves constantly with regard to how they use language for classroom activities and in interactions with students, coworkers, parents, and visitors. In her own teaching this means that Ms. D. thinks about her language choice and language use when planning and carrying out all of her teaching activities, including asking and answering questions, giving directions, and explaining content. She monitors her own language use. She consciously uses both languages for instruction, thus providing opportunities for children to interact both in their native and second languages. Ms. D. allows the children in her classroom to choose whether they will work in English or Spanish, and she encourages working in Spanish. As does Ms. G., Ms. D. provides her children materials, including children's literature, of equal quality in Spanish and English.

Ms. D. takes a definite stance with regard to the Spanish language. She works tirelessly to convince all those she comes in contact with (the children in the classroom, some of the parents and school staff) that the Spanish language is fun and beautiful and that it is worth learning and maintaining. She encourages both native Spanish speakers and English speakers to use Spanish. She especially encourages English speakers to experiment with Spanish, for example, by sprinkling Spanish words in her responses to the children's English language journal entries, and by speaking in Spanish to English speakers. Ms. D. urges the children to take risks with their new language and models risk-taking herself. She also disallows racist remarks of any kind in the classroom (Shannon, 1995).

As you can see, the issue of the role and status of languages other than English in bilingual classrooms is a complex one. It has been our experience that educators working in bilingual settings are committed to valuing and maintaining languages other than English, while simultaneously promoting English proficiency. But are they really able to accomplish this, and, if so, how? As you become a bilingual education professional, we hope that you will reflect on your own work in light of some of the points raised here.

How Do Bilingual Classes Really Function?

We hope that the discussion so far is leading you to wonder about how bilingual classes really operate. Maybe you are wondering about such issues as: How do teachers actually teach bilingually? Is everything done in two languages? If not, how do teachers distribute the time they spend in each language? Do teachers spend their days translating? How do they make sure that the students are learning? Do students have to learn everything in two languages? These and many other questions reflect the complexity of bilingual programs. There are no simple or single answers, because bilingual programs, as you are beginning to see, vary widely in terms of goals, languages, and populations served, personnel and instructional resources available to carry out the programs, community realities, external political pressures, and many other factors. There are many ways in which programs have been designed and implemented (see sources such as Andersson & Boyer, 1978; Ramírez, 1985; Saville & Troike, 1977; Trueba & Barnett–Mizrahi, 1979 for discussions of these options, with an emphasis on elementary school settings). We will consider here some basic ways that a bilingual teacher might work and expand on these ideas in subsequent chapters.

Perhaps the most common bilingual education design at both the elementary and secondary levels is to utilize bilingual teachers in self-contained classrooms, where the teachers are responsible for implementing the curriculum. Some bilingual classrooms contain no or very few speakers of English. Other bilingual classrooms are populated by some monolingual (or dominant) users of a language other than English, some English dominant or English monolingual learners, and some bilingual students (see for example, García, 1991; Marsh, 1995). In such diverse settings bilingual teachers may divide up the day in terms of language in one or more ways; for example:

- They may choose to use one language for instruction on one day and the other language for instruction on the next day (the alternate days model);
- They may use one language for instruction in the morning and the other in the afternoon (alternate times);
- They may use one language for certain areas of the curriculum and another language for other areas (for example, language arts instruction in the native language, mathematics instruction in English);
- They may begin a school year spending almost all instructional time in the native language and, over time, increase the amount of time that is spent in English (Cazden, 1988);
- They may translate content and instructions from one language into the other (as in concurrent translation);
- They may use both languages concurrently (without translation), switching from one language to another depending on the topic and context of the activity (whole class vs. small group). Likewise, teachers may alternate languages while working individually with specific learners to establish rapport or scaffold interaction (Jacobson, 1981; Milk, 1981; Wong Fillmore, 1982);
- They may preview content in one language, switch to the other language for the content presentation, and then review in the first language (Moll & Díaz, 1985; Delgado–Gaitán, 1991). For example, a teacher may decide to read a story in English to a class of Russian and English speakers. She may begin by summarizing the story in Russian, then read the story entirely in English, and then encourage the students to ask questions and respond in both Russian and English;
- They may use English as the medium of instruction but allow the learners to express their understandings in the native language, being careful to translate what they have said into English (as in English immersion);
- They may utilize team-teaching. In most team-teaching situations, one member of the team is a monolingual speaker of English, while the other team member is either bilingual or dominant in the non-English language. This means that the English speaker teaches content in English to all the learners, while the speaker of the other language teaches content in the other language to all the students.

In some bilingual settings, especially where the non-English language is a less common language and where fewer certified personnel are available, a kind of teaming may occur between a certified teacher and an instructional aide. This usually means that the certified teacher presents all content in English and the bilingual aide both translates for those learners who do not understand English and helps the students accomplish their English language school work. While this situation may be necessary under certain circumstances, it is less than ideal, particularly because it presents a view of the native language as useful only for translation and not for substantive learning. It may also present a view of the non-English language speaker as subservient to the English speaker and suggest to learners that only native English speakers may aspire to be teachers. We believe that if instructional assistants are utilized in schools as translators, the school districts involved should develop plans to facilitate these individuals becoming certified teachers.

The content delivery alternatives just outlined may suggest to you that there are clear-cut ways to teach bilingually and that all teachers have to do is decide on an approach and carry it out. However, the reality is a lot more complex, as researchers have discovered when they have examined how two languages are actually used in classroom settings. Several examples of the theoretical or ideal contrasted to the real are provided to illustrate the complexities of bilingual classrooms.

In the alternative days model, languages supposedly are separated from each other according to timeblocks: one day Spanish, the next day English. There is some evidence, however, that, in some classrooms containing both English and Spanish dominant children, English intrudes on Spanish days much more often than vice versa. The reason? There is concern that the English speakers will not understand when content is presented all in Spanish (and in fact the English speakers complain that they do not understand). But there is not a similar concern expressed for the Spanish speakers, and the Spanish speakers do not tend to protest the use of English (Edelsky & Hudelson, 1982).

Many bilingual programs stress separation of the two languages, believing that learners will achieve high levels of proficiency in two languages only if the two languages are separated (Wong Fillmore & Valadez, 1986). But for bilingual people, the concurrent utilization of two languages is a day-to-day reality. Within conversations, it is normal to switch from one language to the other and back again (Grosjean, 1982). Thus bilingual teachers, when instructing in one language, may codeswitch into the other, often without being conscious of doing so. Sometimes switching occurs for instructional reasons, such as assuring that children understand information (see Faltis, 1989, 1997 and the Bilingual Social Studies vignette in Chapter 6 for examples of this kind of switching). There is also evidence that teachers switch out of English and into the home language in order to control learners' behavior, because the home language is associated with respect for adults (Cazden, 1988).

Most bilingual education programs advocate that teachers use the children's native language for subject matter instruction. But there is evidence from the Ramírez study that some teachers in Spanish–English bilingual education programs, especially in the early exit elementary programs, do not have sufficient proficiency in Spanish to teach effectively in that language (Cazden, 1992). This may mean that, in spite of a bilingual design, more content is being delivered through English. The reality of many bilingual teachers' English dominance should not be surprising, because most individuals who are currently teaching bilingually went to school themselves basically in English. And if this is true for Spanish it is probably true for other languages as well, and certainly has an effect on both the quantity and quality of native language use and instruction (see Bialystok & Hakuta, 1994).

Bilingual programs usually stress native language literacy, but in many languages there are limited written resources, such as literature and environmental print, available. Additionally, some non-English languages employed in bilingual programs have only recently been written, so many community members are not literate in them, and controversies exist in some communities over which written version of the language to teach (Edelsky & Hudelson, 1989). These realities need to be recognized because they may influence classroom instruction and have an effect on learners' understandings of and attitudes toward literacy.

Concluding Remarks

In this chapter we hope that we have made you more aware of some of the possible ways that instruction for bilingual and second language learners may be organized. We hope we have raised your awareness of the complexities of what is called *bilingual instruction.* We also hope that you will participate in school and district (and perhaps even state) level discussions about how to provide quality education experiences for the linguistic and culturally diverse learners who populate our schools. As you work with others on this issue, we hope that you will keep in mind the following points made in this chapter:

- Schools with numbers of nonnative English-speaking learners must respond in some way to the special needs of these students, in order that the learners may benefit from education.
- Responses may include the design and implementation of instructional

programs that are bilingual (that make use of the learners' native language) or that provide special English as a second language service.

- Bilingual programs at both the elementary and secondary levels vary in their goals. Most programs are transitional in nature, having as their goal non-English-speaking learners' acquisition of and achievement in and through English. There is also, however, growing interest at the elementary level in enrichment bilingual programs, which have the goal of encouraging bilingualism in all learners, native speakers of English and speakers of other languages alike.
- ESL and sheltered content programs vary in how they are organized to help learners acquire English and learn content through that language.
- There is tremendous variation in how bilingual/second language programs at both the elementary and secondary levels are designed and implemented. There are often also tremendous differences between the theoretical design and the practical reality.
- Nonnative English speakers need considerable time (between four and ten years) before they are able to achieve in English at levels comparable to those of native English speakers. Very often the special services provided by districts and schools do not provide support for the length of time it is really needed, most notably at the secondary level.
- Quality bilingual education programs work well in terms of academic experiences and the English language achievement of non-English speakers. These learners have the added advantage of bilingualism and biliteracy in school language.

In the next chapter, we present our ideas with regard to the need to view bilingual education as a schoolwide issue, and not simply as a special program separate from the rest of the school. In light of this perspective, we examine ways that bilingual elementary and secondary schools recognize an effective plan and implement bilingual education, and we follow this with a section on bilingual schools that we have visited and observed over time. Chapter 3 serves to introduce our framework for bilingual education, a framework that we will elaborate in subsequent chapters.

References

American Institute for Research. (1975). *Identification and description of exemplary bilingual education programs.* Palo Alto, CA: AIR.

Andersson, T., & Boyer, M. (1978). *Bilingual schooling in the United States.* 2nd ed. Austin, TX: National Educational Laboratory Publishers.

Appel, R., & Muyksen, P. (1987). *Language contact and bilingualism.* London: Edward Arnold.

Au, K. (1993). *Literacy instruction in the multicultural settings.* Fort Worth, TX: Harcourt, Brace and Jovanovich.

Auerbach, E. (1993). Reexamining English only in the ESL classroom. *TESOL Quarterly, 28*(1), 9–32.

Baker, C. (1988). *Key issues in bilingualism and bilingual education.* Clevedon, England: Multilingual Matters.

Baker, K., & deKanter, A. (1983). Federal policy and the effectiveness of bilingual education. In K. Baker and A. deKanter (Eds.), *Bilingual education* (pp. 33–86). Lexington, MA: Lexington Books.

Bialystok, E., & Hakuta, K. (1944). *In other words: The science and psychology of second-language acquisition.* New York: Basic Books.

Campbell, R. (1984). The immersion approach to foreign language teaching. In Office of Bilingual Education, *Studies on immersion education* (pp. 114–143). Sacramento, CA: California State Department of Education.

Cantoni-Harvey, G. (1987). *Content-area language instruction: Approaches and strategies.* Reading, MA: Addison-Wesley.

Carlisle, R. (1994). Influences of L1 writing proficiency on L2 writing proficiency. In R. A. DeVillar, C. Faltis, & J. Cummins (Eds.), *Cultural diversity in schools: From rhetoric to practice* (pp. 161–188). Albany, NY: SUNY Press.

Casanova, U. (1991). Bilingual education: Politics or pedagogy? In O. García (Ed.), *Bilingual education: Focusschrift in honor of Joshua A. Fishman on the occasion of his 65th birthday* (pp. 167–180). Amsterdam/Philadelphia: John Benjamins Publishing.

Cazabon, M., Lambert, W., & Hall, G. (1993). *Two-way bilingual education: A progress report on the amigos program.* Santa Cruz, CA: National Center for Research on Cultural Diversity and Second Language Learning.

Cazden, C. (1992). *Language minority education in the United States: Implications of the Ramírez report.* Santa Cruz, CA.: National Center for Research on Cultural Diversity and Second Language Teaching.

Cazden, C. (1988). *Classroom discourse: The language of teaching and learning.* Portsmouth, NH: Heinemann.

Christian, D. (1996). Two-way bilingual programs institute. Session 1. Center for Bilingual Education and Research, Arizona State University. December 7.

Christian, D. (1994). *Two-way bilingual education: Students learning through two languages.* Santa Cruz, CA: National Center for Research on Cultural Diversity and Second Language Learning.

Cohen, A. (1975). *A sociolinguistic approach to bilingual education.* Rowley, MA: Newbury House.

Collier, V. (1997). Two-way bilingual institute. Session 3. Center for Bilingual Education and Research, Arizona State University, February 1.

Collier, V. (1995a). Acquiring a second language for school. *Directions in language and education, 1*(4). Washington, DC: National Clearinghouse for Bilingual Education.

Collier, V. (1995b). *Promoting academic success for ESL students: Understanding second language acquisition for school.* Elizabeth, NJ: New Jersey Teachers of English to Speakers of Other Languages–Bilingual Educators.

Collier, V. (1992). A synthesis of studies examining long-term-language-minority student data on academic achievement. *Bilingual Research Journal, 16*(1&2), 187–212.

Collier, V., & Thomas, W. P. (1989). How quickly can immigrants become proficient in English? *Journal of Educational Issues of Language Minority Students, 5,* 26–38.

Commins, N. (1989). Language and affect: Bilingual students at home and at school. *Language Arts, 66,* 29–43.

Commins, N. (1994). Planning for two-way bilingualism in whole language bilingual programs. Paper presented at the Annual TESOL Convention, Atlanta, April.

Commins, N., & Miramontes, O. (1989). Perceived and actual linguistic competence: A descriptive study of four low-achieving Hispanic bilingual students. *American Educational Research Journal, 26,* 443–472.

Constantino, R., & Faltis, C. (1997). Teaching against the grain in bilingual education: Resistance in the classroom underlife. In H. T. Trueba & Y. Zao (Eds.), *Ethnic identity and power: Cultural contexts of political actions in school and society.* Albany, NY: SUNY Press.

Constantino, R., & Lavadenz, M. (1993). Newcomer schools: First impressions. *Peabody Journal of Education, 69*(1), 82–101.

Crandell, J. (Ed.). (1987). *ESL through content area instruction: Mathematics, science, social studies.* Englewood Cliffs, NJ: Prentice-Hall.

Crawford, J. (1992a). *Hold your tongue: Bilingualism and politics of "English only."* Reading, MA: Addison-Wesley.

Crawford, J. (1992b). *Language loyalties: A source book on the official English controversy.* Chicago: University of Chicago Press.

Crawford, J. (1989). *Bilingual education: History, politics, theory and practice.* Trenton, NJ: Crane.

Cummins, J. (1981). The role of primary language development in promoting educational success for language minority students. In *Schooling and language minority: A theoretical framework.* Los Angeles: Dissemination and Assessment Center, California State University.

Daniels, H. (Ed.). (1990). *Not only English: Affirming America's multilingual heritage.* Urbana, IL: National Council of Teachers of English.

Delgado–Gaitán, C. (1991). Relating experience and text: Socially constituted reading activity. In M. McGroarty & C. Faltis (Eds.), *Languages in school and society: Policy and pedagogy* (pp. 512–528). Berlin: Mouton de Gruyter.

Edelsky, C. (1991). *With literacy and justice for all: Rethinking the social in language and education.* New York: Falmer Press.

Edelsky, C. (1982). Writing in a bilingual program: The relation of L1 and L2 texts. *TESOL Quarterly, 16,* 211–228.

Edelsky, C., & Hudelson, S. (1989). *Contextual complexities: Written language policies for bilingual programs.* Berkeley, CA: Center for the Study of Writing Occasional Papers.

Edelsky, C., & Hudelson, S. (1982). The acquisition(?) of Spanish as a second language. In F. Barkin, E. Brandt, & J. Ornstein–Galicia (Eds.), *Bilingualism and language contact: Spanish, English and Native American languages* (pp. 203–227). New York: Teachers College Press.

Edelsky, C., & Hudelson, S. (1980). Second language acquisition of a marked language. *National Association for Bilingual Education Journal, 5*(1), 1–15.

ERIC Digest (1994). Two-way bilingual education programs in practice: A national and local perspective. Washington, DC: Center for Applied Linguistics.

Escamilla, K. (1994). The sociolinguistic environment of a bilingual school: A case study introduction. *Bilingual Research Journal, 18,* 21–48.

Faltis, C. (1997). *Joinfostering: Adapting teaching strategies for the multilingual classroom.* 2nd ed. New Jersey: Prentice–Hall.

Faltis, C. (1994). Doing the right thing: Developing a program for immigrant and bilingual secondary students. In R. Rodríguez & N. Ramos (Eds.), *Compendium of readings on bilingual education* (pp. 39–47). San Antonio, TX: Texas Association for Bilingual Education.

Faltis, C. (1993a). Critical issues in the use of sheltered content teaching in high school bilingual programs. *Peabody Journal of Education, 69*(1), 136–151.

Faltis, C. (1993b). *Joinfostering: Adapting teaching strategies for the multilingual classroom.* New York: Merrill (Macmillan).

Faltis, C. (1989). Code-switching and bilingual schooling: An examination of Jacobson's new concurrent approach. *Journal of Multilingual and Multicultural Development, 10*(2), 117–127.

Faltis, C., & Arias, M.B. (1993). Speakers of languages other than English in the secondary school: Accomplishments and struggles. *Peabody Journal of Education, 69*(1), 6–29.

Faltis, C., & Hudelson, S. (1994). Learners of English as an additional language in K–12 schools. *TESOL Quarterly, 28*(3), 457–468.

Fishman, J. (1976). *Bilingual education: An international sociological perspective.* Rowley, MA: Newbury House.

Freeman, D., & Freeman, Y. (1994). Whole language learning and teaching for second language learners. In C. Weaver (Ed.), *Reading process and practice,* 2nd ed. (pp. 558–630). Portsmouth, NH: Heinemann.

Freeman, D., & Freeman, Y. (1993). Strategies for promoting the primary languages of all students. *The Reading Teacher, 46*(7), 552–558.

Friedlander, M. (1991). *The newcomer programs: Helping immigrant students succeed in U. S. schools.* Washington, DC: National Clearinghouse for Bilingual Education.

García, E. (1991). *The education of linguistically and culturally diverse students: Effective instructional practices.* Santa Cruz, CA: The National Center for Research on Cultural Diversity and Second Language Learning.

General Accounting Office. (1987). *Bilingual education: A new look at the research evidence.* Washington, DC: United States General Accounting Office.

Genesee, F. (1994). *Integrating language and content: Lessons from immersion.* Santa Cruz, CA: National Center for Research on Cultural Diversity and Second Language Learning.

Genesee, F. (1987). *Learning through two languages: Studies of immersion and bilingual education.* Rowley, MA: Newbury House.

González, L. (1994). Effectiveness of bilingual education: A comparison of various approaches in an elementary school district. In R. DeVillar, C. Faltis, & J. Cummins (Eds.), *Cultural diversity in schools: From rhetoric to practice,* (pp. 233–260). Albany: SUNY Press

Griego–Jones, T. (1994). Assessing students' perceptions of biliteracy in two way bilingual classrooms. *Journal of Educational Issues of Language Minority Students, 13,* 79–94.

Grosjean, F. (1982). *Life with two languages: An introduction to bilingualism.* Cambridge: Harvard University Press.

Hamayan, E. (n.d.). personal communication.

Heath, S. B. (1983). *Ways with words.* New York: Cambridge University Press.

Hewlett–Gómez, M., & Solís, A. (1995). Dual language instructional design for educating recent immigrant secondary students on the Texas–Mexico border. *Bilingual Research Journal, 19*(3&4), 429–452.

Holland, P. (1997). Two-way bilingual institite. Session 2. Center for Bilingual Education and Research, Arizona State University. January 11.

Hornberger, J. (1991). Extending enrichment bilingual education: Revisiting typologies and redirecting policy. In O. García (Ed.), *Bilingual education: Focusschrift in honor of Joshua A. Fishman on the occasion of his 65th birthday,* (pp. 215–234). Amsterdam/Philadelphia: John Benjamins Publishing.

Hornberger, N., & Micheau, C. (1993). "Getting far enough to like it": Biliteracy in the middle school. *Peabody Journal of Education, 69*(1), 30–53.

Hudelson, S. (1992). Reading in a bilingual program. *Canadian Children, 17*(2), 13–26.

Hudelson, S. (1989). *Write on: Children's writing in ESL.* Englewood Cliffs, NJ: Prentice-Hall and ERIC Clearinghouse on Languages and Linguistics.

Hudelson, S. (1987). The role of native language literacy in the education of language minority children. *Language Arts, 64*(8), 827–841.

Jacobson, R. (1981). The implementation of a bilingual instructional model: The new concurrent approach. in P. G. Gonzales (Ed.), *Proceedings of the Eighth Annual International Bilingual Bicultural Education Conference at Seattle.* Rosslyn, VA: National Clearinghouse for Bilingual Education.

Kachru, B., & Nelson, C. (1996). World Englishes. In N. Hornberger & S. McKay (Eds.), *Sociolinguistics and language teaching,* (pp. 71–102). New York: Cambridge University Press.

Krashen, S. (1985). *The input hypothesis: Issues and implications.* New York: Longman.

Labov, W. (1970). The logic of nonstandard English. In F. Williams (Ed.), *The language of poverty.* Chicago: Markham Publishing.

Lambert, W. (1974). Culture and language as factors in learning and education. In F. E. Aboud & R. D. Meade (Eds.), *Cultural factors in learning and education.* (pp. 72–95). Bellingham, WA: Fifth Western Washington Symposium on Learning.

Lambert, W., & Cazabon, M. (1994). *Students' views of the Amigos program.* Santa Cruz, CA: National Center for Research on Cultural Diversity and Second Language Learning.

Lambert, W., & Tucker, R. (1972) *Bilingual education of children: The St. Lambert experiment.* Rowley, MA: Newbury House.

Lindfors, J. (1987). *Children's language and learning,* 2nd ed. Englewood Cliffs, NJ: Prentice-Hall.

Lindholm, K. (1994). Promoting positive cross-cultural attitudes and perceived competence in culturally and linguistically diverse classrooms. In R. A. DeVillar, C. Faltis, & J. Cummins (Eds.), *Cultural diversity in schools: From rhetoric to practice,* (pp. 189–206). Albany, NY: SUNY Press.

Lucas, T. (1993). Secondary schooling for students becoming bilingual. In M. B. Arias & U. Casanova (Eds.). *Bilingual education: Politics, practice, research* (113–143). Chicago, IL: NSSE.

Lucas, T., & Katz, A. (1994). Reframing the debate: The roles of native languages in English-only programs for language minority students. *TESOL Quarterly, 28*(3), 537–562.

Mackey, W. F., & Beebe, V. N. (1977). *Bilingual schools for a bicultural community.* Rowley, MA: Newbury House.

Marsh, L. (1995). A Spanish dual literacy program: Teaching to the whole student. *Bilingual Research Journal, 19*(3&4), 409–428.

Milk, R. (1981). An analysis of the functional allocation of Spanish and English in a bilingual classroom. *CABE Research Journal, 2*(2), 11–26.

Minicucci, C., & Olsen, L. (Eds.). (1992). *Educating students from immigrant families: Meeting the challenge in secondary schools.* Santa Cruz, CA: National Center for Research on Cultural Diversity and Second Language Learning.

Moll, L., & Díaz, S. (1985). Ethnographic pedagogy: Promoting effective bilingual instruction. In E. García & R. Padilla (Eds.), *Advances in bilingual education research,* (pp. 127–149). Tucson: University of Arizona Press.

National Board for Professional Teaching Standards (1996). *English as a new language: Standards for national board certification* (Draft). Washington, DC: National Board for Professional Teaching Standards.

National Council of Teachers of English (1996). *Standards for the English language arts.* Urbana, IL.: National Council of Teachers of English.

Olsen, R., & Leone, B. (1994). Sociocultural processes in academic, cognitive, and language development. *TESOL Matters, 4*(3) 1,18.

Pease–Alvarez, L., & Hakuta, K. (1992). Enriching our views of bilingualism and bilingual education. *Educational Researcher, 21*(2), 7–9.

Pease–Alvarez, L., & Winsler, A. (1994). Cuando el maestro no habla español: Children's bilingual language practices in the classroom. *TESOL Quarterly, 28*(3), 507–536.

Ramírez, A. (1985). *Bilingualism through schooling: Cross cultural education for minority and majority students.* Albany: SUNY Press.

Ramírez, D., Yuen, S., Ramsay, D., & Pasta, D. (1991). *Final report: Longitudinal study of structured English immersion strategy, early-exit, and late-exit bilingual education programs for language-minority children,* vol. 1. San Mateo, CA: Aguirre International.

Ramírez, J. D. (1992). Executive summary. *Bilingual Research Journal, 16*(1&2), 1–61.

Reyes, M., Laliberty, E., & Orbansky, J. (1993). Emerging biliteracy and cross-cultural sensitivity in a language arts classroom. *Language Arts, 70*(8), 659–669.

Rigg, P., & Allen, V. (Eds.). (1989). *When they don't all speak English.* Urbana, IL: National Council of Teachers of English.

Rossell, C., & Baker, K. (1996). The educational effectiveness of bilingual education. *Research in the Teaching of English, 30* (1), 7–74.

Salinas, R. (1992). Sheltered English for teaching content. In C. Minicucci & L. Olsen (Eds.), *Educating students from immigrant families: Meeting the challenge in secondary schools,* (pp. 55–57). Santa Cruz: National Center for Research on Cultural Diversity and Second Language Learning.

Saville M., & Troike, R. (1977). *A handbook of bilingual education,* rev. ed. Washington, DC: Teachers of English to Speakers of Other Languages.

Shannon, S. (1995). The hegemony of English: A case study of one bilingual classroom as a site of resistance. *Linguistics and Education, 7,* 175–200.

TESOL (1996). *Promising futures.* Alexandria, VA: Teachers of English to Speakers of Other Languages.

Thomas, W., & Collier, V. (1995). *Language minority student achievement and program effectiveness.* Washington, DC: National Clearinghouse for Bilingual Education.

Trueba, H., & Barnett–Mizrahi, C. (Eds.). (1979). *Bilingual multicultural education and the professional: From theory to practice.* Rowley, MA: Newbury House.

Turner, E. (1994). *Emerging bilingualism and biliteracy in a primary, multi-age bilingual classroom.* Unpublished Honors Thesis, Arizona State University, Tempe, AZ.

Willig, A. (1985). Meta-analysis of selected studies on the effectiveness of bilingual education. *Review of Educational Research, 55,* 269–317.

Willig, A. (1981). The effectiveness of bilingual education: Review of a report. *National Association for Bilingual Education Journal, 6*(2/3), 1–20.

Wong Fillmore, L. (1991). When learning a second language means losing the first. *Early Childhood Research Quarterly, 6*(3), 323–346.

Wong Fillmore, L. (1982). Instructional language as linguistic input: Second language learning in classrooms. In L. C. Wilkinson (Ed.), *Communication in the Classroom,* (pp. 283–296). New York: Academic Press.

Wong Fillmore, L., & Valadez, C. (1986). Teaching bilingual learners. In M. C. Wittrock (Ed.), *Handbook of research on teaching,* 3rd ed., (pp. 648–685). New York: Macmillan.

3

Bilingual Education as a Schoolwide Concern

In the first two chapters we chronicled the evolution of bilingual schooling in the United States and looked at the kinds of special educational programs educators have developed in response to the needs of learners who are speakers of languages other than English. By now you may be wondering how you will fit into this complicated picture. In order to answer that question, we turn to the challenge of creating and sustaining positive social and educational climates for bilingual and becoming bilingual students in a setting that is particularly meaningful to the majority of educators: the whole school community. In this chapter we briefly examine the literature on effective bilingual schools, and then share the stories of four schools that are committed to high quality education for all students. In concert with the research on effective bilingual schools, a major thrust of this commitment at each of the four schools has been to move away from viewing bilingual education as a program apart from other schooling efforts. Instead, these schools have found ways to restructure their policies and practices to integrate bilingual education in all aspects of the school community by having knowledgeable and caring teachers, teacher-aides, and other staff, and by promoting an accepting and inviting social climate.

We highlight specific schools because it has been our experience that the most significant positive changes in learning environments and opportunities have occurred within individual buildings where teachers, administrators, and other staff have collaborated to improve their service to all learners within the particular site. This is not to say that federal, state, and even district policies, initiatives, and leadership have been unimportant in providing an impetus or a framework for self-examination and change. But it is to assert, as have many who have examined what they term *restructuring* in U. S. schools (see, for example, Hudelson & Faltis, 1993; Merino & Faltis, 1993), that change that makes a difference in terms of the daily lives of learners stems mainly from grassroots efforts, from the bottom up, and that it must involve the participation of the majority of personnel in a school (see Escamilla, 1994, for an example of an elementary school; Minicucci, 1996, for middle school examples; and Olsen, 1992; Lucas, 1992, for high school restructuring efforts).

Effective Bilingual Schools

The Carter and Chatfield Study: Elementary School

The move to restructure schools to make them more inclusive and, at the same time, raise and sustain students' academic performance, has been based primarily on results from studies of effective schools, particularly those in which poor children, both bilingual and English-only, perform very well academically. One of the first studies of this type examined three elementary schools with well-established bilingual programs and very high student outcomes (Carter & Chatfield, 1986). Carter and Chatfield were particularly interested in studying the three schools that had been recognized as effective to identify the features that contributed to their effectiveness. To be recognized as an effective school, a majority of students must have consistently achieved above grade level on national standardized exams. Once the schools were selected, Carter and Chatfield found that in all three settings, there was (1) knowledgeable leadership and direction, (2) continual staff development, and (3) a positive social environment. The schools also stood out academically in a way not characteristic of most bilingual schools: Students in the bilingual program performed as well or better than their English-speaking peers in nonbilingual classrooms.

To understand effective bilingual schools in depth, Carter and Chatfield (1986) focused on one particular school, Lauderbach Elementary School in Chula Vista, California. They were interested in learning how the bilingual program and the school community interacted. What follows is a summary of their description and analysis of this effective bilingual elementary school:

> *The bilingual program is not a separate part of the school but rather participates in, partakes of,* and contributes to *the positive student and educational climate outcomes. It is possible to point to specific aspects of the bilingual program that appear to be especially important: the careful attention given to the issue of reclassification, the coordination between bilingual*

and non-bilingual curricular objectives and materials, the careful monitoring of student progress, the high degree of total staff acceptance of the bilingual program, the strong volunteer program, and so on. The important point, however, is that these features do not act in some simple, linear manner; rather, they interact in a complex way, and they interact with other aspects of school organization and culture that are not specifically bilingual in character. . . . The school does not make the bilingual program effective; neither does the program make the school effective. The program, as an integral part of school activities, contributes to and mirrors the overall effectiveness (pp. 226–227, emphasis in original).

In addition, Carter and Chatfield found that processes, rather than structures or particular curriculum strands, contributed in important ways to the effectiveness of Lauderbach Elementary. Among the processes they found present at Lauderbach were:

- A safe, positive, and orderly school climate;
- Positive leadership, from the principal on down;
- Clearly stated academic goals, objectives, and mission statement;
- Well-organized classrooms;
- High staff expectations for students and a strong demand for academic performance;
- Denial of the cultural deprivation argument and the stereotypes that support it;
- High staff morale.

Carter and Chatfield found that Lauderbach teachers were constantly seeking to improve their teaching, and the entire staff worked together to promote a positive social and academic environment for all children. Nearly half of the teachers at Lauderbach were minorities, and among these, most were Hispanic and bilingual. In addition, the principal was actively involved in all aspects of teaching and staff improvement and had worked hard to hire an ethnically diverse faculty. Carter and Chatfield concluded that the integration of bilingual education into the whole school, combined with the emphasis on processes and having minority teachers, contributed strongly to the effectiveness of the elementary schools they studied.

The García Study: Middle School

A team of researchers and teachers, directed by García (1993), used features found in effective schools with high minority populations (Purkey & Smith,

1983), and in particular, Hispanic students (Carter & Chatfield, 1986; García, 1988; García, Flores, Moll, & Prieto, 1988), to design an instructional plan to enhance academic experiences of fifty-four seventh-grade bilingual Hispanic students attending Pájaro Middle School. When the restructuring began in 1988, Pájaro Middle School, located in Northern California, had 90 percent Hispanic students, 60 percent of whom were non-English speakers, with academic achievement scores indicating that these students were one to two grades below statewide averages.

García and the team identified fifteen principles synthesized from research on attributes of effective schools for Hispanic bilingual students. To get an idea of the kinds of factors they identified and used to develop their instructional plan, here are five principles that address schoolwide concerns:

- School restructuring for language minority students must address all aspects of learning, including social rules of behavior and self-esteem;
- The more linguistically and culturally diverse the students are in the school community, the more the content should be related to the students' everyday lives;
- The more linguistically and culturally diverse the students are in the school community, the more important it is to offer students opportunities to apply what they are learning in a meaningful context;
- The more linguistically and culturally diverse the students are in the school community, the more integrated the curriculum should be;
- The more linguistically and culturally diverse the students are in the school community, the greater the variety of teaching and learning strategies should be, with multiple opportunities to learn from peers as well as the teacher and other adult staff.

Next, they translated the principles into strategies for enhancing reading, writing, and mathematics achievement, and academic self-worth. Once this was completed, the team reorganized the seventh-grade curriculum and schedule for the students involved so that these students would be taught through Project THEME, an interdisciplinary, collaborative curriculum. Project THEME was based on five strategies:

Strategy 1: Use thematic, integrated curriculum and teaching across the content areas;

Strategy 2: Use small group activities with heterogeneous language grouping and peer tutoring, in which learning proceeds from hands-on to presentational activities and then to activities involving more abstract ways of dealing with content process and knowledge;

Strategy 3: Use interactive journals, literature study groups, silent reading, followed by small group discussion, individual- and group-authored literature, and mathematics logs;

Strategy 4: Use cooperative learning strategies emphasizing the equitable participation of each student in processing curriculum materials;

Strategy 5: Address interpersonal inequities related to gender differences with a focus on activities that foster equal status interactions.

After one year of implementation, Project THEME students showed significant gains in reading, writing, and mathematics abilities. Nearly 70 percent of the students had above average grades in language arts and across subject matter content areas. The students also exhibited a positive sense of self and expressed pride in their Mexican heritage. García found that feelings of self-worth and confidence in appearance were high, especially among the girls. These results led García and the team to conclude that the principles and strategies used in Project THEME promoted an effective bilingual middle school community for language minority students.

The Lucas, Henze, and Donato Study: High School

To extend the knowledge about effective bilingual schooling, particularly at the high school level, Lucas, Henze, and Donato (1990) gathered information from high schools recognized as effective by local, state, and federal agencies. From a pool of a dozen school sites, the researchers selected six high schools on the basis of their successful whole school approach to providing a quality education for bilingual language minority students, and because these schools were able to provide quantitative evidence for success; for example, low dropout rates, high daily student attendance, and high standardized test scores. Five of the high schools (organized around grades 9–12) were in California; one was in Arizona. All six sites were predominantly attended by Latino students (mainly students of Mexican origin) who either were becoming or already were bilingual in Spanish and English. Most of the students who were becoming bilingual were newcomers, students who had arrived in the United States between the ages of fourteen and eighteen.

Based on the case studies and their analysis of them, Lucas, Henze, and Donato (1990) came up with eight features present within all the six schools that they believe promote success in bilingual and Latino language minority students:

1. Teachers and school leaders place a high value on the students' languages and cultures;
2. Schools place concrete, high expectations on language minority students;

3. School leaders make the education of language minority students a high priority;

4. School leaders explicitly design staff development to help teachers and other staff serve language minority students more effectively;

5. Schools offer a variety of courses and programs for language minority students;

6. Counseling programs give special attention to language minority students;

7. Schools encourage parents of language minority students to become involved in their children's education;

8. School staff members share a strong commitment to empower language minority students through education.

As Lucas, Henze, and Donato (1990) note, many of these features have been reported in the effective schools literature. (You might try to compare these features with those articulated by Carter and Chatfield [1986] and García [1993].) However, they suggest that some of the particulars within the features may be especially crucial for the success of language minority students. For example, several of the principals hired teachers who understand cultural diversity and the importance of creating a school community. In a majority of the schools, teachers received an extra bonus in their salaries if they gained communicative proficiency in Spanish. One of the ways that several schools demonstrated a commitment to serving students was by employing Latino and Latina counselors. Additionally, a number of schools supported periodic meetings among students, teachers, and parents to exchange ideas about curriculum matters. All of these special features help empower language minority students (Moraes, 1996).

The steps taken by effective bilingual elementary, middle, and high schools mirror the perspective presented in the 1994 version of Title VII, also referred to as the Improving America's Schools Act. The 1994 version of the Bilingual Education Act promotes the policy that "local agencies reform, restructure and upgrade *all elements of an individual school's programs and operation* so as to ensure that the comprehensive educational needs of all of a school's LEP students and their families are fulfilled" (Ohio Bilingual–Multicultural Update, 1994, emphasis ours). The upshot of this new perspective is that bilingual education is a schoolwide concern, not merely one of the students and staff who teach and learn within the program.

Bilingual Education in School Communities

We believe that the new BEA perspective on the benefits of whole school approaches to bilingual education closely reflects earlier findings on effective bilingual schools, and that this is a wise and appropriate direction to take. In the following section, we present four case studies of elementary, middle, and high schools in which we have worked and studied. All names are pseudo-nyms. As you will see, there is no simple formula for success at any level of schooling. Although there are points of commonality, no combination of fea-tures will necessarily produce an effective bilingual school (Lucas, Henze, & Donato, 1990). We have purposefully not presented a discussion of the simi-larities or differences between the effective bilingual schools research and these case studies—we leave this up to your own constructions.

Hamilton Elementary School

Thomas Hamilton Elementary is an elementary school located in the urban core of a southwestern city. Hamilton is situated in a neighborhood of forty- to fifty-year-old single-family homes and more recently constructed two- to three-story apartment buildings, interspersed with small businesses. Fifty years ago the neighborhood was middle-class Anglo American, but it has changed over time and is now predominantly working class Hispanic, with a significant number of families recently arrived immigrants from Mexico and Central America. Hamilton's population of over 800 children is about 70 percent Hispanic, 20 percent Anglo American, and the remaining 10 percent are African American, Native American, and Vietnamese. More than 60 per-cent of the children receive free breakfast and free or reduced lunch, and 60 percent of the school's population has been labeled "at-risk" due to a combi-nation of factors, including family income level, non-English-speaking fam-ily background, history of school dropout by siblings, and test scores.

By the 1980s Hamilton was considered by most teachers in the district to be the least desirable school in which to teach in terms of children's abilities and attitudes. Children were viewed from a deficit perspective. They were a problem, and they did not achieve because they did not speak English. The district in which Hamilton is located had developed a transitional bilingual program, and this program was in place at the school, where it served about a third of the Spanish-speaking children. Children in the bilingual program received initial literacy and math instruction in Spanish, but the stated ob-jective of bilingual education was to transition the learners into all-English instruction as quickly as possible. Aside from the utilization of Spanish lan-guage materials, the program was highly traditional, relying on the same kinds of instructional materials and strategies that had been used in the dis-trict for years. For the native Spanish speakers not enrolled in the bilingual program there was a resource ESL teacher who conducted a pullout program.

The bilingual program was viewed by the non-bilingual education teach-ers as a separate effort that had little or nothing to do with them. When the program ended at third grade, the learners formerly in bilingual classrooms were placed in mainstream classrooms with teachers who had no sensitivity to second language needs and no awareness of their Spanish language strengths.

In 1986 Karen Dillon became the new principal at Hamilton. She brought with her a belief that all children are able to learn and that it is the responsibility of the school to identify children's strengths and abilities and work from there. One of the strengths she saw was the children's Spanish. She believed that Hamilton should encourage the children to develop their Spanish language literacy for its own importance and not simply for its usefulness as a bridge to English. She also operated from a theoretical perspective on language and literacy learning that was radically different from the traditional view in place at the school.

That view, elaborated in Chapter 4 and in the rest of this book, emphasizes children's construction of their own knowledge and their own literacy. It focuses on children and teachers collaborating on projects of interest to them. It advocates children becoming literate through engaging in reading and writing for multiple purposes and through using written and oral language as they engage with content of significance to them. Given her beliefs and understandings Dillon set out both to change the educational philosophy at the school and to reconceptualize and expand the bilingual program.

Dillon began by increasing the number of bilingual classrooms in the primary grades, first increasing the numbers of sections of bilingual kindergarten and, each year thereafter, the number of primary classrooms. This increase meant that a greater percentage of Spanish-speaking children would be able to learn through their stronger language while they developed their English. For the most part Dillon hired bilingual teachers (and monolingual teachers as well) who shared the philosophy of education that she was advocating. As Headstart and preschool three-year-old classes have been added to the campus, these also have been developed to be both bilingual and reflective of the kind of developmentally appropriate, holistic education of the rest of the school.

Dillon and her staff also decided that, given both the number of older Spanish-speaking children who were coming into Hamilton from Mexico and Central America and the research data on the number of years of bilingual schooling needed to achieve proficiency in English (see Chapter 2), that they should extend the bilingual program beyond the third grade. Many teachers at Hamilton were beginning to work with multiage classrooms (for example, teaching a class comprised of five-, six- and seven-year olds who normally would be classified as kindergarten, first- and second-grade children), and the decision was made to organize bilingual fourth- and fifth-grade combination rooms. As teachers retired and/or transferred to other schools, Dillon hired more bilingual teachers. Several of these individuals have teamed with some excellent monolingual teachers already at the school, working together to offer their students opportunities to choose the language of instruction for particular activities and validating their learning through Spanish, while at the same time encouraging the development of English.

An increase in the number of classrooms was coupled with outreach to Spanish-speaking parents by the principal and the new Spanish-speaking teachers, who explained repeatedly why learning in Spanish was beneficial to their children. PTA meetings began to be conducted in both Spanish and English, and teachers urged Spanish-speaking parents to attend. Bilingual education teacher educators joined bilingual teachers in conducting parent meetings in which they shared examples of children's learning in Spanish and illustrated how a firm base in the native language facilitated learning in English.

Dillon also wanted to increase the English-speaking faculty's commitment to and concern for educating all learners, and she wanted to promote faculty development in the area of second language methodology. To that end, she urged her English monolingual faculty to take university classes that would lead to completion of the state ESL endorsement in addition to a regular teaching certificate. She contacted the local university and arranged for some of the endorsement classes to be offered on the Hamilton campus. Hamilton sponsored several second language methodology workshops offered by a local teacher support group, and Dillon paid for a number of Hamilton teachers to attend these workshops. She also sponsored workshops for the entire faculty that dealt with topics in second language acquisition and methodology. She encouraged teachers who were not in agreement with the school's changing philosophy to transfer to other schools in the district. Currently, when new hires are made, only certified and endorsed bilingual and ESL teachers who share the school's educational philosophy are hired.

In addition to the classroom teachers, resource personnel have increased their direct involvement with the bilingual learners. About five years ago, the first Spanish–English bilingual special educator joined the Hamilton staff. She and the other special education teacher team worked with the classroom teachers to provide extra assistance to learners who need more individual attention. Sometimes extra assistance consistent with the kind of classroom instruction that is occurring is provided in a special education resource room, but often the special educators work in the regular classrooms, reducing the student–teacher ratio and allowing the children who need additional help to receive it within the context of their own classrooms. This is a model that special educators have come to call *inclusion.*

Inclusion may mean, for example, that during the daily language arts block the classroom teacher will meet with one group of students to discuss the book they are reading for literature study while the special education teacher meets with another group, some of whom, but not all, are special education students. Or it may mean that the bilingual special education teacher will work in a classroom during math time in order to explain new mathematical concepts to Spanish dominant children who have been identified as needing special assistance in this area of the curriculum.

The same teaming concept has influenced the work of the Title I teachers, whose federally funded job traditionally has been to work with children designated as low-achieving in literacy and/or mathematics due to poor performance on achievement tests. In some settings bilingual students have been excluded from Title I services; at Hamilton this is not the case. As do the special education teachers, the Title I teachers, who share the educational philosophy of the principal and classroom teachers, frequently work alongside the bilingual classroom teachers. There is also an afterschool tutoring program that is staffed by a bilingual teacher. The Title I teachers expend a large percentage of their yearly budget on children's literature to be used in all classrooms, and, in recent years, they have purchased a significant amount of children's literature in Spanish. Title I has sponsored parent workshops conducted in both Spanish and English to emphasize the importance of parents listening to their children read and discussing stories with them.

Along with the special education and Title I teachers, a resource ESL specialist works with selected classrooms. As do the other educators, this individual works in classrooms instead of pulling out children for services. A major challenge in teaming has been planning time; in the last two years specific planning times have been arranged between the classroom teachers and the additional resource teachers.

In 1992, when the school librarian transferred to another school in the district, Karen Dillon hired a woman who had completed an elementary education degree with a concentration in English-as-a-second-language teaching. While not fluent in Spanish, she had been studying the language and was committed to the bilingual education program. She began working with the bilingual teachers to bring increased quality and quantity to the collection of Spanish language books. She has opened the library up to children before and after school and at lunchtime; she has initiated a series of parent–child breakfasts to encourage parents to learn about the library and children's books in both languages. She has attended conferences with bilingual teachers in order to look for books that reflect the linguistic and cultural diversity of the school.

Hamilton School currently operates under a shared decision-model of governance. A parent–teacher–classified staff–administrator council meets monthly to consider issues and policies at the school. Classroom and resource teachers are an integral part of the decision-making with regard to the hiring of new teachers; teachers sit on interview committees and provide their input to the principal. Twice a year the staff meets for a weekend retreat designed to build community and to allow measured consideration of issues that may arise at the school. The teachers themselves have worked together in teams on curricular issues, for example, creating alternatives to the traditional report cards, and presenting a case to the district office that monies the district would automatically spend on basal readers and content area texts be given directly to teachers so that they could purchase literature for their classrooms. Teachers also meet in study groups to examine aspects of the curriculum (for example, science or math) or to study a particular professional book of interest.

Kelso Elementary School

Elizabeth Kelso is a kindergarten through sixth-grade elementary school in the southern quadrant of a suburban school district. For many years this district was basically middle and upper middle class, with a few Hispanic and American Indian students on the southern and eastern fringes. These students, supposedly, were serviced by resource ESL teachers. However, beginning in the middle 1980s and continuing until the present, increasing numbers of Spanish-speaking families have moved into the district. To its credit, the district response has been to state unequivocally that it has the responsibility both to provide a quality education for all its students and to assist classroom teachers in increasing their abilities to work effectively with students whose native language is not English. To meet its commitment the district hired a multicultural resource teacher whose job it has been to work with teachers who are interested in learning about teaching second language learners.

As the school population (at Kelso and other sites) changed so significantly, the district multicultural resource teacher sensed an uneasiness on the part of teachers with regard to what their responsibilities were in terms of the ESL children. She spent time in classrooms, offering suggestions and support. But she soon realized that if teachers were to be asked to integrate non-English-speaking children into their classrooms, they needed some expertise in the field of second language pedagogy. District level administrators agreed with her and agreed to fund graduate work in second language education. This has meant that the district has paid tuition and fees for approximately fifty teachers to earn the state English-as-a-second-language endorsement by completing coursework and practicum experiences. These teachers, for the most part, have become what we termed in Chapter 2 *self-contained ESL teachers*. By district design, their classrooms are populated by a mix of native speakers of English and ESL learners, the goal being to achieve approximately equal numbers of each group.

While for years a small Spanish-speaking population has lived within Kelso's boundaries, in the last ten years its population has shifted from more than 90 percent Anglo American to approximately 40 percent Hispanic and 60 percent Anglo American. At Kelso (and other schools), the resource teacher recruited teachers to undertake the coursework required to add the ESL endorsement to their existing elementary education certificates. In general the teachers who volunteered already had positive attitudes toward working with the second language learners at their school; now they needed the knowledge base and opportunities to experiment with more innovative, interactive instructional strategies. In conjunction with one of the local universities, courses were designed that included field requirements, and coursework was offered at school district locations. As they studied together and carried out group projects on their own campuses, the teachers developed a sense of community, a feeling that they were working together for children. They began to understand how traditional textbook-based learning often did not provide the second language learners with the kinds of direct, contextualized experiences they needed to benefit from school. They began to see that they could make changes in classroom environment, organization, and instruction that would make content more meaningful for all learners and more accessible for ESL learners. They began to acknowledge the importance of allowing children to use Spanish with each other to mediate their learning, even if they themselves did not speak Spanish and even if the school district policy was officially ESL.

When the first teachers completed their ESL coursework in 1991, Kelso's staff included a designated, certified ESL teacher at each grade level, and one teacher who was bilingually certified and fluent in Spanish. This teacher, whose tenure at Kelso predated the influx, had long been an advocate for the Spanish-speaking learners at the school, using Spanish for instructional purposes in his classroom and working to sensitize the other educators in the building to the needs of the children. Recently this individual has been joined by another teacher (who has been studying Spanish in order to pass the state Spanish proficiency exam) who has encouraged the children in his room to use and develop their Spanish (including becoming literate in Spanish) and who has used his own imperfect Spanish in the classroom to demonstrate that it's okay to make mistakes while learning another language. These two individuals also have purchased a significant amount of Spanish language children's literature for officially ESL classrooms, thus acting on a belief in native language literacy by providing opportunities for learners to read in their native language. Their leadership in this area has served to encourage other teachers to make more use of Spanish, and the librarian has purchased Spanish language materials for literature and content study.

Establishing the designated ESL classrooms and mixing native English speakers and ESL learners has not happened without controversy. For several years a small but very vocal group of English-speaking parents protested the changes that were occurring at Kelso. They argued that the ESL learners did not belong at Kelso; they should be sent to another school in the district. They expressed concern that, in the integrated classes, the teachers would need to spend so much time with the ESL learners that their own children would be neglected. They feared that the curriculum would not be as rigorous as it had been because of the need to accommodate the second language children. They questioned whether monies designated to be spent on the ESL classrooms meant fewer resources for the other classes.

Through a series of meetings, the district explained its commitment to all learners and the actualization of this philosophy in integrated classrooms that provided a quality education for all learners. The superintendent made it clear that the district would not back down on what it believed was right. The district federal programs director and the multicultural resource teacher asked educators from the state department of education to join Kelso teachers in open meetings with parents, so that they could answer questions about the design and implementation of the program. The teachers presented a united front in their commitment to what they were doing.

The controversy in the district has diminished but has not disappeared completely. In an effort to reach out to the community, a district-wide multicultural committee, comprised of parents, teachers, classified staff, and university representatives, was formed. This committee has sponsored workshops and conferences for teachers and parents, has encouraged increased parental involvement in school programs, and has promoted a multiculturalization of curricula with a view to having an effect on the Anglo American students as well as the second language learners.

More recently at Kelso the principal of many years retired and was succeeded by an educator fairly knowledgeable about bilingual and second language education. Because of continued concerns about the achievement of the Spanish-speaking children, this individual decided to hire some bilingual teachers to provide greater opportunities for the children to learn through their stronger language. Currently there are bilingual teachers in kindergarten through third grade, as well as the ESL endorsed professionals. The staff is now in the midst of struggling with how to work most effectively with the children who are not fluent in English and the role each of the educators will play.

Green Hills Middle School

The Dry Valley School District opened the doors of Green Hills Middle School in the Fall of 1992. The school featured state-of-the-art school design for middle schools: building and units organized as families to promote togetherness within the school boundaries. Green Hills also opened a new bilingual program and designated it as one of the six major families in the school. The family units shared a home room, and each unit contained English, science, and social studies classrooms. The students affiliated with each family spent half of their day within the family building unit, and the rest of the day taking 55-minute classes throughout the campus with students from other family units.

Two bilingual teachers were hired to implement the bilingual program. One teacher was certified in the area of science, and was in the process of obtaining a bilingual endorsement. The other teacher was certified as a secondary teacher with a specialty in English. Both teachers had some experience teaching in bilingual programs, and both had worked extensively with bilingual students in a variety of settings.

The year Green Hills opened seventy seventh- and eighth-grade bilingual and becoming bilingual students were assigned to the Bilingual Family building unit. All but four of the students were from Spanish-speaking countries, mainly Mexico, and several were born in the United States. Following the family scheduling plan, students in the bilingual unit spent their morning working on ESL and learning subject matter content in Spanish. In the afternoon, they took classes with their English-speaking peers in other buildings across the campus. This design allowed the bilingual teachers to schedule instruction in the major content areas (English, math, science, and social studies) and to devote greater amounts of time to these various subjects. The bilingual teachers favored this arrangement because it enabled them to make decisions about their curriculum and to provide input to the principal on scheduling based on the daily experiences with their students. So, for example, the teachers were able to regroup students by English language and primary language and literacy proficiency throughout the school year without disrupting their own schedule for content areas classes.

As the two teachers moved further and further into the school year, they found themselves constantly adjusting their teaching practices and trying out all sorts of materials. By midyear they were beginning to feel pressure to increase the amount of English they and the students used during instruction within the bilingual family classes. They started to hear complaints from their colleagues that the "bilingual" students were not getting enough English in their family unit classes to prepare them to participate sufficiently in classes outside the family unit. There was also a concern that the eighth graders were not being adequately prepared for the local high school, which offered neither Spanish language subject matter courses nor Spanish for bilingual native speakers. (Spanish for bilingual native speakers is a Spanish class for students who speak and understand Spanish, but who need work on reading and writing in Spanish.) The high school had only a small ESL program.

The two teachers used the pressure to incorporate more English for instruction both as an incentive to organize fellow teachers to insist on the entire school taking a greater role in socially integrating the bilingual students into all aspects of school and as a threat to the bilingual program. Both teachers were fully aware of the need to increase the quantity of English in their classes, but were keenly concerned about the quality of English as well. They wanted to make sure that students who were not yet fully proficient in English could participate in classroom activities that were presented entirely in

English. At the same time, they, along with the school principal, were determined not to allow the school district to dictate how much Spanish could be used in the bilingual classrooms or in the school as a whole. There was a mounting drive by some members of the school board to eliminate the bilingual program at Green Hills, and instead to offer ESL courses there, and at the other two middle schools that feed into the local high school.

Here is what happened: The two bilingual teachers, the principal, and several concerned teachers banded together to plan a way to support the bilingual program by expanding it as a schoolwide effort. In collaboration, they developed a working paper that outlined their arguments about the value of bilingual education at Green Hills, and how they would like to expand the program schoolwide, and presented it to the District Board of Education. The plan called for expanding the program by hiring three additional bilingual teachers and several bilingual assistant teachers to work in mainstream classrooms. In addition, the plan called for the retooling of the English-speaking faculty to make them aware of the language and learning needs of bilingual students. The plan also recommended adding a newcomer center to help brand-new immigrant students prepare for secondary school, and to learn some rudimentary English before coming to Green Hills and other secondary level schools.

As a result of these efforts, the bilingual family unit was not only continued, but several new bilingual staff members were added. The principal vowed that any newly hired teachers would need to have ESL or bilingual endorsements. He also spread the word to faculty, staff, parents, and the school board that immigrant and bilingual students were an integral part of the whole school. That meant that these students' success depended not only on a strong bilingual program, but on a whole school that supported their needs as well. To this end, the entire school, the extracurricular events, the support staff, the front office, and teachers had to become more sensitive to the language and cultural needs of the students in the bilingual family and place high expectations on the students to perform well regardless of their proficiency in English.

How did the school work toward this change in focus? One strategy the principal and staff used was to "think language" (Enright & McCloskey, 1988) whenever they planned events, notices, workshops, and activities. For example, the librarian upgraded the Spanish language book selection and improved the selection of multicultural adolescent literature. The principal adapted his morning talks over the intercom to make them more comprehensible to students who were still learning English.

By 1997, the bilingual program grew considerably, and the principal added three new bilingual content area teachers to the four existing ones, two Spanish-speaking classroom aides, and a bilingual Hispanic Director of Academic Programs. Moreover, he implemented a year-long staff development plan so that all teachers and staff could become more familiar with bilingual methodology and ways of adapting teaching to increase the social and academic participation of bilingual students in all classes.

César Chávez Community High School

Almost one-half of the nearly 4,000 students at César Chávez Community High are recently arrived immigrant students who are adding English to their first language, Spanish. The rest of the student body consists mainly of students of Mexican origin, African Americans, and Anglo Americans. César Chávez High is located next to a major interstate freeway, on the edge of a well-established Hispanic barrio near the downtown of a large city. There is a chain-link fence around the campus, and the buildings are organized around subject matter areas, for example, English, science, math, and social studies.

The bilingual program at César Chávez High was one of the first to be implemented in the city, and it was the first program to have its own Director of Bilingual Education. The hiring of a director was critical to the progress of the program from its inception in the early 1980s. Since that time, the program has changed from a separate, and socially segregated set of loosely organized courses to an integrated curriculum that enables students to take core classes in their native language as well as in sheltered content settings.

The bilingual program started out as an ESL program that offered three levels of English classes (beginning, intermediate, and advanced), plus a conversation and writing class. Students in the bilingual program were not allowed to mix socially or physically with their English-speaking peers. The reason given for this was to reduce the number of gang-related fights and altercations between Mexican immigrant students and U. S.-born Chicano students. The school had a reputation for having members of some of the oldest and toughest gangs in the city.

The Director of Bilingual Education at the school restructured the bilingual program significantly. With support from the Superintendent's office, he hired a number of credentialed Spanish dominant content area teachers and expanded the course offerings to insure that students in the program had access to core courses needed for graduation. All but two of the Spanish dominant teachers were from Mexico and the Dominican Republic; the remaining two were natives of the United States. In addition to offering core courses in Spanish, students with high English language proficiency could select from a number of sheltered content areas classes. He also hired a bilingual counselor to work specifically with students in the program.

One of the important responsibilities of the Director of Bilingual Education was to work with the school principal on making up the class schedules for students in the bilingual program. Before the Director came on board, students were placed in P.E., art, and other noncore area classes for as long as they stayed in school. The Director, with recommendations from teachers and the bilingual counselor, worked to provide access to as many core classes as possible, assigning the beginning bilingual students to Spanish language courses, and the more advanced English proficient students to sheltered and mainstream classes taught in English.

The bilingual program at César Chávez has a long way to go to become a schoolwide effort. Students in the bilingual program are still socially and physically segregated from students in regular content area classrooms for much of their education at César Chávez High. English-speaking teachers in the regular content areas are still weary of having students who are not fully proficient in English placed in their classes. The principal has not placed a high priority on helping regular teachers to become more effective working with language minority students. However, the principal has actively encouraged and helped language minority parents and families to become involved in their students' education at home and in school. The high school offers ESL courses for parents in the evening and on the weekends.

Concluding Remarks

The above descriptions of schoolwide efforts to meet the needs of bilingual and becoming bilingual learners reflect some of the ways that schools are addressing the integration of bilingual education within the whole school community. As you may have noticed, the cases we presented depended on local circumstances and realities, but all of them included features that were found in studies on effective bilingual schools. Accordingly, while the specifics of each school community are different and unique, there are some features that apply across settings and grade levels. They are the following:

1. Leadership at the local level is crucial. There must be a person or persons at the site with a vision for what could be and a willingness to commit the time and effort necessary to effect change.

2. Making significant changes in a school requires the efforts and commitment of many people. One or two individuals cannot effect needed change by themselves; they must recruit and work with others.

3. Significant change takes time. Those who are committed to change must acknowledge that growth in understanding and changes in attitudes and actions do not necessarily happen overnight. Patience and continued efforts are required over a period of years.

4. Knowledge is crucial. It is not enough for educators to have goodwill and attitudes of acceptance toward newcomers and language minority students.

They also need to learn how to work with them in the most effective ways possible and work at creating a positive social and academic climate for learning.

5. Parents and families need to be involved in restructuring efforts. Families need to be informed about plans for their children's instruction. Parental and family support is important to successful programs.

6. Change is a process, not a product. Educators committed to providing the best educational environments and opportunities for becoming bilingual learners are never satisfied, and their programs are not static. There is always something else to be done; there is always a new challenge.

We hope that these cases, coupled with what is known about effective bilingual schools, will provide you with an idea of the complexity of bilingual education, and a personal sense of the role you might play in supporting a school community in your school. In the next chapter, we introduce our theoretical stance on learning and language, with an eye toward providing you with what we believe are principles that can guide you toward these goals as you prepare for bilingual education.

References

Carter, T., & Chatfield, M. (1986). Effective bilingual schools: Implications for policy and practice. *American Journal of Education, 95,* 200–232.

Enright, D. S., & McCloskey, M. L. (1988). *Integrating English: Developing English language and literacy in the multilingual classroom.* Reading, MA: Addison-Wesley.

Escamilla, K. (1994). The sociolinguistic environment of a bilingual school: A case study introduction. *Bilingual Research Journal, 18*(1&2), 21–48.

García, E. (1993). Project THEME: Collaboration for school improvement at the middle school for language minority students. In *Proceedings of the Third National Research Symposium on Limited Proficiency Student Issues: Focus on Middle and High School Issues,* vol. 1, (pp. 323–350). Washington, DC: U. S. Department of Education, Office of Bilingual Education and Minority Language Affairs.

García, E. (1988). Attributes of effective schools for language minority students. *Education and Urban Society, 20*(4), 387–400.

García, E., Flores, B., Moll, L., & Prieto, A. (1988). *Effective schooling for Hispanics: A final report.* Tempe, AZ: Bilingual/Bicultural Center, Arizona State University.

Hudelson, S., & Faltis, C. (1993). Redefining basic teacher education: Preparing teachers to transform teaching. In G. Guntermann (Ed.), *Developing language teachers for a changing world,* (pp. 23–42). Lincolnwood, IL: National Textbook Company.

Lucas, T., Henze, R., & Donato, R. (1990). Promoting the success of Latino language minority students: An exploratory study of six high schools. *Harvard Educational Review, 60*(3), 315–340.

Lucas, T. (1992). High school restructuring and school reform. In C. Minicucci & L. Olsen (Eds.), *Educating students from immigrant families: Meeting the challenge in sec-*

ondary schools, (pp. 39–51). Santa Cruz, CA: National Center for Research on Cultural Diversity and Second Language Learning.

Merino, B., & Faltis, C. (1993). Language and culture in the preparation of bilingual teachers. In M. B. Arias & U. Casanova (Eds.), *Bilingual education: Politics, practice, research,* (pp. 171–198). Chicago, IL: University of Chicago Press.

Minicucci, C. (1996). *Learning science and English: How school reform advances scientific learning for limited English proficient middle school students.* Santa Cruz, CA: National Center for Research on Cultural Diversity and Second Language Learning.

Moraes, M. (1996). *Bilingual education: A dialogue with the Bakhtin circle.* Albany, NY: State University of New York Press.

Ohio Bilingual–Multicultural Update (1994). New Title I provides funding for programs that benefit English language learners. Columbus, OH:Ohio Department of Education.

Olsen, L. (1992). School restructuring and the needs of secondary LEP students. In C. Minicucci & L. Olsen (Eds.), *Educating students from immigrant families: Meeting the challenge in secondary schools,* (pp. 36–39). Santa Cruz, CA: National Center for Research on Cultural Diversity and Second Language Learning.

Purkey, S., & Smith, M. (1983). Effective schools: A review. *Elementary School Journal, 83*(1), 52-78.

4

A Theoretical Framework for Learning and Language Acquisition in Bilingual Education Settings

This chapter is necessarily different from the other chapters in this book. It presents the theoretical framework that we would like you to consider in asking questions and making decisions about bilingual education practices. The other chapters are about bilingual classrooms, teaching practices in bilingual classrooms, and the children and adolescents whose social and academic lives are affected by what happens in bilingual education. This one focuses the discussion on our beliefs about how children and adolescents acquire language and learn in school, and particularly, in classroom settings. It may interest you to know that while we center the discussion about language acquisition and learning in school and in classrooms, you will see that we tie what happens in school and in classrooms to larger contexts and communities beyond these two critical settings. Moreover, while users of the term *language acquisition* often refer exclusively to the acquisition of spoken language, we include both spoken and written language in our use of the term (Weaver, 1994). We do so because we believe that spoken and written language are intertwined and interconnected both in and out of school.

We hope to accomplish three things in this chapter. First, we want to lay out for you our theoretical framework for learning and language acquisition. In doing so, we also present our views on teaching as well. Our framework differs considerably from what you might have read about and discussed in classes on classroom learning and instruction, especially those offered from a traditional educational psychology perspective. We feel strongly that if bilingual education is going to prepare children and adolescents to be successful in school as well as in society, then we must be critical of the status quo in learning research, because much of this research leaves out the social, contextual, and political nature of learning and language acquisition. These aspects of learning and language acquisition are central to the theoretical framework we present in these pages.

Second, we hope to show you how and why our theoretical framework for learning contrasts with the more commonly presented one that drives much of what is done in teacher education and in classroom teaching. The framework that operates in the vast majority of teacher education and classroom settings is based on concepts and ideas from educational psychology and, in the case of bilingual education, on linguistic research. This framework represents what Marilyn Cochran–Smith (1991) calls the Consonance Model. The Consonance Model works under the assumption that what experimental and educational psychologists and linguists present as theoretical models for learning and language acquisition and what happens in school are consistent with each other. In other words, linguistic explanations, which are cognitively based, are compatible with the theoretical models within which experimental and educational psychologists operate. Our theoretical framework rejects the Consonance Model because we believe it is overly dependent on experimental and positivist research paradigms. Accordingly, it minimizes or ignores or marginalizes the role of social interaction, context, and political activity in learning and language acquisition. Moreover, because the Consonance Model seeks agreement at the theoretical level, its users tend to be noncritical of existing practices associated with it.

Third, we want to persuade you to adopt the guiding principles of our perspective on learning and language acquisition because they underpin the practices that we believe you should be using, promoting, or inquiring about in bilingual education. In subsequent chapters, we will provide examples of what happens in classrooms where teachers are struggling to improve learning conditions by paying attention to social, cultural, and political realities.

Some Basic Ideas

Spoken and written language acquisition are at the heart of bilingual education. It is not possible to think about the ways that children and adolescents learn in school without having a good understanding of how they come to use spoken and written language in ways that are appropriate for school and society. This is because the development of knowledge, of social abilities, of feelings, of values, all happen as individuals use language (both spoken and written) while they engage in social interactions first at home, then in school, and, subsequently, throughout life. In other words, children grow up to be knowing, feeling, and socially responsible adults as a result of the way that they have been socialized at home and in school, and a significant amount of that socialization occurs through spoken and written language.

From this perspective, learning and language acquisition overlap to a great extent in the sense that both are social, contextual, and goal-oriented. That is, individuals learn both content and language as they engage with others in a variety of settings and to accomplish specific purposes. To give an example, you are learning about bilingual education practices by reading this book (transacting with the authors and drawing on your own social history), but also by talking with your classmates, your friends and family members, and the instructor. Chances are, too, that you have already considered some aspects of language learning in other discussions, and you may have engaged in considerations of bilingual education before reading this book or taking the course in which it is used. After completing the book and the course, you will undoubtedly talk with others about bilingual education and language learning. In addition, your previous life experiences (related, for example, to bilingual people, bilingualism in general, personal language learning, and school experiences) also influence your views about bilingual education.

All these experiences and instances of talk and exchange of ideas figure prominently in how you come to view language learning and how you come to talk about and practice bilingual education. How you change over time with regard to language learning and bilingual education is also a byproduct of using language that is associated with bilingual education. Accordingly, what you experience and reflect on, what you read and discuss, observe and discuss, write and discuss, all have an impact on what you learn, how you feel, what you practice, and how you talk with others about it.

Now, many of you might be countering the above by arguing that learning is primarily cognitive, and, thus, that it resides inside the heads of learners. This is an expected reaction, and a good one to make at this point, because this is what experimental and educational psychologists have been claiming for the last twenty-five years (Smith, 1988). In fact, much of the vocabulary and many of the concepts that we use to talk about learning come from experimental and educational psychology. The concepts of comprehension, short-term and long-term memory, cognitive processing, input–output, and storage capacity, for example, are all the property of psychology. And, we will see later on in this chapter that psychology has dominated the field of first and second language acquisition as well.

We are not claiming that cognitive processes are uninvolved in learning or in language acquisition. To be sure, learners organize and store information from visual as well as spoken and written language sources and "place" them into meaning systems. Learners also tap into these meaning systems in order to communicate with others. In fact, there needs to be a fairly well-developed meaning system in order for young children to begin to communicate through language. Thus, to a certain extent, language learning requires a pre-existing network of cognitive processes in which objects, events, and ways of referring to or talking about those objects, and events are tied into a meaning system (Bialystok & Hakuta, 1994).

Beyond this, we readily acknowledge that it is "generally accepted that children are creative constructors of their native language, cognitively generating and revising hypotheses about how it works" (Hudelson & Faltis, 1993, p. 29). There is multiple evidence of the child as hypothesis tester in terms of both spoken and written language. For example, an English-speaking child's comment as she watches the departure of a parent will change as the child's knowledge of English develops over time. A very young child might say: "Da go." This utterance later becomes "Daddy going" and still later "Daddy is going," with the child producing utterances that are not only lengthier but more conventional in terms of adult speech (Lindfors, 1980). This same child, over time, expresses the idea of *no* in different ways. Even when she is speaking basically in words, the child may indicate rejection of something as in "No dirty soap" as she pushes away a sliver of soap while being bathed. Later she may make it clear that she doesn't want to do something by adding the word *no* to a sentence as in, "No play that game." Still later, her range of expressing negatives expands to include *don't* and *can't* as she says, "I don't want it" and "You can't dance" (Lindfors, 1980).

Similarly, there is a significant amount of evidence available that many children begin to experiment with written language long before formal literacy instruction in school. A young English-speaking preschool child's earliest letters to her grandmother may be rendered in scribbles and subsequently be refined to a series of wavy lines that resemble adult cursive writing (Baghban, 1984). Later the same child may write using forms that resemble the letters of the language that surrounds her, even though the forms bear no relationship to specific letters and sounds (Ferreiro, 1990; Weaver, 1994). Eventually, in alphabetic languages such as English, the child figures out that the letter forms are related to and in some way symbolize the sounds she makes when she speaks. She will then begin to engage in what has been termed *invented spelling*, spelling that is logical and reasoned even though it does not correspond to adult conventions (Weaver, 1994). Moreover, invented spelling changes over time, becoming more conventional as the child's knowledge of conventional orthography grows. Gradually, the child constructs the orthography of English. These examples should make it clear that we recognize that mental processes are centrally involved in how information is handled and how concepts are formed.

Our quarrel is with the assumption that mental processes are *wholly or primarily responsible* for learning in general or for learning language. We prefer to view the mind as a social phenomenon (Gee, 1992; Vygotsky, 1978) that operates on concepts, abilities, and knowledge systems, which are formed and developed through social interactions and the individual's hypotheses about them. In this manner, learning does not happen exclusively inside the heads of learners; it results from social interactions with others that enable learners to participate by drawing on past and present experiences and relating them to the specific context at hand in some meaningful way (Tudge, 1990; Wertsch, 1984).

If we return to the examples of the children that we have just used, the centrality of social interaction becomes clear. A young child is dropped off at the child care center by her father every morning. Perhaps her father or the center worker says something like, "Daddy's going now. Say goodbye." Language is attached to a real-world event of which the child is an integral part. The child uses language not for the sake of language itself but rather to participate with others in this event, to be an actor in this social situation. Similarly, a young child begins to write letters to her grandmother because she sees her parents writing letters to relatives and friends in other parts of the country or world, because her parents explain to her what they are doing, and because they invite, encourage, and assist her to engage in the same literacy practice. Part of participating in family life, and accomplishing her goals as a family member, then, involves writing and sending her own letters.

The key point here is that learning stems from participating in collaborative social practices, interactions, and situations in which we try out ideas and actions (Lave & Wenger, 1991). Moreover, since language is the means through which learning in the sense we are discussing occurs, it follows that participants in social interaction don't acquire or even construct concepts, knowledge systems, and language in isolation. Accordingly, we would like to propose a fundamentally social perspective on learning, that asserts that learning happens because a community of more capable members invites learners through social means, for example, demonstration and engagement (Smith, 1981), to become constructors, knowers, and users of the concepts, knowledge systems, and language valued and used by that community (Lave & Wenger, 1991). In other words, learning is by invitation, and it is a social event that is always situated in the present, but necessarily evokes the past. Why the past? Because every time an interaction occurs, it relies on knowledge, meaning, feelings, and images that have already happened.

Risky Business

Taking the stance that learning is socially situated and that it requires social interaction that invites the learner into the new discourse is risky because it goes against the grain of what has been widely accepted in the educational psychology literature on learning. In this chapter, we ask you to participate with us as we build our theoretical framework, and at the same time, we want you to challenge us to present a convincing set of arguments for our stance. Part of our argument will be that examining learning, including language learning, solely within the framework of a formalized curriculum based on psychological principles results in a limited perspective of what learning and language are, how learning and language develop, where learning takes place. Supporting this perspective for education is, in the words of Frank Smith, tantamount to placing all of your bets on "the wrong horse" (Smith, 1988, pp. 110–111).

Our commitment to the social, contextual, situational, and political nature of learning and language will be couched in terms of what we consider to be the guiding principles of our theory of learning and language acquisition for bilingual education. We begin by examining learning and language acquisition through the historical lens of psychology and then move on to contrast it with the theoretical platform that we are striving to construct. Our goal is two-fold: (1) to deconstruct the experimental and educational psychology view of learning and language acquisition; and (2) to present an alternative framework that we believe more closely reflects what currently happens in high quality classrooms and schools where children are becoming bilingual and biliterate, critical and inquiring, and socially and academically adept people.

We begin the deconstruction process by examining how learning is presented through the psychology lens. We follow this with a brief inquiry into the way language and the acquisition process have been studied through this same lens.

Learning through the Psychology Lens

Experimental and educational psychologists are interested in studying the mental processes of children and adolescents. They want to know which cognitive processes enable learners to input, organize, and store meaning systems, and to recall and produce meaningful information as needed. Moreover, they are interested in presenting complexities of cognition in as relatively simple terms as possible, and preferably in a model that "explains" cognition and concept formation in universal terms. It is important in educational psychology to present a theoretical model that is *not* affected by content, context, or culture. This kind of model is touted as the most powerful by many within the educational psychology community.

Within the general field of education, many educational psychologists believe that theoretical models that explain the learning process in cognitive terms have great significance for instruction. You can see this particular learning–instruction connection readily in the way that many beginning teachers are taught to break down concepts and knowledge systems they will be teaching into small units of information and present the units one at a time in a predetermined sequence. One assumption behind this view is that the teaching of each part will add up to a coherent whole, that learners need to have what they are learning broken down for them for efficient processing. Teaching will be most efficient and effective when the whole has been analyzed, broken up into, and presented in its component parts (Driscoll, 1994; Gage & Berliner, 1984; Gagné & Driscoll, 1988; Slavin, 1997). Another assumption is that the learner is a passive recipient of knowledge transmitted by the teacher. This is what Paulo Freire (1970) has referred to as the banking concept of education, in which the teacher, the one with the knowledge in his or her head, deposits this knowledge into the heads of students (the depositories).

Many types of school curriculum packages, teaching methods, and assessment systems have been developed based on this view of learning. You can see this view represented in many textbooks produced by large textbook publishing companies. It is fairly easy to detect. In content areas such as science and social science, for example, textbooks often present facts and key vocabulary in isolation, in a bit-by-bit fashion to be studied and recalled on end-of-chapter tests. In beginning reading materials, language is broken down into its components, and instruction begins with the smallest units, sounds and letters. Sounds make up words; words make up sentences; sentences make up paragraphs; paragaphs make up texts. The perspective of these materials is that literacy learning proceeds from part to whole, and that learners need practice with the parts before experiencing the entire text (Weaver, 1994).

Many English-as-a-second-language programs (particularly those at the secondary school level) also continue to operate from part to whole assumptions about second language learning. In addition, they are based in a behaviorist stimulus–response paradigm that suggests that learning occurs through repeated practice, with a focus on accuracy (Freeman & Freeman, 1994). In these programs, students start out with words, phrases, and basic sentence patterns. To these are subsequently added elements such as yes–no questions, information questions, negative formations, and if–then statements. All of this is presented to students in the context of questions and answers meant to be produced with as few errors as possible and practiced as many times as needed prior to moving to the next skill level. These examples serve to demonstrate the influence that the mainstream perspective in educational psychology has on teaching and curriculum development.

It is not the case that all psychologists involved in education or that all educators share the perspective on learning articulated above. There *is* a perspective that is significantly different and that is having an increasing impact on schooling. That perspective is often called *constructivism,* and it is associated closely with developmental psychologist Jean Piaget and his students. Constructivists believe that individuals, both adults and children, learn by constructing knowledge for themselves, by living in the world and working to make sense of it, rather than by being told and shown how the world, broken up into pieces, functions. From infancy learners act on the world, asking questions, observing, formulating hypotheses, and revising these hypotheses over time. Learning occurs through doing; learners must construct their own knowledge and understandings. No one can do it for them, which means that curricula that divide what is to be learned into supposedly "easily masterable" bits are useless, because they violate the ways in which children really learn (Duckworth, 1987; Fosnot, 1989).

The constructivist perspective has influenced educators in a wide variety of fields and has become an accepted view of learning in many of them. Early childhood educators, for example, advocate developmentally appropriate practices that are based on the view that children are constructors of their knowledge (National Association for the Education of Young Children, 1995). In mathematics education, the standards for the profession focus on the need for children to experiment with mathematics concepts so that they build and articulate their own understandings over time, rather than being asked to memorize algorithms, solutions, and so on (Burns, 1991; Fosnot, 1989; Kamii, 1985; National Council of Teachers of Mathematics, 1989). In science education, too, the view of children is that they actively construct their knowledge of the natural world, that their knowledge changes over time, and that they need opportunities to experiment with materials and processes in order to really understand scientific concepts and generalizations (Cohen, Horak, & Staley, 1984; Merino, Hammond, Faltis, & Goldberg, 1994). Mathematics and science materials, activities, and approaches have been developed in response to this altered view of the child as active learner.

Constructivism also has influenced the field of language and literacy education (Ferreiro, 1990; Goodman, 1990; Weaver, 1994). If you think back to the examples of first language learning that we considered earlier, the perspective of the child constructing her own understandings of spoken and written language is evident. The child's earlier hypotheses about language are less conventional and more inventive, but over time they become more and more conventional, more and more like the spoken and written language of those around her (Ferreiro & Teberosky, 1982; Goodman, 1996). Certainly literacy educators who operate from a whole language theoretical perspective have documented children's construction of their literacy (Goodman, 1990; Goodman, 1996). And in the field of second language learning, the term "creative construction" has been used to describe the basic process of acquiring a second language (Dulay & Burt, 1975; Dulay, Burt, & Krashen, 1982). We will return to this later as we argue that construction of knowledge does not and cannot occur in a social vacuum.

Language through the Psychological Lens

Many academics are interested in the study of language. The field of study most often associated with the study of language and language acquisition is linguistics. Modern-day linguistics got its start as a branch of cognitive psychology. Generally speaking, linguists are interested in understanding how language works in an ideal speaker–hearer, and how children and adults acquire it. As a branch of cognitive psychology, many linguists present language as a complex mental construct that resides inside the head of the person generating it for communication. It is to these views that we now turn in order to distinguish them from our view of language as socially shared.

One of the earliest yet still influential views of language as a mental construct comes from the theoretical writings of Noam Chomsky, a preeminent linguist, psychologist, and social activist. Chomsky (1959) proposed that the rules and principles for constructing the grammar of a particular language emanate primarily from a genetically determined faculty for language. The ability to learn language, from a Chomskian perspective, stems from an innate ability that is a "component of the human mind" (Chomsky, 1977, p. 164). This perspective assigns a general, indirect role to social interaction as a source of language competence in children. The central role is that of the individual mind. According to Chomsky, adult caregivers provide the language source from which a Universal Grammar residing in the child's head selects grammatical rules and principles specific to the language the child will eventually acquire. The Universal Grammar contains all of the grammar and sound formation rules for all languages in the world.

In addition to there being a Universal Grammar that learners tap into on hearing the source language, Chomsky also proposed the existence of a Language Acquisition Device (LAD), a mental organ dedicated to the uniquely human capacity to acquire language. Without going into a great deal of detail about what happens inside the LAD and its special relationship to Universal Grammar, we can nevertheless give you an indication of what Chomsky, in dialogue with others, constructed as reality with respect to language and language learning.

Chomsky paid a great deal of attention to the syntax of languages, to how the words of a sentence must be ordered in a string to be acceptable by native speakers of the language in question. He was concerned with constructing a theory that explains how people know what is appropriate and grammatical in a specific language. That is, he was interested in figuring out what it is that people know about language. He was not at all interested in the purposes for which people use language in their daily experiences. In Chomsky's theory of language, the goal is to explain how, with a finite set of abstract rules and principles, an ideal speaker–hearer of a language is capable of generating an infinite set of grammatically acceptable sentences.

For Chomsky, language consists of a set of abstract rules that generate the basic or underlying structure of a sentence. The abstract rules have some formal universality, but they are also particular to the language the learner knows. The Universal Grammar, working in harmony with the LAD, sorts out the appropriate rules needed to communicate in the particular language. Words are then attached to the basic structure to complete the meaning of the sentence. All of this is assumed to be a relatively deep level of abstraction because, in many cases, various changes must be made in the rules in order to produce different kinds of acceptable sentences for communication.

Chomsky's proposals stimulated a tremendous amount of research, in the 1960s and 1970s, by a group of linguists (called developmental psycholinguists) who studied young children's native language development. Beginning with the given that the human child is biologically predisposed or "wired" to acquire language (Lenneberg, 1967), these linguists were interested in figuring out how the child actualized this predisposition by acquiring the particular linguistic system of his or her community. By carefully observing children (mostly Anglo, middle-class preschoolers) of various ages, and recording and examining their language utterances, they began to describe a predictable general sequence of native language development (Brown, 1973), as well as the gradual acquisition of such aspects of syntax as negatives and interrogatives (Brown, 1968; Klima & Bellugi–Klima, 1966). Researchers also investigated how children over time develop the sound and meaning systems of their native language (E. V. Clark, 1973; Clark & Clark, 1977; H. Clark, 1970).

The focus of this research was the individual child's gradual construction of conventional forms of language, the child's activity in using linguistic data from his environment, hypothesizing about particular aspects of the language, and revising these hypotheses over time, ultimately reaching the adult conventional forms. While some proponents of the child's innate abilities as a language learner stressed that the child is born with the possibilities for language already present (McNeill, 1970), others suggested that children were born with the cognitive potential for processing language (Slobin, 1966), and that language learning ability is one manifestation of the child's general cognitive abilities (as the constructivists note, the ability to construct knowledge from the environment).

Chomsky's formal approach to language has since been challenged for ignoring how meaning and intentions are developed from and used for social interaction and communication. Jerome Bruner (1983), for example, proposed that children's language develops through social engagements. He proposed that learners have a LASS (Language Acquisition Support System) that interacts with critical aspects of conceptual development to build a language system of meaning as well as language. Another respected researcher, Jean Berko–Gleason (1989), has argued that language development in the Chomskian sense of formal grammar emerges *only after* a great deal of social interaction and intellectual development has occurred. Many other child language researchers have reached similar conclusions about the progression from social to individual language accomplishments (see Bialystok & Hakuta, 1994 for a discussion of this). The most widely accepted current view of native language acquisition is the one labelled by many as the *social interactionist perspective* (Genishi & Dyson, 1984; Lindfors, 1987; Smith, 1988) with its emphasis on the social nature of language development, including spoken and written language. This view does not reject the idea that language resides in the head of the user, but it does emphasize the absolute need for social interaction if language is to be acquired. This is a view that many, if not most, language and literacy educators use as they work with future and practicing teachers. We ask you to keep this position in mind as we subsequently share our principles.

Extending the Psychological Lens to Second Language Acquisition Theories

According to Michael Long (1993), there are between forty and sixty theories of second language acquisition. As diverse in scope, source, and form as they are in number, nonetheless, many of the theories, like those concerned with first language acquisition, are bound to the idea that language development is a result of complex cognitive processing. Some borrow Chomsky's LAD and give it a central place in acquisition (Krashen, 1981; Dulay, Burt, & Krashen, 1982); others use terms like "latent psychological structure" (Selinker, 1972) and "restructuring" (McLaughlin, 1990) to get at essentially the same phenomenon.

Two psychologically based theories of second language acquisition that have had a widespread impact on the way many people in bilingual education think about language and language acquisition are Stephen Krashen's Monitor Theory and Michael Long's Interaction Model. We acknowledge that Krashen's Monitor Theory and Long's Interaction Model may not be the best theories for explaining second language acquisition (SLA). Nonetheless, we choose to focus on them here because both frameworks for SLA, especially Krashen's, are widely known and revered among practitioners in the field of bilingual education.

Monitor Theory

Krashen first introduced the Monitor Theory in 1977 as a comprehensive theory to explain second language acquisition among adult ESL learners. By the mid-1980s, he had extended the theory to include children (Krashen, 1985). The theory consists of the following five major interrelated hypotheses:

1. The learning–acquisition distinction;
2. The natural order hypothesis;
3. The monitor hypothesis;

4. The input hypothesis;
5. The affective filter hypothesis.

The first hypothesis sets the stage for the remaining four hypotheses because it has to do with the process of internalizing new second language knowledge, storing it, and using it for communication. For Krashen, *acquisition* occurs below the level of consciousness as a result of participating in authentic communicative settings in which the focus is on meaning. Acquired language knowledge is stored in a part of the brain reserved for language, and it serves as the major source of initiating and understanding speech. *Learning*, on the other hand, has to do with the conscious study of the formal features of language. You can talk about the language that you learn, and it is not necessarily stored in language parts of the brain. Language that you learn is available only as a means to monitor your output. Finally, what you learn does not become acquired knowledge, because acquisition and learning are two separate ways of developing language abilities. According to Krashen, our efforts in school should focus on facilitating language acquisition; learning should be downplayed considerably because it has nothing to do with acquisition or with the ability to communicate meaningfully with speakers of the language being acquired (Krashen & Terrell, 1983).

The natural order hypothesis states that individuals who acquire (as opposed to learn) a second language follow a more or less invariant order in the acquisition of formal grammatical features of language. A natural order is evident when the individual is engaged in authentic communication; it changes when an individual tries to perform using learned language.

The monitor hypothesis has to do with how acquisition and learning are used for and in the production of language. The language that we have acquired enables us to initiate talk in the second language. Learned language serves only as a monitor for what we wish to say or have just said. Learning, then, enables us to change the output of our acquired system in order to perform beyond our competence. Krashen (1985) suggests that three conditions need to be met to operationalize the monitor: (1) you must be concerned about correctness, (2) you must know the rule in question, and (3) you must have time to employ the rule.

The input hypothesis is what Krashen introduces as his fundamental explanation for how children and adults acquire a second language. He proposes that children and adults acquire language in one way and one way only: They must receive abundant amounts of comprehensible input, and the internal mechanism (the LAD) must process the input and assign it to the developing order of acquisition. What is comprehensible input? According to Krashen (1985), it is meaningful language presented to the learner that is "a bit beyond" the learner's current level of ability.

Interestingly, Krashen sees absolutely no direct role for social interaction in second language acquisition. That is, he does not believe that trying out the new language in oral or written communication with others facilitates second language acquisition. He does admit to an indirect role for output. As you might have guessed, the role of output is to provide a stimulus for more comprehensible input, which in turn contributes directly to second language acquisition. The role of others is to provide comprehensible input to the learner.

Krashen does, however, see a role for the creative construction process in language acquisition. Once the comprehensible input gets into the LAD, the learner can hypothesize about the way language works, and generate new language on the basis of the hypothesis. In this manner, the learner may produce language that is nonconventional, but likely to be understood (e.g., *I no like that car*).

The final hypothesis Krashen proposes has to do with the role of affect in acquisition. *Affect* refers to the learner's feelings about the new language and its speakers as well as the learner's disposition to becoming like speakers of the new language. According to Krashen, to the extent that the learner has positive feelings about the new language and its speakers, i.e., that the affective filter is down, comprehensible input can reach the LAD and be processed and organized into the developing second language system. Figure 4 1 provides a diagram of the Monitor Model.

Interaction Model

Michael Long's Interaction Model (1981) attaches special importance to the role of the negotiation of meaning in making input comprehensible. Like Krashen, Long believes that comprehensible input is the primary cause of second language acquisition. Long, however, argues that interactional adjustments between more and less proficient speakers is what ultimately provides the best environment for comprehensible input to facilitate language acquisition. In particular, Long says that the negotiation of meaning is better for acquisition than simply providing comprehensible input because it aims to repair interaction when nonunderstanding occurs. In attempting to clarify nonunderstanding, the learner provides feedback to the more proficient speaker on what is being understood, and the more proficient speaker adjusts his or her speech or otherwise lets the learner know that the meaning is clear. In this manner, there is a greater likelihood that the input has been comprehended, which in turn, contributes to language acquisition. For Long, interactive input is more important for second language interaction than noninteractive input (Ellis, 1994). Figure 4.2 illustrates Long's Interaction Model.

Early evidence in support of the role of comprehensible input for second language acquisition came mainly from research in child language development (e.g., Cross, 1977; Snow & Ferguson, 1977), and from logic. The child language research showed that mainsteam mothers and other adult caregivers take the perspective of the child and simplify their language when talking to the child. This simplified language, referred to as *baby talk*, enables

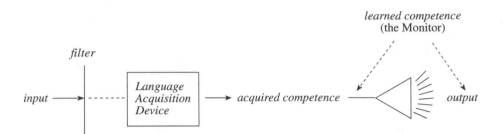

FIGURE 4.1   Krashen's Monitor Model for Second Language Acquisition

Adapted from: Krashen, S., & Terrell, T. (1983). *The natural approach: Language in the classroom.* San Francisco: The Alemany Press.

adults to carry on conversations with young children, and in the process to provide the kind of linguistic and conversational input that promotes language acquisition.

The logical argument for the role of comprehensible input reflects the findings from this early child language development research. The argument proceeds as follows (based on Long, 1985):

1. Because linguistic/conversational adjustments promote comprehension of input, as shown in the research literature,
2. And comprehension of input promotes language acquisition because the LAD is activated;

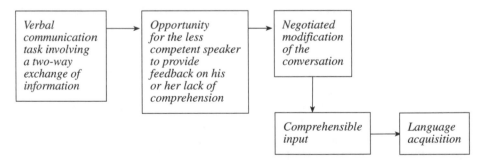

FIGURE 4.2   Long's Interaction Model of Second Language Acquisition

From: Long, M. (1983). Native speaker/non-native speaker conversation in the second language classroom. In M. Clarke & J. Handscombe (Eds.), *On TESOL '82: Pacific perspectives on language learning and teaching* (pp. 207–255). Washington, DC: Teachers of English to Speakers of Other Languages.

3. Therefore, we can deduce that linguistic/conversational adjustments promote language acquisition.

Numbers of studies on the relationship between comprehensible input and second language acquisition have been conducted, but the results have been inconclusive (Ellis, 1994). In addition, several well-respected researchers have critiqued the input hypothesis. Some have suggested that the focus should be on comprehended, not comprehensible, input (Gass, 1988). Others have noted that learner output is critical in the process (Swain, 1985). Still others have argued that second language acquisition occurs as a result of learning to participate in conversations (Hatch, 1978; Peck, 1978; Wagner–Gough, 1975). In spite of these critiques, both Krashen's Moniter Model and Long's Interaction Model appeal to intuition and make sense to many in the field of bilingual education. Why shouldn't they? They are based on empirical evidence coming from psychological and language development research. They both assume the LAD is responsible for organizing and structuring the new language. They both claim to explain how acquisition occurs, and they do so *without having to discuss at all the people who acquire and use language in school and in communities.* We believe that any explanation of language acquisition and learning that excludes social interaction and context undermines two of the most important goals of bilingual education: to produce students (1) who are proficient in two languages, and (2) who can use spoken and written language to participate critically in social and academic experiences and acquire and utilize knowledge that school and society value. Both goals require learners to actively engage in social interaction with peers, texts, and more proficient adults, as opposed to simply receiving comprehensible input from peers, texts, and more proficient adults.

Toward a Different Vision of Language Acquisition and Learning

In contrast to the psychological views presented, we take a strong view that language acquisition and learning depend on two key factors: (1) access to, and (2) participation in, legitimate social activities in which students use multiple forms and functions of language with the goal of understanding and using new discourse appropriately to accomplish their purposes. By discourse, we mean ways of talking or writing within a context, such that the context influences how learners construct what they talk and write about. In our view, students first have to have *access* to what is going on in a particular context, and then, within that context, be able to participate fully. In other words, having access to what is going on is not enough for learning to occur. Students also need to *participate* in discussions and other social activities to make sense of the ideas and concepts and to have opportunities to use language in ways that are authentically associated with those ideas and concepts. That is, rather than meaningful input, students need *comprehensible invite* (Faltis, 1997), oral and written language addressed to them that invites them to participate in the social construction of knowledge.

We believe that the two essential conditions of language acquisition and learning are access to and participation in social activities that enable students to listen to, read, write, talk about, and question what is needed to succeed in school and society. How do access to and participation in legitimate social activities facilitate language acquisition and learning? Rather than invoking a theoretical model based on laboratory experiments and linguistic guesswork, we present our theoretical framework in terms of guiding principles drawn from what we know about the ways that children, adolescents, and adults interact socially in classrooms and communities, and how they use language to create and construct realities from the experiences into which they either stumble or are invited to participate. We would like the guiding principles to serve two purposes. First, they should help you understand language acquisition and learning in bilingual classrooms and communities. We believe that it is important to have a set of principles to use in judging and deciding what is good and useful in bilingual education. Second, we would like you to apply the guiding principles to help you make sense of the ways that we present bilingual education in elementary and secondary schools in the subsequent chapters.

Guiding Principles

Principle No. 1. *Language Is a Socially Shared Meaning System.*

Language is a system for creating and sharing meaning. We start out with this principle not only to underscore the fact that language is profoundly social, but also to set the stage for how it is that socially shared language is acquired and the role of language in learning. In our view of language, the meanings for language are not located in the language itself, nor are they located in the heads of the people who produce it. Rather, language can only mean what its community of users has experienced and has attached to it. Language means what its community of users has decided through use that it means. This is not to say that language cannot be personal, and that individuals cannot use language in personal ways. However, the meaning attached to personal use of language is always social. As Edelsky, Altwerger, and Flores (1991) point out, this is because when we interpret and use language we relate language to social experiences and contexts in which that language figured. Thus the meanings assigned to language have their origins in the experiences and contexts of any given language community.

Edelsky, Altwerger, and Flores also remind us that members of a language community represent meaning through shared conventions of language that are used both consciously and unconsciously. For example, when a child tells or writes a story about her dog, she will follow certain conventions about how to start and end stories, about how to introduce characters, about how to set the location of the story, develop the tension, and so on. The conventions she uses are familiar to her because she has experienced them as she has listened to or read stories within her family and community and perhaps the school. Those listening to her story will construct meaning from it and will acknowledge it as a story if they share the conventions that the girl is using.

Meanings, conventions, and language and literacy practices in both spoken and written language vary from community to community and from setting to setting, for example, the home and the school. Not all communities share the same meanings and conventions and utilize the same practices, and some family and community ways of using language are more congruent with the ways of typical schools than are others (Au, 1993; Gee, 1992; Heath, 1983). To be a member of a particular speech community is to share the meanings and know and use the conventions and practices of that community. Learning a new language thus involves more than learning new vocabulary and rules for forming sentences. Learning a new language entails learning a new set of social and personal meanings, practices, and conventions; it entails learning how to participate successfully in new ways of doing things; it means being socialized into certain ways of being and acting in a new speech community (Gee, 1992; Faltis & Hudelson, 1994).

Principle No. 2. *Learning, Including Language Learning, Is Socially Constructed.*

The traditional educational psychology view of learning is that it takes place inside the individual's head and that it is transmitted from one person to another. In contrast, we believe that learning (including language learning) is fundamentally social. Learners construct their knowledge of the world through engaging with others, some of whom are more knowledgeable than they are, through living and acting in the world. Learning is constructed in relations among people as they engage in activities within social settings, using whatever tools and symbols are appropriate to the particular setting (Warren & Roseberry, 1995). Thus, when a person is hired to work as a receptionist in a doctor's office, s/he learns how to function competently in this setting by observing an experienced receptionist at work; by engaging him- or herself in answering the phone, making and cancelling appointments, responding to questions, and so on; by consulting with the more experienced person to whom s/he is apprenticed; receiving feedback from a supervisor, and so on. The learning is situated within the social setting, and learning occurs within the social practice (Gee, 1992) of being a receptionist.

Similarly, language learning is fundamentally a social enterprise. As children live and participate in families and communities they learn the language (the socially shared meaning system) that surrounds them. This occurs as they observe multiple demonstrations of language use in everyday life; as they engage in using language with others in supportive and collaborative social situations in order to accomplish their ends; as they receive feedback from family and community members; and as they gradually refine their understandings of how to use language appropriately in the social settings in which they find themselves (Smith, 1981; Kucer, Silva, & Delgado-Larocco, 1995). Thus, children learn oral and written language through use, because it is an integral part of community life and functioning, and because it is used around and with them, with the assumption that they will learn it as they live their lives with others (Edelsky, Altwerger, & Flores, 1991). Children learn the meanings, the conventions, the language and literacy practices of family and community as they live and grow within a family and community. Through interaction and collaboration children are socialized into or acquired by their families and communities.

In terms of school, to learn language, whether a first or an additional language, learners need multiple opportunities to try out that language in both spoken and written forms. This trying out of language occurs naturally and meaningfully as learners engage with meaningful content, employing spoken and written language to mediate their learning. Language is a major vehicle for content learning (Genesee, 1994; Vygotsky, 1978). There are multiple disciplines or knowledge systems in school, for example, history, mathematics, science, literature, and so on. Each has its own discourse, that is, its own way of examining the world and constructing knowledge, for example, the discourse of science, the discourse of mathematics, the discourse of history, and so on (Gee, 1992; Lemke, 1990; Short & Burke, 1996).

We believe that learners gain the ability to talk and write about these various ways of knowing by participating in the discourse of knowledge as presented by and through the discipline, by becoming apprentices in the discourse community (Gee, 1992). Thus, learners appropriate the discourse of science or examine the world from a scientific lens, for example, not by memorizing isolated facts or the sequence of the "scientific process," but by participating in communities of scientific practice in which they continually construct and refine their scientific understandings as, using spoken and written language, they pose questions, investigate their questions, develop and argue their evidence, and build and critique their developing theories (Lemke, 1990). Thus, at least part of the curriculum and all of the students' knowledge comes from their own scientific activity. This knowledge is a product of the socially shared interaction and collaboration between teachers and students as well as among students to engage in ways of talking that moves students closer to the community of practice (Lave & Wenger, 1991; Warren & Roseberry, 1995).

Principle No. 3. *What Students Talk, Read, and Write about Matters.*

Social interaction about nonsense and trivial matters begets more nonsense. Along with how they learn, *what* learners learn must be given serious consideration. Learners need to have opportunities to share their own stories. They need to be able to explore issues in their lives and those of their families and communities, including the classroom and school communities. Learners also need opportunities to examine topics and themes of personal interest, to ask questions and look for answers. A major function of schooling is the development of the understanding of learning as inquiry, of asking and seeking answers to questions as the core of learning, not only learning in school but learning throughout life (Short & Burke, 1996). Learners need to see themselves as problem solvers, as engaging in posing and answering questions in order to better understand the world around them (Dewey, 1929). This means that some learner choice in and control over curriculum is essential.

But learners also need to be challenged to look critically at the society in which they live and take note of existing inequality, injustice, racism, sexism, and the like. Having done this, some of the work of school should be focused on contributing to the struggle for justice and equality, changing the world for the better, whether that world is the school, the local neighborhood, the larger local community, the state, the country, or the world beyond the United States (Brady, 1995; Freire, 1970; Peterson, 1989). We believe that a major function of school is to prepare learners for responsible citizenship, and that responsible citizenship includes critiquing and challenging the status quo, and working to see that the reality of life in the United States more closely matches the rhetoric (Shannon, 1994; DeVillar, Faltis, & Cummins, 1994). So what learners learn needs to include critique, social action, and active citizenship (Edelsky, 1991; 1994).

Principle No. 4. *Literacy Is Language; Language Is Literacy.*

Language and literacy cannot be separated. Put another way, both spoken language and written language are language. They are different sides of the same coin. Central to both is the creation and construction of meaning. Both are socially constructed. Both are developed in and through use, as learners generate, test, and refine hypotheses. Mistakes or inventions are an inevitable aspect of both language and literacy learning. Traditional school views of spoken and written language that separate it into listening, speaking, reading, and writing, and suggest "teaching" each process separately and sequentially do not reflect the interdependence and interconnectedness of spoken and written language. Rather, both language and literacy are necessarily and inextricably involved in first and second language acquisition, and both mediate participation in ways of knowing in and out of school settings. Classroom environments should promote the natural and authentic use of spoken and written language, which occurs as learners engage with interesting and significant content.

Principle No. 5. *L₁ Proficiency Contributes to Learning and to L₂ Development; L₁ Interaction Facilitates L₂ Participation.*

Many programs for second language learners in U.S. schools advocate or assume that school learning should occur exclusively in and through English. We reject that position as a denial of learners' basic linguistic rights to their native language (Shannon, 1994; Skutnabb–Kangas, 1994). We also believe that this position reflects a lack of understanding or naivete with regard to the reality that, because knowledge is socially constructed, it follows that learners will be better able to construct knowledge if they are able to do so through a language that they know well rather than through a language that they are still struggling to learn and to express themselves in. When learners exchange ideas in their primary language and participate in various ways of knowing, what they learn can be more easily discussed and written about in the new language, English. Language plays a central role in learning, and we maintain that learners need to be encouraged to use their native or stronger language throughout the school day as they work to make sense of content. Enabling students to use their primary language for learning is a way of inviting students to participate in learning.

In a similar vein, native language literacy benefits second language learners, and native language literacy should be promoted. There is a lot of - evidence that learners who feel confident being literate in their primary language venture into the second language, using or applying their primary language knowledge and abilities for reading and writing in the second language (Edelsky, 1982, 1986; Hudelson, 1987, 1989). Second language learners who have become literate in their native language know what it means to be a literate person; they know what written language is good for, what written language allows them to do within a community of language users.

When learners exchange ideas in their primary language and are invited to participate in various ways of knowing, they can more easily discuss and write about what they learn in the new language, English. Accordingly, they have a much greater opportunity to become fully bilingual and biliterate as a result of their social and academic experiences.

Concluding Remarks

It has been our goal in this chapter to explain to you what we understand and believe about learning and language acquisition. We have done this by contrasting current perspectives on the social/cultural/political nature of language and learning to more traditional, individualistic, and cognitive notions still articulated in much of mainstream educational psychology and still dominant in a significant number of classroom settings. Our theoretical framework for bilingual education classroom practice is based on the following principles:

1. The fundamentally social nature of both spoken and written language;
2. The reality that learning, including language learning, is socially constructed;
3. The importance of intellectually stimulating, culturally and socially relevant, and critical content in school to the creation of bilingual–biliterate learners who will become responsible and active citizens;
4. The interdependence of spoken and written language and the impossibility of teaching listening, speaking, reading, and writing as separate processes or separated from or devoid of meaningful content;
5. The contributions of native language proficiency and literacy to learning and literacy in English.

We have devoted an entire chapter to the articulation of our beliefs for two reasons. First, we want to convince you that our principles are the appropriate ones around which to structure instructional practices. Secondly, we want you to begin to examine and critique bilingual education instructional practices, both those you observe and those in which you engage, in relationship to this set of principles. We do not want you simply to accept the status quo. In Chapters 5 and 6 we invite you to begin this examination and critique as we share multiple classroom scenarios with you.

References

Au, K. (1993). *Literacy instruction in multicultural settings.* Ft. Worth, TX: Harcourt, Brace, Jovanovich.
Baghban, M. (1984). *Our daughter learns to read and write.* Newark, DE: International Reading Association.

Berko–Gleason, J. (1989). *The development of language.* Columbus, OH: Merrill.

Bialystok, E., & Hakuta, K. (1994). *In other words: The science and psychology of second-language acquisition.* New York: Basic Books.

Brady, J. (1995). *Schooling young children: A feminist pedagogy for liberatory learning.* Albany, NY: SUNY Press.

Brown, R. (1973). *A first language: The early stages.* Cambridge, MA: Harvard University Press.

Brown, R. (1968). The development of wh-questions in children's speech. *Journal of Verbal Learning and Language Behavior 7,* 279–290.

Bruner, J. (1983). *Child's talk: Learning to use language.* New York: W. W. Norton.

Burns, M. (1991). *Math by all means.* Sausalito, CA: Math Solutions Publications.

Chomsky, N. (1977). Linguistic theory. In F. Smolinski (Ed.), *Landmarks of American language and linguistics,* (pp. 262–266). Washington, DC: English Language Programs Division, USIA.

Chomsky, N. (1959). *Syntactic structures.* The Hague: Mouton.

Clark, E. V. (1973). What's in a word?: On the child's acquisition of semantics in his first language. In T. Moore (Ed.), *Cognitive development and the acquisition of language,* (pp. 65–109). New York: Academic Press.

Clark, H. (1970). The primitive nature of children's relational concepts. In J. Hayes (Ed.), *Cognition and the development of language,* New York: John Wiley and Sons.

Clark, H., & Clark, E. (1977). *Psychology and language: An introduction to psycholinguistics.* New York: Harcourt Brace Jovanovich.

Cochran–Smith, M. (1991). Learning to teach against the grain. *Harvard Educational Review, 61,* 279–310.

Cohen, H., Horak, J., & Staley, F. (1984). *Teaching science as a decision-making process.* Dubuque, IA: Kendall Hunt.

Cross, T. (1977). Mother's speech adjustments: The contribution of selected child listener variables. In C. Snow and C. Ferguson (Eds.), *Talking to children: Language input and acquisition* (pp. 151–188), Cambridge: Cambridge University Press.

DeVillar, R. A., Faltis, C., & Cummins, J. (Eds.) (1994). *Cultural diversity in schools: From rhetoric to practice.* Albany, NY: SUNY Press.

Dewey, J. (1929). *My pedagogic creed.* Washington, DC: Progressive Education Association.

Driscoll, M. (1994). *Psychology of learning for instruction.* Boston: Allyn & Bacon.

Duckworth, E. (1987). *The having of wonderful ideas.* Cambridge, MA: Harvard University Press.

Dulay, H., & Burt, M. (1975). Creative construction in second language learning and teaching. In M. Burt & H. Dulay (Eds.), *On TESOL '75: New directions on learning, teaching and bilingual education,* (209–233). Washington, DC: TESOL.

Dulay, H., Burt, M., & Krashen, S. (1982). *Language two.* New York: Oxford University Press.

Edelsky, C. (1982). Writing in a bilingual program: The relation of L1 and L2 texts. *TESOL Quarterly 16,* 211–228.

Edelsky, C. (1986). *Writing in a bilingual program: Habia una vez.* Norwood, NJ: Ablex Publishing.

Edelsky, C. (1994). Education for democracy. *Language Arts, 71,* 252–257.

Edelsky, C. (1991). *With literacy and justice for all.* Philadelphia: Falmer Press.

Edelsky, C., Altwerger, B., & Flores, B. (1991). *Whole language: What's the difference?.* Portsmouth, NH: Heinemann.

Ellis, R. (1994). *The study of second language acquisition.* New York: Oxford University Press.

Faltis, C. (1997). *Joinfostering: Adapting teaching strategies in the multilingual classroom,* 2nd Ed. New York: Merrill.

Faltis, C., & Hudelson, S. (1994). Learning English as an additional language in K–12 schools. *TESOL Quarterly 28*(3), 457–468.

Ferreiro, E. (1990). Literacy development: Psychogenesis. In Y. Goodman (Ed.), *How children construct literacy: Piagetian perspectives,* (pp. 12–25). Newark, DE: International Reading Association.

Ferreiro, E., & Teberosky, A. (1982). *Literacy before schooling.* Exeter, NH: Heinemann.

Fosnot, C. (1989). *Enquiring teachers, enquiring learners: A constructivist approach for teaching.* New York: Teachers College Press.

Freeman, D., & Freeman, Y. (1994). *Between worlds: Access to second language acquisition.* Portsmouth, NH: Heinemann.

Freire, P. (1970). *Pedagogy of the oppressed.* New York: Herder and Herder.

Gage, N. L., & Berliner, D. (1984). *Educational psychology,* 2nd Ed. Boston: Houghton Mifflin.

Gagné, R., & Driscoll, M. (1988). *Essentials of learning for instruction,* 2nd Ed. Englewood Cliffs, NJ: Prentice-Hall.

Gass, S. (1988). Integrating research areas: A framework for second language studies. *Applied Linguistics, 9,* 198–217.

Gee, J. (1992). *The social mind. Language, ideology and social practice.* New York: Bergin and Garvey.

Genesee, F. (1994). *Integrating language and content: Lessons from immersion.* Santa Cruz, CA: National Center for Research on Cultural Diversity and Second Language Learning.

Genishi, C., & Dyson, A. (1984). *Language assessment in the early years.* Norwood, NJ: Ablex.

Goodman, K. (1996). *On reading.* Portsmouth, NH: Heinemann.

Goodman, Y. (Ed.). (1990). *How children construct literacy: Piagetian perspectives.* Newark, DE: International Reading Association.

Hatch, E. (1978). Discourse analysis and second language acquisition. In E. Hatch (Ed.), *Second language acquisition* (401–435), Rowley, MA: Newbury House.

Heath, S. (1983). *Ways with words.* New York: Cambridge University Press.

Hudelson, S. (1987). The role of native language literacy in the education of language minority children. *Language Arts 64,* 827–841.

Hudelson, S. (1989). *Write on: Children writing in ESL.* Englewood Cliffs, NJ: Prentice-Hall.

Hudelson, S., & Faltis, C. (1993). Redefining basic teacher education: Preparing teachers to transform teaching. In G. Guntermann (Ed.), *Developing language teachers for a changing world,* (pp. 23–42). Lincolnwood, IL: National Textbook Company.

Kamii, C. (1985). *Young children reinvent arithmetic: Implications of Piagetian thought.* New York: Teachers College Press.

Klima, E., & Bellugi–Klima, U. (1966). Syntactic regularities in the speech of children. In A. Bar-Adon & W. Leopold (Eds.), *Child language: A book of readings* (pp. 152–178), Englewood Cliffs, NJ: Prentice-Hall.

Krashen, S. (1985). *The input hypothesis: Issues and implications.* London: Longman.

Krashen, S. (1981). *Second language acquisition and second language learning.* Oxford: Pergamon.

Krashen, S., & Terrell, T. (1983). *The natural approach.* San Francisco: Alemany Press.

Kucer, S., Silva, C., & Delgado–Larocco, E. (1995). *Curricular conversations: Themes in multilingual and monolingual classrooms.* York, ME: Stenhouse Publishers.

Lave, J., & Wenger, E. (1991). *Situated learning: Legitimate peripheral participation.* New York: Cambridge University Press.

Lemke, J. (1990). *Talking science: Language, learning, and values.* New York: Ablex.

Lenneberg, E. (1967). *Biological foundations of language.* New York: Wiley.

Lindfors, J. (1987). *Children's language and learning,* 2nd Ed. Englewood Cliffs, NJ: Prentice-Hall.

Lindfors, J. (1980). *Children's language and learning.* Englewood Cliffs, NJ: Prentice-Hall.

Long, M. (1993). Assessment strategies for SLA theories. *Applied Linguistics, 14,* 225–249.

Long, M. (1985). Input and second language acquisition theory. In S. Gass and C. Madden (Eds.), *Input in second language acquisition* (377–393), Rowley, MA: Newbury House.

Long, M. (1981). Input, interaction and second language acquisition. In H. Winitz (Ed.), *Native language and foreign language acquisition, Annals of the New York Academy of Science 379,* 259–278.

McLaughlin, B. (1990). Restructuring. *Applied Linguistics, 11,* 113–128.

McNeill, D. (1970). *The acquisition of language.* New York: Harper and Row.

Merino, B., Hammond, L., Faltis, C., & Goldberg, D. (1994). The portability of constructivism: Cases in the implementation of a sheltered constructivist approach to the teaching of science to language minority children. Paper presented at the Annual Meeting of the American Educational Research Association, New Orleans, LA, April 8.

National Association for the Education of Young Children. (1995). NAEYC Position statement: Responding to linguistic and culture diversity: Recommendations for effective early childhood education.

National Council of Teachers of Mathematics (1989). *Professional standards for teaching mathematics.* Washington, DC: National Council of Teachers of Mathematics.

Peck, S. (1978). Child–child discourse in second language acquisition. In E. Hatch (Ed.), *Second language acquisition* (pp.383–400), Rowley, MA: Newbury House.

Peterson, R. (1989). Teaching how to read the world and change it: Critical pedagogy. In C. Walsh (Ed.), *Literacy as praxis: Culture, language and pedagogy,* (pp. 156–182), Norwood, NJ: Ablex Publishers.

Selinker, L. (1972). Interlanguage. *International Review of Applied Linguistics, 10,* 209–230.

Shannon, P. (1994). Patriotic literacy: The intersection of whole language philosophy and the bill of rights. In A. Flurkey and R. Meyer (Eds.), *Under the whole language umbrella: Many cultures, many voices* (85–101), Urbana, IL: National Council of Teachers of English.

Short, K., & Burke, C. (1996). Examining our beliefs and practices through inquiry. *Language Arts, 73,* 97–104.

Skutnabb-Kangas, T. (1994). Linguistic human rights and minority education. *TESOL Quarterly 28*(3), 625–628.

Slavin, R. (1997). *Educational psychology,* 5th Ed. Boston: Allyn & Bacon.

Slobin, D. (1966). Comments on 'developmental psycholinguistics.' In F. Smith & G. Miller (Eds.), *The genesis of language: A psycholinguistic approach* (129–148), Cambridge, MA: MIT Press.

Smith, F. (1988). *Understanding reading,* 3rd Ed. Hillsdale, NJ: Lawrence Erlbaum.

Smith, F. (1981). Demonstrations, engagement and sensitivity: A revised approach to language learning. *Language Arts, 60,* 103–112.

Snow, C., & Ferguson, C. (Eds.). (1977). *Talking to children: Language input and acquisition.* Cambridge: Cambridge University Press.

Swain, M. (1985). Communicative competence: Some roles for comprehensible input and comprehensible output in its development. In S. Goss and C. Madden (Eds.), *Input in second language acquisition* (235–256), Rowley, MA: Newbury House.

Tudge, J. (1990). Vygotsky, the zone of proximal development and peer collaboration: Implications for classroom practices. In L. Moll (Ed.), *Vygotsky and education: Instructional implications and application of sociohistorical psychology,* (pp. 155–172), New York: Cambridge University Press.

Vygotsky, L. (1978). *Mind in society.* Cambridge, MA: Harvard University Press.

Wagner–Gough, J. (1975). *Comparative studies in second language learning.* CAL-ERIC/CLL Series on Language and Linguistics, 26.

Warren, B., & Roseberry, A. (1995) *"This question is just too, too easy!" Perspectives from the classroom on accountability in science.* Santa Cruz, CA: National Center for Research on Cultural Diversity and Second Language Learning.

Weaver, C. (1994). *Reading process and practice: From sociopsycholinguistics to whole language,* 2nd Ed. Portsmouth, NH: Heinemann.

Wertsch, J. (1984). The zone of proximal development: Some conceptual issues. In B. Rogoff and J. Wertsch (Eds.), *Children's learning in the "zone of proximal development,"* (pp. 7–18). San Francisco: Jossey-Bass.

5

Bilingual Education in Elementary School Settings

In Chapters 5 and 6 we move from broader policy-related, organizational, and school building program implementation concerns to a detailed consideration of what goes on in specific classrooms. As you have seen, bilingual education programs have been organized and implemented in both elementary and secondary settings, with the majority of programs in elementary schools. In Chapter 5 we examine bilingual education practices in elementary schools. We define elementary as kindergarten through sixth grade, although we know that some elementary school sites include seventh and eighth grades.

In this chapter we present vignettes from a variety of elementary school classrooms, classrooms chosen because teachers are working from an understanding of and belief in the principles of learning and language acquisition articulated in Chapter 4. The vignettes themselves illustrate some of the ways that elementary school educators have worked to incorporate these principles, whether they find themselves teaching in transitional, maintenance, or two-way bilingual settings, or working exclusively through English as a second language instruction. We introduce each vignette by providing background information on the specific classroom setting, after which we provide a view of part of a typical classroom day. We then discuss each vignette, focusing on ways that the classroom scenes illustrate one or more of the guiding principles discussed in Chapter 4. Thus, we alternate between a description of what is happening and a consideration of what we believe to be good teaching and learning, based on our guiding principles.

Before presenting the vignettes, we want to remind you of the principles we articulated in Chapter 4.

1. Language is a socially shared meaning system (language socially shared);
2. Learning, including language learning, is socially constructed (learning socially constructed);
3. What students talk, read, and write about matters (centrality of meaningful content);
4. Literacy is language; language is literacy (language and literacy intertwined);
5. L_1 proficiency contributes to learning and to L_2 development; L_1 interaction facilitates participation (importance of L_1 proficiency/literacy).

You will have noticed that a short phrase appears in parentheses after each principle. These phrases appear in our discussions of each vignette as we relate classroom instruction to the guiding principles. As you read each vignette, we encourage you to think about each scenario in relation to the guiding principles. Before you read each discussion section, you may want to think about how you would answer the following questions:

How does the teacher in the vignette teach as if language is socially shared and constructed?

How does the teacher in the vignette teach as if learning is socially shared and constructed?

What kinds of meaningful content do the children study?

How are the children using and developing their abilities to talk, read, and write?

How is the native language and native language literacy promoted?

What evidence is there that the native language and native language literacy are used to facilitate second language acquisition?

Bilingual Kindergarten

The first classroom vignette comes from a half-day bilingual kindergarten in a school district located in the urban core of a large city. The school population is about 65 percent Hispanic, 30 percent Anglo, and 5 percent African American and Native American. For more than ten years a transitional Spanish–English bilingual program has been available at the school.

Because the numbers of Spanish dominant kindergarten learners are greater than the numbers of English dominant kindergarten children, some of the bilingual classes, such as the one in this vignette, are made up entirely of Spanish-speaking children. This class has twenty-three children in it. All come from homes where Spanish is used almost exclusively. About two-thirds of the children attended a bilingual preschool or Headstart program prior to kindergarten. Those with previous formal schooling experiences are more familiar with English than those children who have not been to school before, but all of the children are more comfortable using Spanish than they are English.

The children's teacher, Ms. Moreno (Ms. M.), is an educated native speaker of Spanish, born, raised, and schooled through secondary school in Mexico. In the United States, she has earned both undergraduate and graduate degrees in early childhood education, with a focus in her graduate studies on bilingual early childhood education. Her classroom practice reflects a strong commitment to bilingual education, along with advocacy for developmentally appropriate instruction in early childhood settings. She emphasizes experiential, hands-on learning in which children actively construct their own understandings of phenomena and processes (National Association for the Education of Young Children, 1991).

For a variety of reasons (the length of the school day, the multi-year nature of the bilingual program, the program's commitment to native language literacy, the children's language strengths), Ms. M. and the children spend more time learning in and through Spanish than they do English. However, their use of English increases steadily over the course of the school year.

The vignette shared here takes place in April of the kindergarten year and includes writing and story time, two significant features of this classroom. On this particular day, the children are clustered at several tables and on the floor with their journals and writing folders, chatting, sharing their work and seeking assistance from each other. One of the children, Cecilia, is illustrating a story about her dog. Cecilia has written a draft of the story, spelling the words using her own predictions about and understandings of sound–letter relationships in Spanish (Hudelson, 1981–1982). Thus, for example, Cecilia has written one of her ideas; *Mi perro estaba corriendo* [My dog was running], as *Mi perro stava corendo*. Because Cecilia has decided that she wants to publish this story for the classroom library, her teacher has retyped it on the computer in conventional Spanish, so that she can create illustrations to accompany the print. Cecilia has most of the text in memory so that she is able to, as one of her classmates puts it, *"leer sin ver"* [read without looking], meaning she can retell the contents of each page without hesitation and without focusing on the graphophonic display, what some might call "pretend reading" (Carger, 1993).

However, as Cecilia begins her work today, she looks intently at the typed page in front of her and begins, laboriously, to sound out each of the words that previously she has read smoothly from memory: *Mmm iiiiii p p p eeerrrrrrroo eeee sttaaaa baaaaaa*. Her determined sounding out and exclusive emphasis on pronouncing the sound each letter makes demonstrate to Ms. M., who has been listening in, that Cecilia has made the critical connection between letters and sounds that will allow her, eventually, to read whatever she chooses to read. Ms. M. gives Cecilia a big hug and tells her that what she has done is very important, that she is figuring out how to read on her own. Then she moves away to work with another child, leaving Cecilia to continue her work.

At another table Diana is working on her own story. She is writing about an imaginary playmate, Erica. Diana is not yet using sound–letter correspondences when she writes. Instead she produces strings of letters to which she attributes meaning (Goodman, 1993). As Ms. M. sits next down to Diana she asks: *¿Qué estas escribiendo?* [What are you writing?] Diana responds: *A Erica le gusta el chocolate*. [Erica likes chocolate.] Diana already has written the word *Erica* (the name of one of her cousins) from memory. She then asks Ms. M. to help her spell the word *le*, and she brings out a small Spanish alphabet chart that many of the children use to help them when they are spelling on their own. Ms. M. pronounces the word *le* slowly, emphasizing the first sound, and asks Diana how she thinks *le* begins. Diana replies *-l l l- ele de libro* [the "l" of libro, meaning 'book']. Diana then picks up the alphabet chart, says *ele de libro* again and points at random to the letter *p*. Ms. M. points to the letter *l* and tells Diana that this letter is the one she is looking for. Diana writes down the *l* and then says *e de elefante* [*e* of *elephant*], after which she goes to the alphabet chart, makes a circle in the air with her finger, and brings it down on the letter *c*. Ms. M. shows her which letter is *e de elefante* and Diana writes it. Ms. M. realizes that Diana understands that representing her ideas includes representing sounds with letters, but she does not know which sounds represent which letters. So she needs help in connecting sounds with their corresponding letters. In the notebook she carries with her, Ms. M. jots down that she needs to sit with Diana as often as possible in order to assist her. She also decides to ask some other children who know which letters represent which sounds to help Diana.

As writing time comes to a close, Ms. M. asks the children to put their work away and sit on the rug. Two learners, Daniel and Laura, have signed up to share their stories. Ms. M. reminds the children that they need to sit quietly and listen to their classmates and that when each author has shared his or her story the others may offer compliments, what they liked about the story, and ask questions if they have any. Following sharing time, Ms. M. announces that it is story time.

There are three events on tap for story time today. The first is reading aloud a story in Spanish. Ms. M. has chosen Joe Hayes's version of *La Llorona* (1987). She begins by asking the children if they have ever heard of *La Llorona*.

Several of them nod their heads yes, and others raise their hands eager to share what they know. Ms. M. calls on three of the children to share their knowledge and then reads the story. When she finishes she asks the children for any comments they may want to make. Again multiple hands shoot up as the children share parts of the story they liked (*A mí me gustó cuando el ranchero entró al pueblo,* and so forth) [I liked it when the farmer came into town], and compare their own versions of the legend to this one).

When the children have finished sharing their impressions of the story, Ms. M. invites Adrián to come and sit in the chair (*El Sillón del Lector*) [the Author's Chair] reserved for someone who is going to read aloud to the class. Adrián has brought a book that his mother bought him at the local grocery to share with the class. Using the pictures, Adrián tells the story and shares the pictures with the class, much as he has seen his teacher do. At the end of his rendition, Adrián receives a warm round of applause.

The final item on tap for story time today is the rereading and dramatization of *Caps for Sale* (Slobodkina, 1940), a predictable book that the children enjoy having read in English. Ms. M. brings out the book and reads it through once, encouraging the children to join in with her. She then assigns several small groups of children to play the role of monkeys who respond by imitating the peddler's actions as he jumps up and down, or wags his finger, or throws his cap down and says to them, "You monkeys you. Give me back my caps!" As Ms. M. reads through the story a second time, the groups of children play their parts. On a third reading, one of the children assumes the role of narrator and another speaks the lines of the peddler while the rest continue to be monkeys. The children frequently use Spanish to negotiate their understandings of how to participate in this choral reading/readers' theatre activity, and they help each other with their English parts.

Discussion:

Writing is a central feature of Ms. M.'s curriculum, both because it provides the children opportunities to share their ideas and experiences and because, as they work to express themselves through written language, the children come to understand how written language functions and how it is produced. Through seeing demonstrations of writing provided by Ms. M. and through engaging in writing themselves, the children learn both how to write (their writing becomes more conventional) and what purposes writing can serve (Goodman, 1996). As they generate and test out their hypotheses about how written language works, they are involved in the natural and authentic use of both spoken and written language (**Principle 4: language and literacy intertwined**). In addition, Ms. M. encourages children to write in their native language, both because she knows that children will construct meaning more easily in a language they are comfortable in, and because she knows that native language literacy will contribute to later second language literacy (**Principle 5: importance of L$_1$ proficiency/literacy**).

Reading aloud also is central to Ms. M.'s curriculum. Ms. M. understands that if she demonstrates reading, and if she engages children in rereadings and in constructing their interpretations of stories, eventually children will become readers themselves (**Principle 4: language and literacy intertwined**). And as children discuss stories, they jointly construct meaning and create richer meanings and interpretations (**Principle 2: learning socially constructed**). Ms. M. reads aloud daily for multiple purposes, and she chooses the books read aloud with care. She selects some books for the quality of the story and the potential for group discussion, to promote children's transactions with and interpretation of literature (Peterson & Eeds, 1990). Some titles relate to content children are studying. Ms. M. chooses other books for one or more elements of predictability, which make the books particularly powerful as sources of comprehensible input for the learners.

Early in the year Ms. M. usually reads in Spanish. As the children become more comfortable both with responding to literature and listening to English, however, Ms. M. uses more stories in English. However, the children continue to share their interpretations in Spanish, and Ms. M. uses Spanish along with English to make sure that the children are constructing meaning from the selections (**Principle 5: importance of L$_1$ proficiency/literacy**).

There is a constant buzz of activity and conversation in Ms. M.'s room. Children constantly consult each other, use each other as resources, and work together on projects. Ms. M. believes strongly that children learn through active participation in hands-on activities, and through asking and answering their own questions. She understands that children learn more if they work together than if they work in isolation, and that they learn both content and language from and with others (**Principle 2: learning socially constructed**).

First Grade/Two-Way Bilingual Program

The second vignette comes from a first grade classroom that is part of a developmental, two-way bilingual program in a semirural working class neighborhood that is within the city limits of a major metropolitan area. The neighborhood is almost exclusively Hispanic. More than half of the families are second- or third-generation neighborhood residents, but there is a sizeable community of recent immigrants from Mexico and Guatemala. The school's original bilingual program began with a transitional philosophy. Five years ago, however, the principal, several teachers, and a group of parents began talking about the possibility of developing and implementing a two-way bilingual program, so that the English-speaking Hispanic children would be able to learn Spanish, as well as the Spanish speakers learn English. Funds from Title VII enabled school personnel to design their program. Given the normal hegemony of English (Shannon, 1995), the bilingual team decided that, in the early grades (K, 1, 2), all of the children needed to be immersed in Spanish nearly all day, with English receiving increasing prominence from third grade on. Therefore they adopted the 90/10 two-way model described in Chapter 2. The children learn through Spanish almost exclusively in kindergarten and first grades. In second grade the amount of English is increased to about 20 percent, in third grade to about one-third of the day, and from fourth grade on learning is half in Spanish, half in English.

All of the twenty-two children in the first grade class are Hispanic, but seven are native speakers of English and fifteen are native speakers of Spanish. Their teacher, Señora Coronado, is a native Spanish speaker, schooled basically in English, but whose family continued to use Spanish and to encourage Sra. Coronado to use her home language and to be proud of it. Sra. Coronado studied Spanish formally at secondary and university levels and received her undergraduate degree in elementary bilingual education. She has since earned a master's degree.

The vignette we share occurs on a chilly March morning. The first graders in Sra. Coronado's room are clustered around the door to their room. Sra. Coronado has been called to the office, and the children stand shivering awaiting her return. When an adult visitor approaches, one of the children asks, "Do you speak English?" When the adult responds affirmatively, the same child asks, "Do you speak Spanish?" The adult again answers in the affirmative and asks the child if he speaks Spanish as well. The child says, "*Sí*," and several other children volunteer that they do, too. At this point Sra. Coronado reaches the door, and the children cluster around informing her that the visitor speaks both Spanish and English. "*Qué bueno*," [how neat] comments Sra. Coronado.

As the children enter the room, they move to tables where their seats have been assigned. Above each table is a cardboard cutout of a geometric form: a square, a circle, a triangle, a rectangle, an oval. As the children take their seats, they chat in both English and Spanish. The tardy bell rings and the public address system asks the children to stand and salute the flag. The principal then makes some announcements. When he concludes, Sra. Coronado calls one table at a time to sit on the rug, referring to the tables as "*la mesa del rectángulo, la mesa del círculo*," and so on. No English is used. The rug is situated in front of a chalkboard and calendar display. The calendar reads *marzo* and the days have been filled in through March 7, today. When the children have gathered, Sra. Coronado asks one of the children, Ana, to help her with the opening exercises. Ana uses a ruler to point to and read the following sentences that appear on the chalkboard:

Hoy es _____ [Today is]

Ayer fue _____ [Yesterday was]

Mañana será _____ [Tomorrow will be]

Hoy vamos a educación física [Today we will be going to physical education]

The group consults the calendar in order to complete the sentences chorally. Pointing to the number line that snakes around a significant portion of the classroom, Mrs. Coronado asks, *"Por cuántos días hemos estado en la escuela?"* [How many days have we been in school?]. Ana responds, *"ciento veinticinco,"* [125], after which she turns to the groupings of popsicle sticks underneath the calendar and points to a grouping of a hundred sticks (*una centena*), two groups of ten sticks each (*dos decenas*), and five single sticks (*cinco unidades*). Sra. Coronado helps all the children count the sticks: *ciento, ciento diez, ciento veinte, ciento veintiuno, dos, tres, cuatro, cinco. Ciento veinticinco días.* [100, 110, 120, 121, 2, 3, 4, 5, 125 days].

Then Sra. Coronado points to several weather cards placed below the calendar and asks: *¿Qué clase de día es?* [What kind of a day is it?]. One of the children replies, *"Hay mucho sol,"* [It's really sunny] and Sra. Cornonado writes that sentence on the board. Another child says "It's windy" and points to the card that pictures the wind and is labelled *Hay viento*. Sra. Coronado responds, *"Sí, tienes razón. Hay viento. ¿Hay mucho viento?* [Yes, you are right. It is windy. Is there a lot of wind?]. When several of the children answer *Sí,* [Yes.] Sra. Coronado writes *Hay mucho viento*, pronouncing the words as she writes. A third child raises her hand and offers, *"Hace frío"* [It's cold]. Sra. Coronado holds her shoulders as though shivering, repeats *Hace frío,* and writes the sentence. She and all the children then read the sentences together.

Next Sra. Coronado directs the children's attention to a story problem written on one of the blackboards and illustrated with stick figures. She reads, *"Tony tiene 11 Power Rangers. Rita le dió uno más. ¿Cuántos Power Rangers tiene en total?* [Tony has 11 Power Rangers. Rita gave him one more. How many does he have in all?]. She asks the children what they think the answer is. One child guesses *doce* [12] and another *diez* [10]. To solve the problem, Sra. Coronado brings out some plastic figures that represent the Power Rangers. She and the children go through the problem, the real Tony and Rita acting out the operation. When they have finished everyone agrees that the answer is 12.

Before journal time, Sra. Coronado announces that she wants to share something from Lucy's journal. She has written part of a recent journal entry on an overhead projector transparency and now displays it. It reads:

Yo le ayudo a mi mamá. A mi mamá le duele la espalda. Y yo digo que pasa. *[I help my mom. My mom's back hurts her. And I say what happens.]*

Sra. Coronado points out that Lucy is using periods at the end of her sentences and capital letters at the beginnings of sentences. She then points to the words *que pasa* and tells the children that when authors are writing the words that someone actually said (*las palabras que salieron de la boca de Lucy*), they use marks around the words (*estas marquitas que se llaman comillas*), and she puts quotation marks around the words. Sra. Coronado also points to her own mouth as she indicates what a quotation is and quickly draws a stick figure with a quotation balloon coming out of its mouth. She then gives a couple of other examples of sentences that include direct quotations and how quotation marks may be used. She tells the children that if they are writing the actual words that someone has said they may want to use these marks in their writing. This week's helpers then distribute the children's journals.

While the children begin to work, Sra. Coronado walks to a corner of the room where a table and chairs are set up, along with a toy cash register, a notepad and paper, and a small chalkboard. There are also several envelopes containing play coins and some paper plates. A sign reads *Restaurante* (Restaurant). Sra. Coronado writes *papitas* [potato chips] 15 c on the blackboard. She places the bag of potato chips that Rosie, a native English speaker, has brought to school by the cash register and calls Rosie and three other children to the restaurant. She then walks away. Three of the children sit around the table and Rosie gives them envelopes of play money. Rosie then picks up the notepad, asks what they will have, takes their order, brings them *papitas*, takes their money, and makes change if necessary. While the intention is that this activity will take place in Spanish, both languages are used, especially when some of the children, Rosie for example, are not fluent in Spanish. Sra. Coronado takes no part in the activity once she has called the first group of children. When the first children finish eating, each goes to another child in the room and indicates that it is that child's turn to go to the restaurant.

During journal time Sra. Coronado sits with individual children, listening to them read what they have written, making comments on and asking questions about what they have drawn, writing back to some of them, and helping some articulate what they want to say. For example, she sits with Tony, a child who comes from a home where Spanish is spoken but who entered this first grade classroom speaking almost no Spanish. On one page Tony has drawn a picture of several people and has written:

Child's writing	English translation
Mi papa tiene una foodarama	My dad has a foodarama
Mi hermano tiene un carro	My brother has a car
Mi mama tiene un perro	My mom has a dog
Yo tiene un perro	I have a dog
Yo tiene un Batman	I have a Batman

Sra. Coronado is pleased that Tony has written several sentences in Spanish about his family. She tells him that he is learning so much Spanish. To herself she notes that he is using a pattern that he knows (*X tiene*) to construct his sentences in Spanish, even though this pattern does not produce a conventional Spanish sentence when Tony writes about himself (he should have written *yo tengo*). She remembers having read about young second language writers using patterns in an ESL context (Hudelson, 1989). She recognizes that Tony has used the pattern from sentences the children have created about one of their classmates, Juan, featured in a photo display and in print as *El Niño/La Niña de la Semana* (Child of the Week). Child of the Week is a regular classroom activity that highlights a different student each week. The children dictate sentences to the teacher about the child. Some of the sentences about Juan read: *Juan tiene una hermanita chiquita. Juan tiene un perro que se llama Oso.* Sra. Coronado writes to Tony:

> Yo no tengo un Batman [*I don't have a Batman*]
> Tengo un gato y tengo un perro [*I have a cat and I have a dog*]

She reads him these sentences before moving on to work with Marcos. Marcos is a child who knew virtually no Spanish at the beginning of the school year. When Sra. Coronado sits next to him, he shows her a picture of a whale that he has drawn and tells her in English about the picture. Mrs. Coronado responds in Spanish, repeating in Spanish what Marcos has said, and then points to a slash of red on the whale's body, asking in Spanish what Marcos is coloring red. Marcos explains in English that a knife has cut the whale and that blood is coming out. Sra. Coronado repeats what Marcos has said in Spanish, pointing to the parts of his picture as she talks and emphasizing words such as *sangre* [blood] and *navaja* [knife], and leaves him to his work.

As the children finish their journal entries, they return their journals to the box in which they are stored and select a book from the bookshelf. A few children choose to read with a partner, others by themselves. The most popular books seem to be those that Sra. Coronado has read previously to the class, especially those that are highly predictable, such as *La Señora Lavandera, De Quién Eres, Ratoncito,* and *Los Tres Osos.* After a few minutes, Sra. Coronado announces that it is time for physical education and the children line up at the door.

Discussion:

A major goal of this two-way program is that all children will use the Spanish language, both for social interactions and for learning. Sra. Coronado knows that if the children in her room use spoken and written Spanish to participate in classroom events and to create and share their meanings and learnings with each other, their abilities with both the spoken and written language will increase. Thus she has worked to create a classroom community in which Spanish is the expected language. Sra. Coronado's goal is to promote a speech community in which participating in community life in and through Spanish is the norm, a community in which children need to use Spanish to accomplish their intellectual work, to be successful classroom participants and learners, and choose to use Spanish for social, as well as, academic purposes. The Spanish language needs to be an integral, central, necessary part of classroom life (**Principle 1: language socially shared**).

Because not all of the children come to her room producing Spanish, however, Mrs. Coronado needs to be careful to organize her classroom so that those less fluent in Spanish will be able to observe Spanish used naturally and authentically; to try out the new language while others support their efforts; and to receive feedback on what they have produced to enable them to refine their understandings and abilities. The non-Spanish-speaking children will learn Spanish as they use it to participate in the life of the classroom community (**Principles 1 and 2: language socially shared, learning socially constructed**).

One of the ways Sra. Coronado has tried to accomplish this is through a set of daily/weekly routines (the calendar, the daily weather, counting the number of days of school, the math problem, the child of the week, and so on) that, by virtue of their repetition, have become familiar to, understood by, and comfortable for all the children. The language in these routines/events also has become familiar, comprehensible, and predictable to all the children, thus facilitating linguistic participation in the activities. Sra. Coronado contextualizes the language she uses with gestures, pictures, and real objects, to better insure children's understanding and participation, to make it comprehensible (Krashen, 1982) and inviting (Faltis, 1997). She encourages group participation, so that the children who are more fluent in Spanish can help the others, and so that the non-Spanish speakers can try out the new language in the safety of a group. She accepts the children's attempts to use Spanish, expanding and extending their Spanish if they use unconventional and incomplete forms. She allows the use of English, but then she provides the Spanish, thus modelling the language once again. Because she stays in Spanish, she challenges the children to try to use the new language.

Because Spanish is being used for nearly all classroom activity, the children see that there are real uses for the language, that it is necessary to use spoken and written Spanish to participate fully in classroom life. Charts around the room depict topics that children have studied and demonstrate that Sra. Coronado has structured activities so that children may contribute to group work with whatever Spanish they are able to offer, or even with a picture. Some of the charts are titled: *¿Quiénes son los miembros de tu familia?* [Who are the members of your family?] *¿Dónde vive tu familia?* [Where does your family live?] *¿Cuál es tu comida favorita?* [What is your favorite food?] (**Principles 2 and 3: learning socially constructed, centrality of meaningful content**).

When Sra. Coronado works with individual children on their journals, she accepts the children's productions, but she also provides examples of conventional written language through her own writing. In the minilesson on quotation marks, Mrs. Coronado focuses briefly on a convention of written language, a convention chosen because of what she has seen in the children's writing. She thus demonstrates the natural and authentic use of this convention (**Principle 4: language and literacy intertwined**).

Mrs. Coronado serves as a Spanish language model for the children and encourages them to experiment with the language. But children also need to use the language with each other. The restaurant activity provides an opportunity for peer interaction and for children to become more proficient in Spanish by using the language with each other (**Principles 1 and 2: language socially shared, learning socially constructed**).

Second/Third Grade Combination Bilingual Class

The next classroom scene comes from a primary, multi-age bilingual classroom that is part of a maintenance bilingual program in a large city. In recent years the school's population has become increasingly Hispanic and Spanish-speaking. The class of twenty-seven children is divided into about 60 percent native Spanish speakers and 40 percent native English speakers, with about equal numbers of children who are in second and third grades. Most of the children have been in the bilingual program since kindergarten or first grade, but there are four who are recent arrivals from Mexico and understand and use less English than do many of the other children.

The children's teacher, Ms. Vernon, is a native English speaker with fourteen years of teaching experience and a master's degree in bilingual education. She has been studying Spanish since her undergraduate education and talks frequently with the children about the importance of being bilingual and working to know and use two languages. A native Spanish-speaking instructional assistant who completed secondary school in Mexico works part-time in Ms. Vernon's classroom.

The afternoon activities we examine took place in April. A sign on the door of Ms. Vernon's room reads *Estamos en computadoras*/We are at the computers, and the class is just returning from the computer lab where they have been using the Internet to search for information on ocean animals. These second and third graders are involved in a study of the ocean with a fourth and fifth grade bilingual class, and cross-age teams of children are preparing presentations about the animals they have chosen to research. Some of the children arrive with computer printouts, which they deposit in their cubbies for use at the next group meetings. As the children settle in, Ms. Vernon announces that it is mathematics time and that the children are going to divide into three groups to work. Using a list, Ms. Vernon assigns some of the children to work with her aide, Sra. Cárdenas, some to work with her, and the others to work with Mrs. Davis, a Title 1 educator who, because the school has adopted an inclusion model for special services, spends about forty-five minutes a day in Ms. Vernon's room working in mathematics. All of the groups contain some children who use only English, some who are fluent bilinguals, and some who are more comfortable in Spanish. Especially in the group facilitated by Mrs. Davis, who does not speak Spanish, the bilingual learners translate for both teacher and Spanish-speaking children when necessary.

Ms. Vernon asks the members of her group to bring their math notebooks with them. Each child receives a plastic container of wooden triangles, of different sizes and kinds (equilateral, isoceles, right angle). Using two triangles, Ms. Vernon explains that the children are going to choose any two triangles and compare them to each other. How are they alike? How are they different? She elicits possible answers from the children. After a few children have responded in English, Ms. Vernon switches to Spanish and asks: *¿Cómo son iguales? ¿Cómo son diferentes?* [How are they the same? How are they different?] and encourages some of the Spanish-speaking children to answer. She then directs the children to choose two triangles, compare them, trace them, and write down their comparisons/contrasts in their notebooks.

Ms. Vernon observes their work and gradually begins to interact with each of the learners. She challenges the children to prove their answers and helps them to articulate their observations. She also provides some of the mathematical terms for the children's descriptions. For example, when one of the children points to the bases of two triangles and says that these parts are the same, Ms. Vernon asks the child to prove this assertion. After the child puts one triangle on top of the other, matching the bases, Ms. Vernon notes, "You proved that the *bases* of the two triangles are the same *length*. They are *equal* in length."

One child contrasts the amount of space inside two triangles and Ms. Vernon labels this the area, and also labels it in Spanish. As another child contrasts what she describes as "a tall and fat triangle" (equilateral) with "a tall but not fat triangle" (right triangle), Ms. Vernon points out the angles, that one has what is called a right angle and one does not. She directs the children to look at the size of the angles to see differences. She also makes protractors available, because some of the children previously have been experimenting with them on their own, using them to draw angles. Ms. Vernon continues to interact with individual children. She closes the session by asking each child to choose two triangles and share with the others how they are alike and different.

While Ms. Vernon has been working on triangles, Sra. Cárdenas and her group have been creating a train using a set of wooden shapes (circle, triangle, diamond, square, pentagon, hexagon) that come in two different sizes and thicknesses and three different colors (red, yellow, blue). Each child's task is to add to the train by choosing a shape that is like the previous one in three ways and different in one way. If one child, for example, puts down a large, thick blue triangle, the next child may put down a large, thin blue triangle, or a large, thick blue diamond, or a large, thick green triangle, and so on. As each child adds to the train, s/he has to explain why a particular piece was chosen: How the piece is like the previous one and different from the previous one. Sra. Cárdenas encourages each child to explain his or her choice, allowing them to use whichever language they prefer. If a child is not able to articulate a decision, Sra. Cárdenas supplies the language.

The group of children working with Mrs. Davis is sitting close to the chalkboard, and Mrs. Davis is asking them to solve two-digit addition equations. At first glance, this resembles traditional addition practice. But Mrs. Davis stops at each equation and asks one or two children to explain how they arrived at their answers. For example, for the problem 37+45 one child begins in the tens column and adds 3 tens and 4 tens to get 7 tens or seventy. The child then adds 7 and 5 to make 12, and adds 70 and 12 to arrive at 82. Another child begins with the 37 and adds 3 to get 40. The child then takes three from 45, gets 42, and adds 40 and 42 for a total of 82. Mrs. Davis does not speak any Spanish, and at times the bilingual children in the group assist their Spanish dominant friends with their explanations.

As the math groups conclude their work, Ms. Vernon asks the class to form a circle on the rug (also the location of daily opening and closing exercises, class meetings, and problems/compliments time). She reminds them that the previous day they had conducted experiments in pairs. Then she asks: What's an experiment? Several children respond: "*Es hacer algo, una cosa, que inventaste*" [It is doing something, some thing, that you invented]. "You try something out and see what happens." "You try more than once and somebody else should be able to do it." "Another person can do it—what you did—and get the same results." Ms. Vernon tells the children that they will be doing experiments again today with specific materials. Their job is to create and carry out an experiment and be prepared to share their experiment and to explain what they learned. Ms. Vernon divides the class into pairs and trios and gives each group a tray containing scissors, paper clips, elastic bands, paper, clay, bar magnets, a piece of wire, and some iron filings. She sets the class to work and slowly moves among the children, observing the work, asking what their experiments are, and helping them to articulate what they are doing. The children use both Spanish and English, and Ms. Vernon restates what they have said in Spanish or English.

After a work period, Ms. Vernon calls the class back into the circle and asks each group to share its experiment. As the children demonstrate what they did, Ms. Vernon restates their articulations in more formal terms. For example, one group has tried to pick up both paper clips and the wire with the bar magnet. The magnet picked up the paper clips but not the wire. The presenter's comment was, "We tried to pick up these and these. The wire didn't pick up." Ms. Vernon notes, "So your experiment was to see if the magnet would lift both the wire and the paper clips. What happened? Why do you think the magnet didn't pick up the wire?"

Another group has rubbed the bar magnet on some of their paper clips but not all. They have discovered that the magnetized clips stick together while the nonmagnetized clips do not (according to the child presenter, "We rubbed the magnet like this. *Y se pegaron*" [and they stuck together]). They also have tried to pick up iron filings with the paper clips. The magnetized clips have picked up the filings, the nonmagnetized clips have not.

Throughout the sharing, Ms. Vernon articulates their procedures and their discoveries ("So you want to know if you will still be able to cut paper when the clips are hanging on the scissors. What happened?"). After all of the groups have presented, the children clean up their experiments, putting all the materials away and preparing to go home.

Discussion:

Ms. Vernon believes strongly in a curriculum that is both meaningful and intellectually stimulating to her students. She maintains that becoming bilingual learners are as capable and competent as any other learners, and that they need to be pushed and challenged and provided opportunities to learn through discovery and investigation (**Principles 2 and 3: learning socially constructed, centrality of meaningful content**). Her math curriculum has been influenced by her graduate study and by the National Council of Teachers of Mathematics (NCTM) Standards (National Council of Teachers of Mathematics, 1989), which extend beyond number concepts and operations to explorations of geometry, measurement, probability, estimation, statistics, and functions. The NCTM standards also highlight the importance of learners articulating their mathematics reasonings, learnings, and understandings in oral, visual, and written forms, and Ms. Vernon emphasizes this in her teaching, as her work with mathematics notebooks and with children's explanations of their reasonings illustrates (Fortescue, 1994). Ms. Vernon's work with number operations is based on the work of Constance Kamii (1985) and other math educators, who have demonstrated that children are able to construct their own understandings of operations and that their teachers need to acknowledge children's ways of doing arithmetic.

As with mathematics, Ms. Vernon believes that children need to approach science as problem-solving, which necessarily involves: asking questions, making predictions, observing, seeking to answer the questions that have been posed, articulating ideas, and defending one's ideas. She also believes that children need time to explore materials and processes informally (to "mess around") before adults impose a lot of structure. Ms. Vernon views her job as one of providing materials, posing questions, challenging learners to explain processes and products, and, at times, attaching more formal mathematical and scientific language to children's work and ideas. She hopes to introduce children to scientific and mathematical discourse by beginning with their own ways of expressing their learning (**Principle 2: learning socially constructed**). Ms. Vernon knows that young children's mathematics and scientific understandings do not correspond to conventional adult understandings, but that their understandings and perspectives are important; that they reflect children's conceptualizations at certain points in time; and that understandings grow and change over time if children receive opportunities to engage in meaningful activity.

As children engage with mathematics and science they necessarily use both spoken and written language and thus language develops along with content knowledge (**Principle 4: language and literacy intertwined**). For becoming bilingual children, engagement with content naturally happens in both the native and second language of the learners. Ms. Vernon encourages children to use their native language to mediate their learning, even if she is using English, because she knows that this will assist both their language and content learning (**Principle 5: importance of L_1 proficiency/literacy**).

Ms. Vernon also believes that children learn both language and content from each other as they work together. So she organizes many activities in which children must work cooperatively. However, she recognizes that the teacher also must take an active role in children's learning, by observing and assisting small groups (Jacob, Rottenberg, Patrick, and Wheeler, 1996).

Third Grade/Transitional Bilingual Program

The vignette that follows takes place in a third grade bilingual classroom that represents the final grade of a transitional bilingual program in an urban elementary school. In the last several years the numbers of Spanish-speaking children in the district have increased dramatically, and the schools have responded by offering bilingual education in the primary grades. The campus on which this class is located is now 60 percent Hispanic, with 45 percent of those children evaluated as in need of bilingual educational services. This class of twenty-nine children is almost evenly divided between English and

Spanish speaking children. Eleven of the Spanish speakers have been in the bilingual program since kindergarten; three arrived less than six months ago from Guatemala.

The teacher, Sandra Thomas, is a native English speaker who majored in Spanish in college. After earning her degree in Spanish, she decided that she wanted to teach and returned to school to earn a teaching credential. She has been teaching for five years, all of them at this school.

It is mid-October, and the weather invites outside activities. The sound of children's voices floats down the walkway of the third grade wing. A group of six Spanish-speaking children is sitting under a tree with the bilingual special education teacher, copies of *La Bruja Mon* open to a page of the story that they are discussing. Three more groups of children are working inside the classroom, one in Spanish with the instructional assistant, and two in English, one with the classroom teacher, and one with the Title 1 teacher. In each group, children are engrossed in talking about a story that they have read. Ms. Thomas's group is just finishing up their talk about Leo Lionni's *Alexander and the Wind-up Mouse* (1989), with one child remarking, "I think the story tells you you need to be happy with who you are." "Yeah," says another, "like Alexander He can see it's good to be a real mouse." Another child adds, "And he also helps Willy." Ms. Thomas holds up the last page of the book and notes that Alexander and Willy look very happy dancing at the end of the book. She says that for her what was important was that Alexander saw that he had a good life, that he was content with what he had, and that he helped Willy to have that life, too. Then she asks the children to get out their literature study notebooks and write to her about how they felt about the book. She reminds the children that the letter is something personal between each child and her. Whatever the children want to write is fine. She also reminds the children that she will read their letters and write back to them. One of the girls, Juanita, takes out her notebook and writes:

> *Dear Ms. Thomas*
> *This book is a nice Book. I liked the part when Alexander med is wich to change Willy in to a ril mouse and he got is wich. Ms. Thomas I Didn't understand when Alexander was goin to mick a wich he was goin to wich to meick him in to a wind-up mouse like Willy but in steed he sed to change willy in to a ril mouse.*
> *Juanita*

Conventional English:

> *This book is a nice book. I liked the part when Alexander made his wish to change Willy into a real mouse and he got his wish. Ms. Thomas I didn't understand when Alexander was going to make a wish. He was going to wish*

to make him[self] into a wind-up mouse like Willy but instead he said to
change Willy into a real mouse.

When Juanita finishes her letter, she drops her literature study notebook into the inbox on Ms. Thomas's desk. She finds a book to read until the end of literature study time, when all of the groups finish their work. Juanita is one of the children in the classroom who began her literacy instruction in Spanish. She has been reading in both English and Spanish since second grade, but she only began to try to write in English in August, when she started third grade.

Ms. Thomas then asks the children to get out their writing folders. Juanita has been working on a story about her family titled "Just My Brother My Sister and Me." Her draft reads this way:

One day my mom and my dad wher going to see a dace and me and my
brother and sistes stayd home aloen. We ear junk food like cooki n ice crim
and soda like soda and ice crem in it and milk whith water in it and it was
good and then we med a big mes. I spild water in the floor My sister spillde
coke in the kichen and at 3:00 in a morning my mom and my dad came back
and my and my brother and my sister wher like a coarton we wher clining
da house and we breli med it. We trnd off the lit and thid like if whe wher
asleep and then the other they let us aloen again.

Juanita has requested a conference with her teacher to read over her story and get some suggestions. Ms. Thomas asks Juanita to read the whole story. She laughs at the end and says, "You mean they didn't catch you? They let you stay alone the next time they went out?" Juanita nods and laughs. Ms. Thomas shares that she enjoyed the way that Juanita described what the children did while their parents were gone. She shows Juanita a place where she was confused as Juanita was explaining what the children ate. She also suggests that Juanita may want to read her piece through carefully and perhaps remove some of the "ands" she has used throughout. She also suggests that she read the piece out loud and think about where the sentences begin and end so that she can insert periods and capital letters.

After telling Juanita how proud she is of her that she is trying to figure out how to spell words in English, Ms. Thomas indicates that when Juanita has made whatever changes she chooses, the two of them will sit down and look at some of the spelling in the piece. As Juanita goes off to work on her piece, Ms. Thomas writes in her anecdotal records that while earlier more of Juanita's spellings seemed to come from spelling words in English using Spanish orthography, her current spelling reflects attention to English orthography. Before writing ends for the day, Juanita comes up with the following changes in her story:

Home Aloen

One day my mom and my dad wher going to a dace. Me and my brother and sister stayd aloen. We eat junk food like soda and ice crem in it and milk whith water in it and it was good. Then we med a big mes. I spild water in the floor. My sister spillde coke in the kichen. Then at 3:00 in the morning my mom and my dad came back and and me and my brother and my sister wher like a coarton. We wher clining da house and we breli med it. We trnd off the lit and did like if whe wher asleep. Then the other they let us aloen again.

the end

At the conclusion of writing time, it is time for the class to go to lunch. Since Ms. Thomas does not have duty today, she stays in her room, eating lunch and answering the letters the children have written her in their literature study notebooks. In response to Juanita's letter, she writes:

Dear Juanita:
 I think that Alexander changed his mind about being a wind up mouse after he found Willy in a junk box. Alexander saw that the little girl did not want to play with Willy anymore. What do you think?
 Ms. T

Discussion:

As a third grade teacher, Ms. Thomas often feels ambivalent about the use of Spanish and English in her classroom, because the school district policy is that all children will enter English-only classrooms in the fourth grade. On the one hand, she knows that some of the Spanish speakers in her room still need some time to develop as proficient readers and writers in Spanish, so that they can apply their understandings about literacy to their second language (**Principle 5: importance of L$_1$ proficiency/literacy**). She also has experienced Spanish-speaking children refusing to use Spanish or even acknowledge that they know it, and she wants to counteract this attitude. So she wants to persuade her Spanish-speaking students that Spanish is of value to them and that they should continue to read Spanish and use the language for social and academic purposes. On the other hand, she knows she also needs to encourage the use of English and provide children opportunities to become comfortable using the language to learn. And she sees learners such as Juanita, who are eager to add on English literacy. She works to balance these conflicting demands in several ways.

During the morning literacy block, Ms. Thomas consciously makes literature in both Spanish and English, and at a variety of difficulty levels, available for the children, both for independent reading time (DEAR—Drop Everything and Read) and for adult-led literature study groups (Peterson & Eeds, 1990). Each week, as she introduces the book choices for literature study, she comments on the importance of becoming a good reader in both Spanish and English, and she often suggests to children who have been reading in only one language that they try reading a book in the other language. Because this school has adopted an inclusion model for services such as special education and Title 1 (see Chapter 3 for a discussion of inclusion), she is able to bring additional educators into the room during literature study time, which makes it easier to provide small discussion groups and to provide for groups in both Spanish and English. During daily read aloud time, Ms. Thomas also makes sure that two readers are available, one reading in Spanish and the other in English, so that the children have an option to listen in the native or second language.

One of the criteria Ms. Thomas uses in selecting some of the books utilized for literature study and read aloud experiences is that of relevance to the children. Ms. Thomas views response to literature as one avenue for children to explore issues in their own lives (**Principle 3: centrality of meaningful content**). Books such as Patricia Machlachan's *Arthur for the Very First Time* (1980) or Juan Farias's *El Hijo Del Jardinero* (1987) (both of which concern, among other things, the changes that occur in families with the coming of a new sibling) exemplify the kinds of books Ms. Thomas seeks to include in her literature program. Ms. Thomas has elected to use literature study, a strategy in which children read a book of their choice independently and then come together to discuss their responses to it, because she believes that individual understandings of a piece of literature are enriched through the sharing of responses (**Principle 2: learning socially constructed**).

Ms. Thomas also makes use of both languages in her writing program. One of her aims with writing is to show children that writing can take different forms and serve different functions, and that people become more proficient writers by engaging in the practice (**Principle 4: language and literacy intertwined**). When children write letters to their adult literature study partners, they use writing mainly to state their own opinions and to ask questions. When they create personal narratives in what is referred to as writing workshop (Calkins, 1994), they write to share their own experiences and to entertain others. As with reading, the children have a choice of which language to work in. Ms. Thomas encourages some learners to continue writing in Spanish, explaining that once they have learned to write well in one language, writing in the other language will be easier (**Principle 5: importance of L_1 literacy**). Ms. Thomas encourages children like Juanita in their English writing, because she knows that children can write in their second language while they are still learning the language (Hudelson, 1984; Peyton, Jones, Vincent, and Greenblatt, 1994). But she also reminds the children that they may want to write in Spanish from time to time, especially when they are writing to someone who is more comfortable using Spanish. As the year progresses Ms. Thomas will encourage more English writing and reading because the children will be faced with English language environments in the fourth grade.

The children's writing in both English and Spanish is not yet completely conventional, and Ms. Thomas responds to this in different ways. Rather than marking up the children's literature response letters, Ms. Thomas demonstrates conventional written language in the letters that she writes to the children. In dealing with the issue of conventionality in the children's narratives, Ms. Thomas focuses initially on the drafting of the stories, on the content of what children wish to relate. When the young writers are comfortable with the content, she then works with them on language conventions, much as many professional writers do (**Principle 4: language and literacy intertwined**). Depending on the children's expertise, the number of unconventional features, and the purpose for the writing, Ms. Thomas may or may not require that the final written version be entirely conventional (Hudelson, 1989; Labbo, Hoffman, & Roser, 1995). Ms. Thomas also uses writing workshop because she believes that the children have important stories about their lives to tell and to share with each other, and that a significant part of the school curriculum needs to come from the children themselves (**Principle 3: centrality of meaningful content**).

Fourth/Fifth Grade Bilingual Class

The classroom practices described here take place in a combination fourth/fifth grade in a K–5 elementary school in the urban core of a large city. Over 70 percent of the students at this school are Spanish-speaking. Many are from families who have immigrated to the United States in the last five years. In this class, 75 percent of the children are native Spanish speakers, ranging from those who use both languages easily to others who have been in the United States only a year and are still much more comfortable in Spanish than in English. The recent arrivals have attended school in their native countries and enter U. S. classrooms literate in Spanish. There have been tensions at the school, and in this class, between the Spanish speakers native to the city and the recent arrivals (often referred to by others as *wetbacks* or *mojados*). About 25 percent of the children in this class of twenty-nine are native English speakers. The children's teacher, Donna Morgan, is just completing her third year of teaching. While she is not a native speaker of Spanish, she does have substantial proficiency in the language, and she spends part of every summer in Mexico, working with children and improving her language abilities. Her undergraduate degree is in elementary bilingual education, and she has continued to take courses, particularly in the areas of mathematics and computers, to assist her in her classroom. She is one of the teachers at the school that makes the most regular use of computers, including the extensive computer lab, and there are two computers set up in her room. Frequently parents and Donna Morgan's mother volunteer in the room.

It is the last Tuesday of the school year and Donna Morgan is preoccupied with cleaning and dismantling the classroom in preparation for the end of school. But the children in her class know that it is Tuesday and that Tuesday is Community class time. They insist that this activity go forward even if it is the last week of school. And so Ms. Morgan and her children gather in a circle on the rug. Community class begins with the ritual reciting of a poem. One of the children carries two tagboard sheets containing the poem "I Am an Individual" and its Spanish translation (*"Soy un Individuo"*) to the circle and leads the children in reciting it in both languages. Although this child is a speaker of English, she feels comfortable with both versions of the poem because the children have used this work many times. Virtually all of the children participate in the poetry reading.

Another ritual, instituted to help build a sense of community (Peterson, 1992), is the singing of a song. Ms. Morgan asks one of the boys to choose a song for the group to sing. He chooses Chicana folksinger Tish Hinojosa's bilingual *"Bandera del Sol*/Flag of the Sun" and retrieves the version written on tagboard chart paper while Ms. Morgan finds the audiotape. The class sings along with enthusiasm.

Following the poem and song Ms. Morgan asks if there is any community news that anyone wants to share. Children share their news, some in English and some in Spanish. There is no group translation after each child speaks. Rather, bilingual children in the class are seated next to those children who speak only one language, and they translate quietly for children who have difficulty understanding. One of the children has brought in an article from the newspaper that explains that there is going to be a march in Washington, D.C. for children, sponsored by the Children's Defense Fund, and that a few local people are planning to attend the march. This piece of news stirs the children's interest, and they ask for more information: What's the march for? Who's going to it? What's going to happen? Soon the discussion evolves into a group decision to create posters in support of the march and rally. In addition, some of the children want to compose a letter to Marian Wright Edelman, Children's Defense Fund Executive Director, explaining what they have done locally, because they can't go to the march. Ms. Morgan agrees that this seems like a reasonable activity for the last Community class, and she asks several children to retrieve the necessary supplies from the back of the room.

The children form six working groups of four or five each. Two girls approach Ms. Morgan to ask if she thinks it is a good idea to create bilingual posters. She thinks so but stops the class to ask the others. Because the general concensus is yes, Ms. Morgan asks what that means for the working groups. The children note that they will need to have both English and Spanish speakers in each group, and some of the groups reorganize to make sure that both languages are represented. As the children start to work, the noise level increases with the sound of conversations. Among themselves, the children negotiate what will go on each poster and who will carry out what part of the task.

As the Community class time draws to a close, Ms. Morgan asks the children to bring their posters back to the circle to share them. Along with their brilliantly colored illustrations of young people, the groups have created texts such as these:

Todos los niños tienen el derecho de vivir en paz
All children have the right to live in peace

No importa el color que seas
It does not matter what color you are

Kids have rights too
Los niños tienen derechos también
Kids First   School is Cool

Later in the morning a group composes a letter to send to Marian Wright Edelman, which includes this observation, "We think a lot of people think that kids don't think. You do." At lunch recess two of the groups head for the library to consult the librarian about the address of the Children's Defense Fund. Returning to the classroom, they announce that they have found both the street address and the Children's Defense Fund e-mail address, and immediately the letter is transferred to e-mail and sent out.

The Community Kids project is one that Ms. Morgan has carried out in her classroom for an entire year. Its goal has been to help children become active participants in their communities. The project began with a focus on creating community in their own classroom and then connecting with and serving the local community around the school. To create community within the classroom, Ms. Morgan set aside a two-hour block of time each Tuesday for what came to be called Community class. At the beginning of the year, after the opening ritual of poem and song, the children got to know each other better by sharing their own personal stories. Some shared in English, some in Spanish, and some used both languages. Ms. Morgan asked the more bilingual children to sit next to their monolingual counterparts and assist them with translations as needed.

Once the children knew each other and the adults better, the focus shifted to the community around the school. To help children learn more about the community, over several weeks' time the class constructed a hand-drawn map of the neighborhood around the school. Each week the children had an assignment to (1) observe carefully some aspect of the neighborhood (for example, places where people gather, places for children to play, places where graffiti is prevalent, places where families can receive assistance); (2) come prepared, every Tuesday, to share what they had found; and, (3) in small groups, to add to the map.

In addition, each week children were invited to share news about what was happening in the community, both the community within the school and that of the neighborhood around the school. While some of the accounts depicted robberies and drive-by shootings, children also reported on such aspects of community life as graffiti painted buildings (including their own school building), activities at local churches and the senior citizens center, the preschool for homeless children that was close to the school, and the like.

The children's growing awareness of issues around the school and neighborhood turned into multiple opportunities for projects for the class. In this way, the children were beginning to see themselves as having some control over their own lives, as being able to make a positive difference in their own surroundings. The children also began to see that, even if they had very little themselves, there were a lot of people with much less than they had, and that they could help others; they could contribute to the betterment of their community.

Some of the children in the class, for example, were distraught that their classroom building, set at a considerable distance both from the school office and from the main street, had graffiti all over it. They responded to this situation by writing to the school principal asking that the building be repainted and volunteering to assist with the task. The principal responded that paint had been purchased quite a long time ago, but that the school maintenance personnel were too busy with their own tasks to get the job done. This resulted in the children deciding that they needed to recruit painters for a Saturday painting party. From the school staff and their parents, they organized a Saturday work day, and their building was repainted.

As part of their community mapping project, the children had learned about social service agencies and educational facilities in addition to their school. One that they discovered was a preschool program that served the homeless children in the area. As they talked about this situation, several children suggested that the class visit the preschool and read to and play with the preschoolers. Arrangements were made for this visit, and the class became involved, on a regular basis, with this group of youngsters. Among other activities, the fourth and fifth graders organized and put on holiday parties for the preschoolers and created and sent them cards. The older children became involved in the lives of their young friends.

Discussion:

The original impetus for the Community class was Ms. Morgan's belief in the importance of building community in the classroom. In order for children to work together and learn from each other (**Principle 2: learning socially constructed**), Ms. Morgan understood that she needed to nurture the development of a group of children who knew each other well and who respected and cared about each other. Respect included attitudes of acceptance for languages and cultural practices different from one's own.

As the class members coalesced into a classroom community, Ms. Morgan's agenda of involving the learners in examining the local community and contributing to its betterment (**Principle 3: centrality of meaningful content**) became more prominent. For Ms. Morgan the children's community and community responsibilities needed to move beyond the classroom to the real world around them (McCaleb, 1994). One of the functions of school was to challenge children to engage with the world and contribute to its betterment. Naturally and authentically, children use both spoken and written language as they work to accomplish their social goals (**Principle 4: language and literacy intertwined**). This is illustrated both by the group work on the posters and by the letter written to Marian Wright Edelman.

Fourth Grade Bilingual Class

The scenario that follows takes place in an intermediate classroom in an urban school made up almost entirely of Latino children. Because of increasing numbers of newly arrived Spanish children in the upper grades, this school has extended its bilingual program beyond the primary years. The children in this particular class vary from English-speaking to bilingual to Spanish dominant. Seven of the thirty-one learners have been in the United States less than a year, and another ten less than two years. All of them attended school in their home countries and are literate in Spanish.

The children's teacher, Sandra Pérez, was born in Colombia but raised in the United States. She spoke Spanish in her home growing up and has studied it at the university level. Just completing her fourth year of teaching, she is currently working on a graduate degree. She is interested in computer technology and is committed to exposing her students to the kinds of things that they can do with computers. Currently she is involved in a special externally funded computer utilization project in her district, which has meant that five computers have been placed in her room, four terminals for the children to use and one for her, set up with a large screen monitor so that she can provide demonstrations.

It looks as though an exercise class is about to start as Mrs. Pérez asks the fourth graders to find their pulses on their necks and count the number of beats in fifteen seconds. Once this has been accomplished, the children pair off and see how many sit-ups, jumping jacks, and push-ups they can do in a minute. They record their results on charts they have been using for the last three weeks, and examine their charts to see if they are getting stronger. Mrs. Pérez puts on an audiotape and the children follow the leader in a variety of exercises, after which they take their pulses again.

On returning to the classroom, Mrs. Pérez asks one of the children what her pulse was before and after exercising. She graphs the two figures on a large-screen computer so that the children can see that Alicia's pulse after exercising was almost twice as fast as before exercising. She then asks: Why is there a difference? As children respond, for example, because blood is entering and leaving the heart very fast, she asks further questions: Why is the blood moving faster? Why does the blood need to get to your body? What are you using when you are exercising? What is happening to your body? Mrs. Pérez asks questions in both English and Spanish, using Spanish with the children who are themselves using Spanish and who seem to have trouble following the discussion in English.

She then uses a portion of a videotape that shows how the valves of the heart open and close, how blood flows to and from the heart, and how the speed of all of this varies depending on whether the body is at rest or is active. One child comments, "It looks like it [the heart muscle] is going to tear." When Mrs. Pérez hears this child's comment, she rewinds the videotape and asks the child to point out what he saw. She then asks the children if they think that the heart is going to tear, and why or why not?

Mrs. Pérez directs the children to get into their working groups. Different groups have been studying various organs of the body and are working to prepare presentations for the class. Before she lets the group begin work, she reminds them that each group will be making a presentation, and she suggests that they try to think of how they will present their information. She holds up some of the groups' work and notes that most have created posters and written pieces to decribe what they have learned. However, there are other ways to present information. She asks Juan, who has been studying the intestines, how he could help the others understand just how long the intestines are. He says that he could measure how long the intestines are on the floor. Mrs. Pérez asks him how he will be able to show the others how long the intestines are if he can't leave his measuring tool on the floor. He thinks a minute and then says that he could cut a piece of yarn the proper length. Mrs. Pérez agrees.

When she releases the children, there is a flurry of activity as they begin to work. The larger groups quickly subdivide so that boys are working with boys and girls with girls. Children move to work on their posters, to use the four computers in the room to write up what they have learned, to consult the model of the human body with its removable organs, or to read some of the many books available in English and Spanish.

Juan gets out the meter wheel and measures off seven meters, the length of the small intestines, which he then measures again with purple yarn. He shows Mrs. Pérez his length of yarn and she asks him what about the large intestine. Would he like to show the others how long the large intestine is as well? He readily agrees and measures off two more meters, this time using green yarn. Mrs. Pérez suggests that some children will understand the length better if he uses the measurement unit of feet rather than meters, and she helps him convert his meter measurements to feet.

Alex, who has been in the United States for two years, has used Netscape to find out some information on the brain and to print out three pictures of the brain that are of such good quality that they resemble photographs. He is busy pasting them and his report on the brain on to a large sheet of poster board. His report reads:

El Cerebro

Your brain tells your body what to do. When you get hit around your brain you can't see much. The brain looks like a bunch of veins and it is all slob-bery It is not like a circle. When you see your head it looks like a circle but it's not a circle. The brain is kind of big.

El cerebro parece tripas. Cada cerebro es diferente.
[The brain looks like intestines. Each brain is different.]

Three girls, who have been in this country less than a year, sit at one of the computers negotiating the wording of their report on the heart. They examine their notes and the poster of the heart they have created. One of the girls composes on the computer as the others dictate:

El corazon esta en medio de los pulmones.

El corazon sirve para vivir porque si no tuvieramos el corazon no podriamos vivir. El corazon tiene dos ollitos por donde pasa mucha sangre. Por una entra y por otra sale. Si no haces ejercicios puedes tener un ataque de corazon.

[The heart is located between the lungs. The heart is necessary for life because if we didn't have the heart we couldn't live. The heart has two holes through which passes a lot of blood. The blood enters through one hole and exits through the other. If you don't exercise you may have a heart attack.]

Today's science time ends with children from two of the groups presenting their projects.

Discussion:

Ms. Pérez has a major concern that her classroom be one that is rich in content, particularly in mathematics and science. She believes that her students are intelligent and that they need to be challenged by a curriculum that is meaningful and interesting to them (**Principle 3, centrality of meaningful content**). She also believes that children will learn more content and more language (both spoken and written) if they have some choice in what they study (**Principle 2: learning socially constructed**). And she wants the children in her room to understand that they can use technology to help answer some of the questions that they pose.

Early in the year Ms. Pérez asked the children to suggest some topics of interest to them. The human body was one of their suggestions. Ms. Pérez took their suggestion and began this unit of study by using the K (what we know) W (what we want to learn) L (what we have learned) strategy and asking the children to generate a list of things they knew about the human body and a list of things they wanted to learn (Weaver, 1994; see Wink, 1996 for variations of the KWL strategy). As the children did this, Ms. Pérez collected lots of print and nonprint materials relating to the human body. She also thought carefully about several hands-on activities in which the learners could engage (for example, doing the exercises, examining the stomach, liver, intestines, and brain of a cow). She was especially concerned to provide lots of visual materials to help make the verbal input more comprehensible to the children. As the children work, Ms. Pérez allows them to use their native language, as well as English, to mediate their learning. She believes that the children often need to work through new content in their stronger language (**Principle 5: importance of L_1 proficiency/literacy**).

Fifth Grade Class with Significant Numbers of ESL Learners

The classroom scene to be described below is becoming a common one for elementary school teachers: an educator with no background in working with second language learners teaching a class that includes numbers of nonnative English speakers in it. In this case, about half of the class of thirty-one speaks a native language other than English. Of these children, five are new to the United States this year, while the others have been in this country from three to seven years. The new arrivals vary in terms of how much schooling they had in their home countries. The school of which this class is a part includes children from more than fourteen different countries. Because of the diversity of languages and the lack of bilingual personnel, the school has not been able to implement a true bilingual program. Instead, a full-time ESL teacher both works in a resource room setting with small groups of the children newest to English and assists classroom teachers with questions about how to include the second language learners in ongoing classroom activities. In addition, part-time native language tutors assist some of the learners once or twice a week. But tutors are not available for the speakers of all the languages represented in the school.

The fifth grade in the vignette is taught by Betty Hamilton, a woman with ten years teaching experience at the elementary school level, but with no particular education in working with second language learners. A former Peace Corps volunteer, Ms. Hamilton empathizes with the becoming bilingual children because she has found herself in a similar situation. She is patient and encouraging and makes concerted efforts to see that the children who are learning English are included in all class activities. She believes that this is the best way for them to become more proficient in English. Much of her curriculum would be viewed by many as skills-based and traditional, a fact that Ms. Hamilton acknowledges and explains by noting that the fifth graders need to achieve specific scores on specific skills tests before they are able to enter middle school for sixth grade. However, Ms. Hamilton is open to trying out some more innovative practices, and she is especially interested in experimenting with the children doing more of their own writing.

It is a warm, humid April evening, and children and parents are heading to Ms. Hamilton's room on the top floor of the sixty-year-old school building. Tonight the children are going to share a project that they have worked on over the last three months. As everyone takes seats, Ms. Hamilton moves to the front of the room to detail how the autobiography project was carried out. She explains that she had introduced the idea of autobiographies by reading portions of several published biographies and autobiographies (for example, simplified autobiographies of Jane Pittman and Benjamin Franklin, Jane Goodall's story of her life, a biography of Martin Luther King, Jr., and others). Then she shared parts of her own life and created a personal timeline so that the children would see an example of picking certain times from a life to write about. The children then constructed their own personal timelines and, over a period of several weeks, wrote narrations of events depicted in their timelines. As the children worked on their chapters, Ms. Hamilton met with them individually to assist them in revising and editing their work. Ms. Hamilton and some parent volunteers typed the final versions, which the children illustrated and bound.

With this introduction completed, Ms. Hamilton notes that she and the children decided that they wanted to share their work with their parents and that each child has chosen one or two chapters of his or her autobiography to share. Ms. Hamilton then turns the program over to two children, who call each of their classmates to the front of the room. As each child finishes reading, there is enthusiastic applause from the audience. Two of the second language learners who have been in the United States for only a year are especially nervous about sharing, but they receive encouragement from the others and do read. Daphne from Taiwan shares this chapter:

> *When I am in second grade my mother let me learn how to play the piano. I am really tired, because I want go play. Everytime my mother tells I go play the piano. I get angry I just sitting there looking my mother. My mother get angry she says" I give you money let you learn how to play piano. You can't do this way for your mother!"*

And Cao from Vietnam reads this chapter:

> *I in the 1983. My uncle he's friend help my brother and me can swim. One day he came to my home call my brother and me go to swim pool. We say yae. He say you dont want can swim. We say no we want. He say ok we go to swim pool by bus. We in the swim pool. Off the bus going to swim pool. We buy three card give to the door's porcen. We in the swim pool. I say I cant swim. He say don't wory let me help you. He help me what swim thirty minutes I can swim I very glad. I swim in the swim pool. He say good let me help you are brother. My brother he can swim too we are very glad. we are swim in swim pool five minutes Time is up we go back home say we have a good day.*

When all of the children have shared, refreshments are served, and Ms. Hamilton announces that copies of the children's books will be placed in the school library for others to enjoy. At the end of the school year the children will take their originals home.

Discussion:

Prior to the beginning of the academic year, Ms. Hamilton had done some reading about children's writing development. She had become interested in the ideas that children, both native speakers of English and those learning English as a second language, become better users of English and better writers by engaging in writing, and that children can and should write from their own personal experiences (**Principles 2, 3, and 4: learning socially constructed, centrality of meaningful content, language and literacy intertwined**). She believed that the autobiographical writing would provide all the children in her room the opportunity to write out of their own lives.

As Ms. Hamilton worked with the ESL children on their narratives, particularly those that were recent arrivals to this country, she began to see that the children's products reflected their English language development, that the children were using the English that they knew at a particular point in time to try to express themselves. Often the children were not comfortable making revisions to their pieces, because they were still struggling with basic meanings. She also discovered that she needed to be careful with the quantity of editing she engaged in with the writers, in order to keep what she and each child did meaningful and manageable for them as language learners. She did not expect the products that the beginning ESL children produced to be the same as those of the native speakers. But she did discover that the children could engage in the process of writing and share what they had written (Hudelson, 1989; Peyton and Reed, 1991; Peyton et al., 1994).

ESL Resource Room, Grades 1–6

The final vignette comes from a resource room setting where children identified as being at beginning and intermediate stages of second language learning come for small group sessions of about half an hour. About thirty percent of the children at this particular suburban elementary school are nonnative speakers of English, and, when not in the ESL resource room, they are students in regular elementary school classrooms where the language of instruction is English. The largest concentrations of children are Korean, Taiwanese, Vietnamese, and Spanish speakers. Many of the Korean and Taiwanese families are in the United States in order for their parents to earn degrees at the local university.

The resource room teacher, Mr. Jackson, is a second-year teacher who is certified in both elementary education and English-as-a-second-language teaching. He has studied both Mandarin Chinese and Spanish, but he is not fluent in either language. He also has travelled extensively in Southeast Asia. In the resource room, Mr. Jackson tries to provide the children with opportunities to use English that complement the work of the classroom teachers. In the following description, for example, Mr. Jackson shares some high quality literature with two groups of children. He does this not only because he enjoys literature but also because the classroom teachers at this school use literature regularly, engaging in daily read aloud sessions and using literature for independent reading and literature studies. Mr. J., as the children call him, wants the second language learners to feel comfortable responding to books and to become aware that they can use their own personal experiences and the story illustrations, as well as the words, to construct meaning from the stories.

The morning opening exercises have been completed, and the first group of the day enters the ESL resource room, ten sixth graders, three of whom are Vietnamese, two Bosnian, and five of Mexican origin. Three of the learners speak almost no English; half can respond to simple questions; three can ask and answer questions. Mr. J. invites the children to bring chairs and sit around him as he reads a new book. He holds up Gary Soto's picturebook *Chato's Kitchen* (1995), reads the title, and asks the children what they think the book is about. They respond, cooking and eating, and Mr. J. asks them to examine the cover picture and make some more predictions. After a careful look at and conversation about the cover and the title, Mr. J. begins reading the story.

He stops every couple of pages to call the children's attention to the pictures and to ask them to make guesses about what will happen next. If a child responds with a gesture or a single word, Mr. J. expands what the child has said to create a longer utterance. At the conclusion of the story, Mr. J. asks the group: What did you like about the book? Three of the students respond, "I don't know." The others are silent. Mr. J. waits a few seconds and then opens the book to the picture of the characters eating the delicious food that Chato has prepared. He says, "This is the part that I like best—the part about the food." Then he hands the book to one of the children and asks her to find the part that she liked best. When she points to the picture of the mice riding on the dog's back at Chato's house, Mr. J. says, "Oh you liked the part where Chorizo the dog gave the mice a ride. He was their car. I thought that was fun too." He encourages several children to point out parts of the story that they liked and to articulate what they can in English. Mr. J. then rereads the book, showing the learners the story page by page and encouraging the children to retell the story in their own words. Some children use their native language with each other before they contribute to the retelling in English. When the retelling is complete, Mr. J. announces that they will use this book again and dismisses the group.

A few minutes later a group of seven first graders enters the resource classroom. Four of the children are Mexican American, two are Vietnamese, and one is Navajo. All of them have attended kindergarten in the United States and have been categorized as being at an intermediate level of English language ability. Mr. J. invites the children to sit with him and brings out Carmen Lomas Garza's book *Family Pictures/Cuadros de Familia* (1990). This book is a compilation of short narratives about growing up in a Mexican American community, beautifully illustrated with the artist's paintings. Mr. J. holds up the book cover and reads the title. The children begin to comment on family members that are on the cover as well as in their own families.

Mr. J. tells the children that he is going to read two of the stories today, and he turns to one titled "The Birthday Party." As he holds up the illustration of a blindfolded child trying to hit a piñata, one of the children comments that it's a birthday party. Several others agree. Mr. J. asks how the children know it is. Two of the Mexican American children share that they have had piñatas at birthday parties and that they have attended birthday parties where piñatas have been broken. The Navajo child remembers that his first-grade class had a birthday party for several children in the room (actually for all of the children who had celebrated birthdays during the summer when school was not in session) and that the children broke a piñata. After the children have finished their comments, Mr. J. reads the narrative. As he reads the children continue to comment, relating the author's words to their experiences. When he finishes, Mr. J. asks the children what they liked about the story, and they share their impressions.

The children ask for another story and Mr. J. holds up the book so that they can see one titled "Hammerhead Shark." One child comments that it is a "jaw story," and several others agree. As Mr. J. reads the children make contributions related to the illustration, to personal trips to the beach, to being afraid (or not) of a shark, to recollections of movies with sharks. The children listen to each other carefully and build on each other's comments. As they comment, Mr. J. listens respectfully and encourages everyone to participate in the conversation and to listen carefully to each other. The children talk more than he does.

Discussion:

Mr. J.'s undergraduate coursework in language and literacy learning had emphasized that children learn their second language as they engage in using it to meet their social and academic needs (**Principles 1 and 2: language socially shared, learning socially constructed**). But he has learned from some of the classroom teachers that, in their regular classroom settings, some of the second language learners seem intimidated about using their new language and reluctant to participate in classroom activities. So Mr. J. has conceptualized the resource room as a place where ESL learners can participate in some of the same kinds of activities as the regular classroom, but in a more sheltered environment, with smaller groups of children all of whom are still learning English.

Whatever the content of the lesson, Mr. J. tries to provide an environment in which (1) students talk with each other, as well as the teacher, and students talk more than the teacher (**Principles 1 and 2: language socially shared; learning socially constructed**); (2) the focus is on the speaker's conveying meaning rather than on grammatical accuracy; (3) the topics are often controlled by the students and related to student experiences and interests (**Principle 3: centrality of meaningful content**); (4) the teacher supports the students as they experiment with the new language by listening carefully and prompting learners to talk (Ernst, 1994a; 1994b). Thus, Mr. J. envisions the ESL resource room as a place where English language learners have multiple opportunities to use their new language and to build up their confidence and their willingness to take risks with that language.

Concluding Remarks

In this chapter we have shared slices of life from some of the elementary school classrooms we have been privileged to spend time in and learn from. Most of our own work has been in places where the largest group of speakers of a language other than English has been Spanish-speaking. This is not so surprising considering that the home language of more than half of the more than 32 million speakers of non-English languages in the United States is Spanish (Cisneros & Leone, 1995). So we write from our own experiences. But as professionals working in bilingual/second language education, we also attend conferences, read professional publications, and share with our colleagues. We know that similar kinds of practices, adapted to reflect and respect diverse linguistic and cultural realities, occur in schools and classrooms across this country (Leone & Cisneros, 1995).

We have, for example, read descriptions of Southeast Asian children's literacy development (Lim & Watson, 1993; Rigg & Enright, 1986; Samway, 1992; Samway & Whang, 1994; Samway, Whang, Cade, Gamil, and Phommachanh, 1991; Urzúa, 1987, 1992). We are familiar with work being done with indigenous North American peoples (Goebel, 1996; Hartley & Johnson, 1995; Lipka, 1991; Lipka & McCarty, 1994; McCarty, 1993; McCarty, Wallace, Lynch, & Benally, 1991). We know of many situations where children from widely diverse linguistic and cultural backgrounds learn together (Samway & Taylor, 1993; Taylor, 1990; Taylor & Samway, 1992; Wink & collaborators, 1995).

What the educators in these diverse settings have in common is an understanding of some or all of the principles articulated in Chapter 4. These understandings have resulted in classroom practices that we believe exhibit the following characteristics:

1. Respect for learners' experiences, including learners' cultures and languages;
2. Opportunities for learners to ask their own questions and construct their own knowledge and understandings on their own and with the assistance of others;
3. Engagement of learners with significant content across all areas of the currriculum;
4. Belief in children's ability to learn both content and language.

In our view, the teachers whose practices we have just described are similar to those studied by García (1991), who wanted to identify attributes that characterize effective teachers serving language minority students. García found the following about the classroom practices of teachers identified as exemplary: (1) The teachers adopted an experiential stance toward instruction, which focused on what was meaningful to the children, and which utilized science and social studies themes as vehicles for language and literacy development; (2) The teachers provided opportunities for active learning, often through hands-on activities carried on in collaborative groups; (3) The teachers encouraged collaborative and cooperative interactions among the students, organizing classroom instruction so that children could work in heterogeneously organized groups. García also found that these teachers had high expectations for their students, were open to new ideas and never complacent about what they were doing, were committed to classroom practices that reflected the cultural and linguistic backgrounds of their students, and communicated clearly to parents and others what they were doing in the classroom.

We have suggested in Chapter 3 that the most significant improvements in educational opportunities for becoming bilingual children may occur when educators at individual school sites collaborate and reform occurs at the school level. Recently, Beryl Nelson (1996) examined four elementary schools considered exemplary because of the programs that educators within them developed to meet the needs of elementary school English-as-a-second-language learners. Nelson discovered that these schools shared the following characteristics:

1. The expectation that all the students would achieve a commitment to both spoken and written English proficiency, and providing a challenging core curriculum;
2. A valuing of the languages and cultures of the students and innovative involvement of parents and communities in the schools;
3. Utilization of the students' primary languages, either for literacy development or as a tool in delivering content, or both;
4. The creation of learning environments where students work both in heterogeneously organized cooperative groups and independently;
5. The delivery of a rich and varied curriculum to second language learners;
6. Implementation of literature-based approaches to literacy development, approaches that encourage students to read, write, and speak about topics relevant to their culture and experience, in addition to the utilization of more traditional strategies.

Nelson's conclusions are similar to those reached by Collier (1995, 1997) as she reviewed work done on effective instructional practices for elementary learners who are becoming bilingual.

The teachers whose classes and teaching practices you have read about are working to realize the principles articulated above, both in their own teaching and within their school communities. We hope that these glimpses of what classroom life can be have left you both with questions and with the determination to reflect on your own classroom experiences, on the kind of teacher you strive to become personally, and on the kind of school climate that you choose to contribute to.

References

Calkins, L. (1994). *The art of teaching writing,* 2nd Ed. Portsmouth, NH: Heinemann.

Carger, C. (1993). Louie comes to life: Pretend reading with second language emergent readers. *Language Arts, 70*(7), 542–548.

Cisneros, R., & Leone, B. (1995). Introduction: Critical descriptions of classrooms and programs. *Bilingual Research Journal, 19*(3/4), 353–368.

Collier, V. (1997). Two-Way Bilingual Institute. Third Session. Center for Bilingual Education and Research. Arizona State University, Tempe, February 1.

Collier, V. (1995). *Promoting academic success for ESL students: Understanding second language acquisition for schools.* Woodside, NY: Bastos Educational Books.

Ernst, G. (1994a). Beyond language: The multiple dimensions of an ESL program. *Anthropology and Education Quarterly, 25*(3), 317–335.

Ernst, G. (1994b). Talking circle: Conversation and negotiation in the ESL classroom. *TESOL Quarterly, 28*(2), 293–322.

Faltis, C. (1997). *Joinfostering: Adapting teaching for the multilingual classroom,* 2nd Ed. Upper Saddle River, NJ: Merrill.

Farias, J. (1987). *El hijo del jardinero.* Madrid: Ediciones Anaya.

Fortescue, J. (1994). Using oral and written language to increase understanding of math concepts. *Language Arts, 71*(8), 576–581.

García, E. (1991). Effective instruction for language minority students: The teacher. *Journal of Education, 173*, 130–141.

Garza, C. L. (1990). *Family pictures/Cuadros de familia.* San Francisco, CA: Children's Book Press.

Goebel, B. (1996). Honoring native cultures: Reflections and responsibilities. *Primary Voices, 4*(3), 3–10.

Goodman, K. (1996). *On reading.* Portsmouth, NH: Heinemann.

Goodman, K. (1993). *Phonics Phacts.* Portsmouth, NH: Heinemann.

Hartley, A., & Johnson, P. (1995). Toward a community-based transition to a Yup'ik first language (immersion) program with ESL component. *Bilingual Research Journal, 19*(3/4), 571–586.

Hayes, J. (1987). *La llorona.* Santa Fe, NM: Four Winds Press.

Hudelson, S. (1989). *Write on: Children writing in ESL.* Englewood Cliffs, NJ: Prentice-Hall.

Hudelson, S. (1984). Kan yu ret an rayt en ingles: Children become literate in English as a second language. *TESOL Quarterly, 18*, 221–238.

Hudelson, S. (1981–1982). An introductory examination of children's invented spelling in Spanish. *NABE Journal, 6*, 53–68.

Jacob, E., Rottenberg, L., Patrick, S., & Wheeler, E. (1996). Cooperative learning: Context and opportunity for acquiring academic English. *TESOL Quarterly, 30*(2), 253–280.

Kamii, C. (1985). *Young children reinvent arithmetic: Implications of Piagetian thought.* New York: Teachers College Press.

Krashen, S. (1982). *Principles and practice in second language acquisition.* New York: Pergamon.

Labbo, L., Hoffman, J., & Roser, N. (1995). Ways to unintentionally make writing difficult. *Language Arts, 72* (March), 164–170.

Leone, B., & Cisneros, R. (Eds.). (1995). The ESL Component of Bilingual Education in Practice. Special issue of *Bilingual Research Journal, 19*(3/4).

Lim, H., & Watson, D. (1993). Whole language content for second-language learners. *The Reading Teacher, 46*(5), 384–393.

Lionni, L. (1989). *Alexander and the wind-up mouse.* Boston: Houghton Mifflin.

Lipka, J. (1991). Toward a culturally based pedagogy: A case study of one Yup'ik Eskimo teacher. *Anthropology and Education Quarterly, 22*(3), 203–223.

Lipka, J., & McCarty, T. (1994). Changing the culture of schooling: Yup'ik and Navajo cases. *Anthropology and Education Quarterly, 25*(3), 266–284.

Maclachlan, P. (1980). *Arthur for the very first time.* New York: Harper and Row.

McCaleb, S. (1994). *Building communities of learners: A collaboration among teachers, students, families and the community.* New York: St. Martins Press.

McCarty, T. (1993). Language, literacy and the image of the child in American Indian classrooms. *Language Arts, 70*(3), 182–192.

McCarty, T., Wallace, S., Lynch, R., & Benally, A. (1991). Classroom inquiry and Navajo learning styles: A call for reassessment. *Anthropology and Education Quarterly, 22*(1), 42–59.

National Association for the Education of Young Children/State Departments of Education. (1991). National Association for the Education of Young Children (NAEYC) and National Association of Early Childhood Specialists in State Departments of Education Guidelines for appropriate content assessment in programs serving children ages 3 through 8. *Young children, 46*(3), 21–38.

National Council of Teachers of Mathematics. (1989). *Curriculum and evaluation standards for the teaching of mathematics.* Washington, DC: NCTM.

Nelson, B. (1996). *Learning English: How school reform fosters language acquisition and development for limited English proficient elementary school students.* Washington, DC: National Center for Research on Cultural Diversity and Second Language Learning.

Peterson, R. (1992). *Life in a crowded place.* Portsmouth, NH: Heinemann.

Peterson, R., & Eeds, M. (1990). *Grand conversations: Literature study groups in the classroom.* Scarborough, Ontario: Scholastic TAB.

Peyton, J., Jones, C., Vincent, A., & Greenblatt, L. (1994). Implementing writing workshops with ESOL students: Visions and realities. *TESOL Quarterly, 28*(3), 469–487.

Peyton, J., & Reed, L. (1991). Profiles of individual writers. In J. Peyton and L. Reed (Eds.), *Dialogue journal with nonnative English speakers: A handbook for teachers,* (pp. 35–56). Alexandria, VA: TESOL.

Rigg, P., & Enright, S. (Eds.). (1986). *Integrating perspectives: Children becoming literate in English as a second language.* Washington, DC: Teachers of English to Speakers of Other Languages.

Samway, K. (1992). *Writing workshop for ESL children.* Washington, DC: National Clear-
    inghouse for Bilingual Education.
Samway, K., & Taylor, D. (1993). Inviting children to make connections between read-
    ing and writing. *TESOL Journal, 3,* 7–11.
Samway, K., & Whang, G. (1994). *Literature study circles in the multicultural classroom.*
    York, ME: Stenhouse.
Samway, K., Whang, G., Cade, C., Gamil, M., Lubandina, M., & Phommachanh, K.
    (1991). Reading the skeleton, the heart and the brain of a book: Students' per-
    spectives on literature study circles. *The Reading Teacher, 45*(3), 196–205.
Shannon, S. (1995). The hegemony of English: A case study of the one bilingual class-
    room as a site of resistance. *Linguistics and Education, 7,* 175–200.
Slobodkina, E. (1940). *Caps for sale.* New York: Scholastic Books.
Soto, G. (1995). *Chato's Kitchen.* New York: G. P. Putnam's Sons.
Taylor, D. (1990). Writing and reading literature in a second language. In N. Atwell
    (Ed.), *Workshop by and for teachers: Beyond the basal,* (pp. 105–117), Portsmouth, NH:
    Heinemann.
Taylor, D., & Samway, K. (1992). The collected letters of two collaborative researchers.
    In S. Hudelson and J. Lindfors (Eds.), *Delicate balances: Collaborative research in lan-
    guage education,* (pp. 67–92), Urbana, IL: National Council of Teachers of English.
Urzúa, C. (1992). Faith in learners through literature studies. *Language Arts, 69,*
    492–501.
Urzúa, C. (1987). 'You stopped too soon': Second language children composing and
    revising. *TESOL Quarterly, 21,* 279–304.
Weaver, C. (1994). *Reading process and practice: From sociopsycholinguistics to whole lan-
    guage.* Portsmouth, NH: Heinemann.
Wink, J. (1996). *Critical pedagogy: Notes from the real world.* New York: Longman.
Wink, J., & collaborators. (1995). A picture of diverse language groups and ESL pro-
    grams. *Bilingual Research Journal, 19*(3/4), 641–660.

6

*Bilingual Education in
Secondary School
Settings*

Bilingual education has been an option for middle, junior high, and high schools, the three main divisions of secondary school, since its federal inception in 1968. As you know, the Bilingual Education Act was intended to fund both elementary and secondary schools to develop programs designed to meet the needs of students who could not speak English, but were otherwise completely eligible for school. However, until 1990, the majority of all programs that had been designed, funded, and implemented focused on the elementary school-age child, and the lion's share of research on the effectiveness of bilingual education has been conducted at the elementary level (Faltis & Arias, 1993). Nonetheless, there are teachers and educators at secondary schools who have worked diligently to plan and implement bilingual programs that incorporate some or all of the guiding principles we presented in Chapter 4, and they have done so within the structural and pedagogical conditions that distinguish secondary from elementary schools.

In this chapter, we present a series of classroom and program level vignettes to illustrate some of the ways that middle and high school teachers have worked to incorporate our guiding principles for learning and language acquisition. We begin the chapter with a brief overview of the bilingual program options for secondary schools to give you an idea of the structural complexities these bilingual teachers face, and to provide a context for the vignettes that we present. Part of the fabric of the vignettes will be a discussion of the ways teachers invite students into the discourse of their subject matter knowledge, while at the same time they endeavor to facilitate their literacy and language acquisition. As you shall see, this is no easy feat at the secondary level, where many teachers interact with up to 150 students a day, prepare and teach several different classes (quite possibly in different subject matter areas), and work with students on extracurricular activities as well. Our aim, as in Chapter 5, is to alternate between what is happening in certain secondary classes and what we would like you to consider as good practice in bilingual teaching and learning. In other words, we will move back and forth between what is and a discussion of the principles and stances that we would like you to learn as you become bilingual teachers.

Framing the Context

There is an old saying in education that elementary teachers teach children, and secondary teachers teach content. Like most folklore, there is some truth to the saying. Elementary teachers typically have self-contained classrooms and are responsible for the same children all day for the entire academic year. Secondary teachers, in contrast, usually teach out of a home room and have students who are assigned to them for a fixed time period each day. A major purpose of the time teachers spend with their students each class period is to teach them certain subject matter content; hence, the saying. In reality, however, secondary teachers are no less teachers of students than are elementary teachers; they interact with more of them throughout the day. As Faltis (1993) points out,

> *teachers in [m]iddle and high schools teach students who are in the process of becoming adults, of learning responsibility, and of understanding the meaning of friendship, groups, gangs, moods, and humor and tragedy. Part of the mission of the secondary school, therefore, is also to pay attention to the social, personal, and emotional needs of learners who are very much in the transition from childhood to adult reality (p. 103).*

So, although secondary teachers identify themselves as content area specialists who teach and assist adolescents to learn the knowledge and abilities that they will need to graduate from high school, they are also very much concerned with helping adolescents become caring, productive, and thoughtful adult citizens.

Secondary education is sometimes synonymous with high school, grades 9 through 12. However, as many of you are already thinking, not all high schools offer four years of study. Some have only grades 10 through 12. Likewise, middle school and junior high vary from district to district. In some school districts, middle school comprises grades 6 through 8; in others,

6 through 9. Junior high schools can be grades 7 and 8 or grades 7, 8, and 9. Rather than fretting about all of the combinations, we will present scenarios from middle and high schools, and simply tell you what the grade organization is. For our purposes, the two major features that connect as well as distinguish middle, junior, and high schools, regardless of their grade organization, are that teachers are hired because of their endorsement as content area specialists, and that students travel from one class to another to study different subject matter.

Before going any further, we would like to remind you of a significant structural difference between middle and high schools that has occurred nationwide in the last decade as a result of restructuring efforts. Many middle schools, especially small and medium-sized campuses (400 to 800 students), have been restructured into family units or teams, with students being housed either in a separate building or assigned to a set of classrooms. Students belong to a family unit in the sense that they have a home room, they are encouraged to identify with the family unit, and spend up to half of their school day attending classes taught by family unit team teachers. The rest of the day, students venture out to other family units to take classes from non-family teachers and are likely to study with students who belong to other family units. This particular design acts as a means to build group identity, while simultaneously preparing students for high school, where taking individual classes in relative isolation is the norm. Middle schools organized into family units with more than one hundred students who are adding English as a second language tend to assign the English learners to one family unit, often known as the bilingual family (see Minicucci & Olsen, 1992; Minicucci, 1996). Students spend much of their school day with the same set of teachers and peers, studying subject matter in their native language when possible, and in English. Students travel outside the bilingual family unit to other families to participate in other classes and activities the rest of the day. We described one such middle school in Chapter 3.

Bilingual Program Options

Basically, four types of bilingual programs operate in secondary schools (see Figure 6.1). Within each type there can be courses taught in the students' primary language, courses taught bilingually, in the students' primary language and English, and courses taught in English. The courses taught in English can be sheltered content courses or English-as-a-second-language courses. The first type of program is best described as a set of within-school courses that are developed within the existing time block schedule of 45–55 minutes. Students typically take one or more special courses designed for them. The program, in this case, is an array of special courses ranging from ESL classes and content area classes, taught bilingually or as sheltered courses, to language arts and literacy classes taught in the students' native language. In many schools, although the selection of special classes may not cover all of the content areas taught in English, students nonetheless have the same number of classes as their English-speaking counterparts. In this type of program, there are few systematic teacher-to-teacher shared exchanges about how students are faring in other classes, about what does and does not work, and about improving teaching and curriculum sequences.

The next type of program also offers special courses in some or all of the subject matter areas including ESL, but has a person who serves as a program leader and is responsible for coordinating the schedule of courses across grade levels. The program coordinator can schedule classes to integrate subject matter across the curriculum and may even reorganize classes into longer blocks of time, or more traditionally, as single subject matter courses but in longer blocks of time. Having longer blocks of time enables teachers to regroup students by English proficiency throughout the semester or year without disrupting the schedule of content area classes (Lucas, 1993). The program is a self-contained instructional unit within the secondary school. Accordingly, this often means that special program teachers meet together several times a week to discuss how students are progressing and to coordinate themes, lessons, and activities. Physically speaking, this type of program can be housed within a particular building, as in the "families" found in many middle schools, or it can be spread out among several classrooms within the school grounds.

A third type of secondary bilingual program assigns students who are adding English as a second language to a building or buildings at a site away from the regular school grounds. The program operates on the same daily schedule as the main campus, with classes scheduled either in 45–55 minute periods or for longer blocks of time. However, coursework offerings are limited. The program does not offer a full range of courses needed for graduation, and, thus, is considered to be a satellite of the main campus. The program has a director who reports directly to the main campus building principal.

ESL vocational programs are an example of this type of program. ESL vocational programs are typically designed for boys, and offer training in areas such as automotive repair, body shop work, air-conditioning and heating repair, and building construction. Students attending the specialized school ordinarily take a bus to and from the program site, attending the program for only a part of the day.

The final type of program option provides a learning center or an entire school designed exclusively for students who are adding English as a second language. There are two alternatives within this option: (1) newcomer schools

FIGURE 6.1   Bilingual Program Types

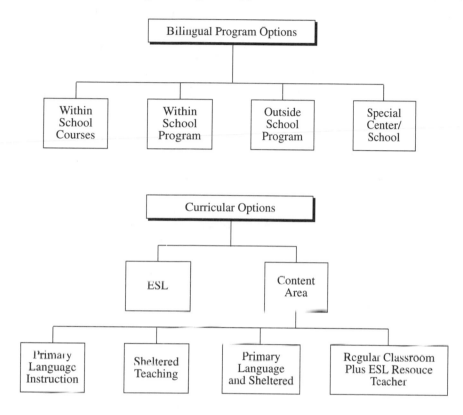

and centers, and (2) comprehensive high schools. Recall from Chapter 3 that newcomer centers are schools that recently arrived, non-English-speaking students attend for a limited time period before enrolling in a regular secondary school. Newcomer centers may be located on the school grounds of a particular school site as was the case at Liberty High School in New York (see Chapter 3) or at a separate site. Most students stay in newcomer centers for less than an academic year (Freidlander, 1991).

The less traditional and rarest type of bilingual program is the comprehensive bilingual school, in which the entire school has been designed exclusively for English learners. Only one such comprehensive bilingual school exists in the United States, the International High School at La Guardia Community College in New York City (The International High School, 1991). The high school includes many of the features of a newcomer center, but also

More Traditional/Common Features	Less Traditional/Common Features
Fragmentation	
• daily schedule	• integrated curriculum
• content area scheduled into 45–55 minute classes	• content scheduled into longer, more flexible blocks of time
Isolation	
• no teacher collaboration	• teacher teams/collaboration
• few opportunities to communicate with administrators and other staff members	• multiple opportunities to communicate with administrators and other staff members
Hierarchy	
• top-down decision-making	• shared decision-making
Specialization	
• by content areas	• integration of content areas; interdisciplinary teams
• by teacher speciality area	• teachers use multiple specialties
• by roles and responsibilities	• teachers/staff have multiple roles

FIGURE 6.2   More Traditional/Common and Less Traditional/Common Bilingual Program Features

Adapted from Lucas (1993), p. 118.

offers a full schedule of classes so that students can fulfill graduation requirements in four years. There are no separate ESL language classes offered at this particular high school. Rather, teachers integrate English language and content area teaching in all classes, using sheltered English and content-based ESL approaches throughout the curriculum.

According to Lucas (1993), the first two program options are more traditional, meaning you are more likely to find them in secondary schools than the latter two program types. Lucas considers the latter two types as nontraditional because the entire campus is devoted to students who are adding English as a second language. Figure 6.2 provides a graphic representation of the types of program options placed along a continuum from more traditional/common to less traditional/common.

Bilingual Seventh Grade Class

The first vignette depicts a bilingual seventh grade classroom in a middle school located in a suburb of a large city. The population of the middle school, which comprises seventh and eighth grades, has approximately 600 students, of whom some 40 percent are Hispanic, 3 percent African American and Chinese, and the rest Anglo. Most of the Hispanic students are native speakers of Spanish with varying levels of proficiency in English. There are nearly one hundred students in the bilingual program, which is designated as the Bilingual Team. All except two of the students are native Spanish speakers. There is one student from Romania and one from Taiwan. These two non-Hispanic students are highly literate in their native languages, and have had parallel schooling in their home countries. Among the Spanish-speaking students, however, there is a wide range of variation in literacy and schooling experiences.

This particular school is designated as the bilingual middle school program in the district. The school receives non-English-speaking students from three elementary schools in the district, and in turn, it feeds into a high school where the only special support for English learners is a small offering of ESL courses. Accordingly, teachers in the bilingual program feel some pressure to prepare students for coursework that will be taught exclusively in English. One of the goals of the program, therefore, is to transition students to mostly English instruction in the eighth grade.

The seventh grade class in this vignette has thirty students, all of whom are native speakers of Spanish. One student is from the Dominican Republic, two are from Puerto Rico, and the rest are from Mexico, mainly the northern states of Chihuahua and Sonora. About half of the students have had at least one year of formal schooling experiences in U. S. schools; the other half are recent immigrants and first-time students in U. S. schools. Five of the students were born in the United States, and have had schooling experiences in both the United States and Mexico, and are still considered to be ESL students. Most of the students have literacy abilities that are well below what most teachers would consider to be average for a seventh grade student.

Four or five of the male students are thought to be gang members or young gang initiates. None of these boys are recent arrivals. Rather, they have all been in elementary schools in the United States for at least three years, and they have relatively good oral abilities in English. Nonetheless, the boys are well behind in literacy abilities in both Spanish and English.

The seventh grade bilingual teacher, Ms. Thompson (Ms. T.), learned Spanish as a second language in college, and has spent several summers in Mexico. Her specializations as a secondary teacher are science and English. She has also earned an endorsement in bilingual education. As part of the endorsement, she took and passed an oral and written examination in Spanish. Ms. T. teaches what is called bilingual science, bilingual language arts, sheltered science, and sheltered language arts.

The vignette that we share here takes place in the bilingual science and language arts classes around the beginning of October. Although the classes are referred to as *bilingual,* most of the oral and written interaction is conducted in Spanish. Ms. T. usually begins to introduce English into her exchanges with students after the winter holidays, and then she uses code-switching strategies (discussed below in bilingual social studies vignette) to ease the transition into English.

On this particular day, the students are all facing the front of the class to see what Ms. T. has in store for them with several items that she has placed on a table. The class is fairly noisy, with students talking back and forth in Spanish about what is going to happen. Students in this class sit in tables of four students per table and students are encouraged to talk to one another about activities and tasks at various times throughout the day. One student calls out to Ms. T., "*Miss, Miss, ¿para qué son esas cosas que trae en la mesa?*" [Teacher, teacher, what are those things for on the table?]. Ms. T. responds in Spanish, telling her to wait a minute until she has everyone's attention and she will let the whole class know.

Ms. T. begins by asking the students to look at the four items she has set out on a table in the center of the class in Spanish. The items are a can of hair spray, a can of aerosol paint, a can of aerosol deodorant, and a pump-action water sprayer. Several of the students identify the objects, calling out their names, and looking around for approval from their peers. Ms. T. checks with the entire class to see if everyone is in agreement about the identity of the items. She then asks each table to put their heads together to figure out how the items are similar or different.

Going around the tables, Ms. T. listens to the students as they share ideas among themselves. At one table, Leticia suggests that all of the objects are alike because they spray something. Gilberto adds that it might be that the hair spray, the paint, and the deodorant are all sticky, while the water is not. Ms. T. pats him on the shoulder, and with a smile says: "*Estás pensando muy bien. ¿Qué más les puedes decir?*" [You are really thinking. What else can you tell the group about the items?] Leticia chimes in saying, "*Yo sé. Yo sé. Es posible que haya algo adentro de estas tres* [pointing] *y que tenemos que usar una bombita pa' sacar agua de aquella.*" [I know. I know. It might be that there's something inside these three and that we have to use a little pump to get water from that one.] Ms. T. asks the group to think about what Leticia has proposed, urging them to make some guesses about what might be inside the three items. She then heads for another table to see what kind of ideas other students have come up with.

After fifteen minutes or so, Ms. T. gathers the groups' attention and begins to write out on the whiteboard some of the ideas that students have generated. She writes the ideas on the board as a representative from each group offers one. She plans to refer back to these ideas later in the lesson. Next, Ms. T. introduces the concept of the ozone, and its role in preventing the harmful rays of the sun from burning our skin. After a brief introduction, she asks the entire class to step outside the classroom for a few minutes. Once outside, she asks the students to look up in the sky and see if they can see the ozone. *"¿Dónde está la zona o?"* [Where is the ozone?] she asks the students. After a chorus of *"Yo no sé"* [I don't know] she invites the students back into class to work on figuring out where the ozone is and why it is important. She also reminds the students to think about the four items that she placed on the table.

The lesson continues with students watching a short film about the ozone and its depletion. The film is in English, so Ms. T. turns the sound off and explains to the students in Spanish what is happening in the story line. The film specifically mentions the kinds of chemicals that humans release into the air that are responsible for the depletion of the ozone. Because Ms. T. has previewed the film, she had a list of all of the chemical words and expressions that students would most likely find difficult, and that she did not know in Spanish. She had these on a handout that she distributed before showing the film. After viewing the film, and listening to Ms. T.'s narrative of it, the students work in pairs to respond to several questions about the ozone, and the relationship of the four items to the ozone. Ms. T. also asks the students to draw a picture of how the ozone protects the earth from deadly sun rays, and how certain chemicals may be gradually reducing the layer of protection the ozone provides.

Following the two-hour science class, the students have a short break before beginning their language arts class. Most days, Ms. T. begins the language arts class by reading a short story or a poem written in Spanish, and sometimes in Spanish and English. Today, she was reading the third of a series of poems by Carmen Tafolla, called "Los Corts 3" (la pachuquita) (Padilla, 1992). She had already read "Los Corts 1 and 2," and these generated a lively discussion about how hard their parents have had to work, and about growing up in Mexico. In today's "Cort," students listen to a poem about La Dot, a teenage girl who is complaining about La Silvia, another girl who is trying to take away La Dot's boyfriend. The poem uses hip language that many of the students in class identify with, and the focus on teenage romance problems captures their attention. Several of the girls in the class giggle, and look at each other, as if to say *"Así somos a veces las niñas"* [That's how we girls are sometimes]. To Ms. T.'s question, "Why do people fight over other one another?" one of the boys calls out that *"Tenemos que protejer lo nuestro"* [We have to protect what is ours]. Ms. T. continues the discussion, focusing on the physical violence aspect of protection, and tries to help students think about nonviolent ways of solving these kinds of problems.

After the reading and discussion, which takes about forty-five minutes, the students spread out to work on a variety of projects. Some are working on writing projects, using the computer to compose and produce graphics for their stories. Others are reading from books and magazines of their choice. Ms. T. has tried to build her classroom library with Spanish language books appropriate for adolescents, but the selection is still rather slim. She has had to bolster the collection with Spanish language children's books and magazines. Fortunately, because many of the students have low reading abilities in Spanish, the children's books at least enable them to read for pleasure stories that are often culturally relevant, as well as easy to understand. Ms. T. believes that students should choose the reading materials they want, and she gives them reading time every day.

Discussion:

The students in Ms. T.'s class enjoy a wide range of learning experiences that are based on shared and individual discovery and that enable them to participate in the discourse of knowledge systems in their L_1 (**Principles 2 and 5: learning socially constructed, importance of L_1 proficiency/literacy**). There are ample opportunities for students in Ms. T.'s class to gain understanding of the subject matter from interacting with her and other students (**Principle 2: learning socially constructed**). For example, in the ozone lesson, students negotiated the meaning of the ozone and its importance to life on the planet through various channels: visually with realia and a film, by talking, reading and writing about the process and issues, by brainstorming, and questioning. All of these ways of knowing use language to help students share in the creation of a meaning system about a relatively complex biological process (**Principle 1: language socially shared**).

Literacy plays an important role in Ms. T.'s class. She believes that students need to develop strong native language abilities, especially in the areas of reading and writing (**Principle 4: language and literacy intertwined**). She uses a free voluntary reading program (Krashen, 1993) to help turn her students into readers. Free voluntary reading means that, throughout the day, students can freely choose from a wide selection of adolescent-appropriate stories, comic books, and magazines that are available in certain locations in the classroom. With respect to writing, Ms. T. tries to incorporate writing into almost every activity, keeping in mind that students need to write for a variety of audiences. Some of the writing that students do is as an exercise, to give them practice in controlled writing. This is the boring stuff, because it is straightforward, already known information that has to be practiced. Many students in secondary school expect this kind of writing and want to see and understand what their errors are (Reyes, 1991). But students also write for other audiences: among themselves, to themselves, to the teacher as a trusted adult, and to unknown audiences interested in their stories.

Ms. T. has students use writing during the time they spend with her to help them understand subject matter, but also to assist in their language development (**Principle 4: language and literacy intertwined**). She knows that writing supports interaction about subject matter and vice versa. Plus, writing for a variety of audiences gives students an opportunity to talk, think, and write about ideas that matter to them (**Principle 3: centrality of meaningful content**).

Another way to understand what was happening in this middle school bilingual classroom is to compare it to what García (1993) and Minicucci (1996) reported in their studies of exemplary bilingual middle schools. García, you may recall from Chapter 3, used principles synthesized from research on effective schools for language minority students to develop a set of strategies to maximize academic learning in Project THEME, a bilingual collaborative, integrated middle school curriculum. As in Project THEME, Mrs. T. used thematic lessons, small group work, and a variety of reading and writing activities. She stressed the value of peer learning and meaningful learning experiences.

Minicucci examined several middle schools recognized as effective with language minority students. She uncovered three features that cut across all the programs, especially in the areas of science and mathematics: (1) inquiry-based and thematic teaching; (2) high-quality oral and written language development practices integrated with content learning; and (3) extended time periods for social studies, language arts, and science. These three features were present in Ms. T.'s classes. Ms. T. invited students to construct their own understandings of science-related topics through a sustained period of time, using multiple language means to support an in-depth study of the ozone. Her language arts class was also inquiry-based in the sense that students were encouraged to question readings and social practices that were brought out in the readings. Thus, not only did the students in Ms. T.'s language arts class discuss and inquire about the readings, they also participated in literacy activities that facilitated language development.

High School Bilingual Social Studies Class

This vignette describes a sophomore and junior level social studies class, Bilingual World History, which takes place in an urban high school in a large metropolitan area of the southwest. The high school has nearly 4,000 students, 47 percent of whom are language minority students. More than half of these are becoming bilingual in a school within a school bilingual program that has Spanish language content area courses, sheltered content courses, and ESL courses across all of the grades. The bilingual program at this school enables English learners to take up to half of their required core courses in either their native language (Spanish) or through sheltered content classes. The ESL courses do not count toward credit for graduation. The program was featured as a visitation site for the National Association of Bilingual Education annual conference in 1992.

Mr. Márquez, the teacher of the class we are going to visit, is of Mexican–Apache origin. He is a native speaker of Spanish, Apache, and English. He is most fluent, however, in English, as the major portion of his academic preparation occurred in English. Mr. M. is also the track coach, and he prides himself on bringing many of his Hispanic students into track and field events. He has been teaching at this school for fifteen years, and became the designated bilingual social studies teacher five years ago.

All students in the class are recent arrivals from Mexico, with varying degrees of experience in U. S. and Mexican schools. Most students are literate in Spanish, but many were below grade level. Accordingly, Mr. M. makes an effort to engage students in myriad discussions about the readings, and uses writing and artwork to enhance communication and language development.

On the day that we describe the students are reading out of a Spanish language textbook on the interaction between states' rights and the federal government. They have just completed a close reading of a section on states' rights. A close reading is when students, working in groups of three to four, take turns reading one sentence at a time of a particular section in the book they especially liked or felt strongly about. After the student reads the sentence, he or she discusses with the group what the sentence means. One of the main ideas of the section is that individual states cannot make laws that go against federal laws. The context of the lesson and close reading is the United States in the early twentieth century, when newly formed states were negotiating with the federal government about their right to sovereignty.

Jaime, one of the students, has just asked his partners: *"A mí se me hace estúpido que los estados no tengan derecho de hacer sus propias leyes"* [I think it's stupid that states can't have their own laws]. Rosa replies, *"Yo también, no creo que sea justo"* [I don't think it's fair either]. Consuelo disagrees, saying *"Sí, pero, ¿qué tal si una ley va en contra de la ley federal? Por ejemplo, si la ley dice, este, que es contra la ley discriminar contra los mexicanos no más porque somos mexicanos, un estado no puede tener una ley que nos discrimina y no nos da los mismos derechos a los demás del estado. ¿Qué les parece?"* [Yes, but, what if a law goes against a federal law. For example, if a law says, like, that it is against the law to discriminate against Mexicans just because we're Mexicans, a state can't have a law that discriminates against us and doesn't give us the same rights as everyone else in the state. What do you think?]. The discussion continues in this and other groups along the same lines. Mr. M. then opens up the discussions to the whole class, and works to pull out ideas from individual members of all of the groups.

One of the interesting features of the discussion between Mr. M. and the students is that Mr. M. is a code-switcher, alternating from Spanish to English and back with a natural fluency characteristic of many Mexican Americans who have grown up using two languages for a variety of purposes (Valdés–Fallis, 1976). Mr. M. uses three kinds of code-switching strategies common among bilinguals who have grown up using two languages with other bilinguals. When he doesn't know the word in Spanish for a technical term or when he feels like a word is more suitable to be rendered in English than in Spanish he switches momentarily to English. For example:

Mr. M.: *¿Quién me puede decir lo que significa "yellow journalism"?* [Who can tell me what "yellow journalism" means?]

Mr. M.: *¿Quiénes eran los "Rough Riders"?* [Who were the "Rough Riders"?]

The terms "yellow journalism" and "Rough Riders" are not easily translatable to Spanish, and, in fact, the book the students are using gives the terms in English along with an explanation in Spanish.

Mr. M. also uses two other code-switching strategies, called *intra-sentential* and *inter-sentential switches*. *Intra-sentential* means that he speaks one language and then starts speaking another within the context of a sentence. Here is an example from Mr. M.'s talk on states' rights:

Mr. M.: *Una de las cosas que estamos viendo más y más* are gambling casinos on the Indian reservations. [One of the things that we are seeing more and more of are. . .]

Mr. M.: Do you think it's right *que el gobierno federal pueda controlar los* gambling casinos? [Do you think it is right that the federal government can control the gambling casinos?]

Notice that in the second example, Mr. M. made two switches, one at the phrase level (gambling casinos) and one at the clause level; yet both were within the confines of the sentence.

Mr. M. also spoke one language or the other for long stretches of time before he switched from one language to the other. This is called *inter-sentential code-switching* because the alternation comes between two chunks of meaning, which come out as a series of connected sentences. Because the students in this class were much more proficient in Spanish than English, Mr. M. rarely switched inter-sententially from Spanish to English. Moreover, among the students in this class, we observed very little code-switching, other than an occasional insertion of an English word into an exchange. And, more than likely, a student producing the word in English would use Spanish language sounds. This is because the students had not yet been socialized into code-switching as a means of communication. At this point in their developing bilingualism, most of their daily interactions were still in Spanish and with other Spanish speakers.

As the lesson moved along to a discussion of Cuba and yellow journalism, students began asking a number of questions about Cuba today, and why the United States has no diplomatic relations with the island. One of the first steps Mr. M. took to enter the discussion was to have the class establish where Cuba is on a map. Going to front of the room, Mr. M. pulls down the large map of the western hemisphere and asks a student if she can come up to map and locate it for the class. She points to the right vicinity, but can't distinguish Cuba from Puerto Rico. Another student eagerly comes up and locates the island correctly.

"*¿Por qué se metieron los Estados Unidos en Cuba, maestro?*" [Why did the United States intervene in Cuba?] asks a student from the back of the class. "*Hay que pensarlo un poquito,*" replies Mr. M. "*¿Qué clase de negocios había en Cuba en ese tiempo? ¿Alguién tiene idea?*" [Let's think about it a bit. . . . What kind of businesses were there in Cuba in those days?] After a lot of guesses, Mr. M. throws out the idea of gambling casinos and prostitution, which really grabs the students' attention. The discussion continues with a fairly long exchange between the students and Mr. M. about why the United States had an interest in preserving the U. S.-owned businesses in Cuba at the expense of the Cuban people and the nation's economy.

A historian, Mr. M. enjoys telling lots of stories from his own experiences that relate to key points in the lesson. For example, during the discussion about gambling casinos in Cuba, Mr. M. sidetracked into a story about his childhood on the Apache reservation. He compared the United States wanting to control its interests in gambling to having to learn English as a child. He told the class that he didn't have a choice about having school in Spanish or Apache; it was English only. This story then quickly moved on to the English-only movement to focus on the question of whether there should be only one language in the United States. This question brings forth a good deal of discussion from students. Because this is an issue that matters to them, he was happy to continue the discussion because it provided students an opportunity to strengthen their ability to use persuasive language. During the discussion, one of the students declares that language is one thing that no one can take away. Mr. M. cautions the student and the class in general that language is power, and poses the following question: "*¿Cuál idioma tiene más poder? ¿Inglés o español?*" [Which language is more powerful? Spanish or English?] Mr. M. uses these kinds of question-and-answer exchanges to help students socially construct ideas that are important to them. While all the students agree that English is the language of power, several also point out that developing strong abilities in Spanish, their native language, holds the key to becoming proficient in English.

On another occasion during the class discussion, Mr. M. asks students to relate the issue of states' rights to immigration. He wants them to consider what role they feel the federal government should have in protecting immigrants' rights to education. Mr. M. points out that in California, the voters decided, via an election, that schools are not responsible for educating school-age immigrant children. He frames the discussion so that students have to discuss the issue in terms of federal versus states' rights. This discussion also prepares students for the culminating activity.

For the final twenty minutes of the class, Mr. M. invites the students to create a political cartoon similar to ones presented in their books. Mr. M. asks students to design a cartoon that has one or more of the characters saying something with a double meaning, and with a statement about a politically charged social issue. This is an assignment that the students thoroughly enjoy. Most students choose issues around immigration and language rights.

Discussion:

A major goal in Mr. M.'s class is to help students understand that people make their own history by retelling the past (**Principle 2: learning socially constructed**). Students engage in a host of discussions and activities that support this goal. While he orchestrates many of the discussions with students in a whole class setting, he also invites students to participate through exchanges of meaning that happen in small group work. In the lessons we visited, the students examined topics that mattered to them, as the interaction among Jaime, Rosa, and Consuelo and the themes students selected for their political cartoons demonstrated (**Principle 3: centrality of meaningful content**).

Mr. M. also tries hard to model and interact with students with the kinds of discourse that historians use to relate and analyze significant events that shape history (**Principles 1 and 2: language socially shared, learning socially constructed**). His concern at this point in the year is not so much to have students write history, but rather to read and talk about it, to see how current events are tied to past events. Mr. M. knows that many of the students in his class carry lots of knowledge in their heads. Their literacy is based primarily on oral language, with some support from written language. Accordingly, Mr. M. uses written texts sparingly and always in the service of building a shared understanding of key ideas in the lesson (**Principle 4: language and literacy intertwined**). For example, having the students do a close reading of the text and then discussing it in small groups not only helped students make sense of academic language, it pushed them to respond to ideas orally using the discourse of history (**Principle 1: language socially shared**).

In this class, history comes alive because the students and Mr. M. bring in their own experiences. Moreover, Mr. M. knows the language and culture of his students, which means that he can interact with them in ways that are culturally and historically relevant (**Principles 1 and 2: language socially shared, learning socially constructed**). The stories that Mr. M. shares with the students involve topics that not only relate to the issues at hand, but to the students' lives as well (**Principle 3: centrality of meaningful content**).

High School Sheltered Science Class

This vignette takes place in a classroom with a teacher who has been recognized and has received awards nationally and locally as an outstanding science teacher. This particular class is part of a group of sheltered content classes offered to tenth and eleventh grade students who have reached at least intermediate levels of English oral and written proficiency. These students are eligible to enroll in this particular class, a sheltered language arts class, a sheltered algebra class, and a sheltered social studies class. This set of classes is part of a loosely organized bilingual program at this particular urban high school of 2,500 students. Approximately 800 students are adding English as their second language, and nearly all of these are native Spanish speakers. There are some forty students who are speakers of languages other than Spanish or English. These students study ESL and then take as many sheltered content classes as possible before moving into regular content area classes.

The teacher of this class, Mr. Sinclair, has been a science teacher for eighteen years. In recent years, he was selected to attend special science teaching workshops at Harvard University and Dartmouth College. An avowed constructivist, he believes strongly that students learn by figuring out solutions to problems that he presents to them and they figure out through scaffolded interaction and an abundance of good guessing (see Merino & Faltis, 1993, pp. 183–184). Mr. S. has taken several classes in bilingual education as part of his coursework toward a doctorate in science education. He is very interested in working with students who are becoming bilingual, and tries to teach at least one sheltered science class each academic year. He also teaches honors biology and general biology. He understands some Spanish, and knows several words and phrases. He encourages students to use Spanish during group work, but wants them to use English when talking to the whole class or to him within a whole-class setting. The classroom is adorned with posters, science equipment, three aquariums, and models of human bones and animals. The class described below is part of an ongoing biological investigation of plants, with energy and seeds the topic of focus.

In the lesson we visit a class of some twelve students are trying to figure out why one plant grew and another one didn't. Both plants had been placed in a dark cupboard for a week; they both received water and had identical containers and dirt, but neither received any light. The question Mr. S. poses to the students is "What enabled one plant to grow?" On the whiteboard, he has written out the word *hypothesis,* and asks the students to propose a hypothesis or "good guess" about what might be contributing to the growth. Knowing that the word *hypothesis* might be difficult for students, he tries to give lots of examples using more familiar language and situations, and has the students think about "good guessing."

Armando, a boy in the front of the class, raises his hand to give his guess: "I think is because the dirt is better in one." Marisol disagrees, and says, "I think it is in the plant. Maybe the plant don't need light." Mr. S. writes out both hypotheses on the board, without correcting the students' nonconventional English, and reminds the class that the hypotheses are guesses that can be confirmed or rejected.

Next, Mr. S. tells the class that he has an ancient Yaquí Indian legend that he is going to read to them, but that he is going to leave out the ending. He wants them to guess what has happened. He tells them to listen for words they don't understand, and that he has anticipated places in the story where the wording may be difficult. But, first, he asks the students what the difference is between a legend and a story. A girl starts to answer, but Rudolfo butts in, saying "an old story." Mr. S. assents, repeating, "An old, old story, right. And what do legends do, what are they usually for?" Rudolfo continues, saying, "to tell us about something, maybe why something happens."

Mr. S. seems certain that students understand the meaning of legend, and moves on. Holding up a watermelon, he asks, "Does anyone know what kind of fruit that is?" "Watermelon," says Carolina, the girl Rudolfo cut off a few minutes earlier. This time, Mr. S. makes sure to acknowledge her, doing so by moving closer to her and says, "It's a watermelon, yeah, and what do you see in the watermelon?" All of the students answer, "Seeds!" "Yeah, that's right," says Mr.S., "and now we are ready for the legend. Listen and see if you can guess what will happen."

The legend is about horses in a pasture, and a person who puts a patch of mud from the field on the back of a horse that has developed a sore, over the winter months, from rubbing against the saddle. As springtime arrives, something starts to appear on the back of the horse. The sore has healed, but the horse looks peculiarly different. Throughout the legend, Mr. S. stops and asks students if they understand certain words, for example, *pasture* and *saddle.* Moreover, he uses his hands and facial gestures as well as simple artwork on the whiteboard to enhance understanding. Near the end of the story, Mr. S. stops reading and asks the students to write out how they think the story ends, adding that because it is a legend, they can let their imaginations run wild. "You can finish the story the way *you* think it ends," he invites them.

While the students are busy writing in English and talking in Spanish about the legend, Mr. S. prepares each table for an experiment. On each table he places a bowl with several one-sided razor blades, a bag full of bean seeds, several paper towels, and two bottles of a red liquid. Next, he wanders from table to table looking at what the students are writing and helping them with unfamiliar words, such as *underbrush.* He also utters high praises for clever endings, and because students showed understanding.

Almost all of the students guess that some kind of plant started growing out of the horse's back. Mr. S. uses this opportunity to bring up a key question: "Where did seeds on the horse's back get their energy to grow?" After several seconds of thought-time, Mr. S. continues with a set of leading questions: "Remember yesterday we were looking at some plants and these plants had grown? Where were they?" He looks directly at Ramona, who answers, "In the dark, Mr. S." Mr. S. acknowledges her answer with a smile and a nod, and adds:

> *And one of them had grown more than the other. They were both the same age, planted at the same time, grown in the dark, and we compared them with the ones over there (points to the back of the room) grown in the light and we saw that these were taller, and where does the energy come from usually, where do plants get their energy?*

"Light," blurts out Marisol. "From the light, yes Marisol, but these were grown in the dark. Where did the energy come from?" replies Mr. S., repeating the question. "If we looked at the soil and said that the energy was coming from the soil, then what would you expect, would these both be the same?" Several students say, "No."

"Wait a minute," says Mr. S., holding his hands in the air. "Same soil, same bean? Wouldn't they be the same? We are going to do an experiment to find out where that energy comes from and that allows that [pointing to plant] to grow. Let's look at the introduction [referring to a sheet of paper with instructions for the experiment]."

Mr. S. goes on to explain the procedure. At each table, the students have several seeds that have been in water to soften them up. They also have test tubes that they will be using the next day to grow the seeds in. However, before the students grow their seeds, they will be operating on them. Mr. S. tells students they can cut the seeds anyway they like, at this point in the lesson. But, before allowing any of the students to start the experiment, Mr. S. asks the class to draw pictures of each of the steps in the procedure so that he can tell that they have understood the directions and can explain them back to him.

Basically, the procedure calls for students to cut open a seed using a razor blade, examine it on a paper towel, and then stain the seed with iodine. Mr. S. quizzes the class about why they are using iodine. "What does iodine tell you?" he asks. Carlos raises his hand, and, on being selected, says, "Iodine tests for starch or something like that." "Yes, it does test for starch. And what do you see on the seeds when you put iodine on them?" "It turns the starch yellow," answers Rudolfo. "Not exactly. It's yellow now, but if there is starch in the bean, what color will it turn? Ramona?"

Ramona looks at her seeds and says, "Black?" "Black, yeah, very dark. Almost a dark brown or a black. It is yellow now, but you want to see if it turns dark," replies Mr. S. "But, the question now is—Did the whole seed turn dark or just certain parts of the seed?" At this point in the lesson, Mr. S. is trying to get students to pay attention to what happens to parts of the seed and to different types of seeds. Working with several students, he elicits the idea that when part of a seed becomes very dark after placing iodine on it, that means that part of the seed does not have starch.

Going up to the whiteboard, Mr. S. writes out that part of the seed has starch, and says to the entire class, "OK, so part of the seed has starch. What about the rest of it? Did you notice the part that is still white?" "Yeah," reply several students. Mr. S. then invites the students to consider the reason: "Okay, everybody: What does that mean?" Marisol answers somewhat hesitatingly, "No starch?" "Exactly," acknowledges Mr. S.

Pleased that the students seem to be understanding, Mr. S. asks students what they would like to call the two parts of their seeds, the part with starch and the part without starch. Marisol suggests "starchy part." Rudolfo adds, "Call the other, the not-starchy part." Mr. S. writes both names on the board, and tells the class that they can change the names later, to give them more scientific names if they'd like.

Mr. S. now focused the class's attention on the not-starchy part of the seed, asking, "Have you noticed anything else about it? What does it look like?" He walks around the room with a not-starchy seed part in the palm of his hand showing each of the tables of students, and asking questions along the way. At this point, he is trying to get the students to guess the function of the not-starchy part that he holds up for all of the students to see.

Next, Mr. S. poses the question, "What does this not-starchy part look like?" One student calls out that it looks like a "tail," but Mr. S. ignores that answer. Marisol raises her hand, and Mr. S. calls on her, "It could be a baby plant," she surmises. Mr. S. is visibly pleased and continues the exchange with Marisol: "Ahh. Now what do you call the baby when the baby is inside at the very early part, do you know the word?" After trying several strategies to elicit the word, Mr. S. finally has to tell them that the concept is an "embryo." A chorus of students calls out "Oh" in unison to indicate "yeah we've heard that word before." "So, then, what do you think, what is the function of the embryo?" asks Mr. S. quickly to tie in a key idea. Carlos, who hasn't talked in a while, answers timidly: "To grow."

Mr. S. immediately goes to the whiteboard to add the hypothesis that the embryo in the seed will grow. Still at the whiteboard, he asks if there is anyone in the class who still wants to keep the hypotheses that there is something in the dirt or that maybe it has to do with the light." After a few seconds of silence, the entire class says, "No, Mr. Sinclair." "Okay, then, class, we have a new hypothesis that says the embryo will grow. What about the starchy part, what does it do?" Mr. S. points to the dark part of the bean to make sure that all students understand the question.

Rudolfo suggests that "it turns into the root." "Interesting idea," says Mr. S. "Are you saying that if the embryo is going to be the top part, the starchy part is going to be the bottom part?" "Yeah," replies Rudolfo. "What do you think, Yolanda?" "The starchy part could be like energy or something." "That's another good hypothesis, Yolanda. Did you all hear that. Let's put that on the board as another hypothesis," says Mr. S. as he walks slowly to the whiteboard. Yolanda is visibly pleased.

The interaction continues in this manner to the end of the class. Mr. S. asks the class again what the main question is that they are trying to answer. Ramona responds, "Where does the energy come from to grow the plant?" In the final moments of the class, Mr. S. talks with students about ways to experiment using the materials and tools before them in order to test the hypotheses and answer the big question. After several exchanges, Marisol suggests that the class try cutting part of the starch part away from one seed, and compare how it grows with another seed that has all of the starchy part intact. "Fantastic suggestion," says Mr. S., "let's try that one out tomorrow."

Discussion:

This is a class in which students are actively involved in constructing the meaning of big ideas in biology and life science. The teacher, Mr. Sinclair, worked to engage students in exchanges about complex ideas in both whole-class and small group settings. During small group work, he encouraged students to talk about the task or problem in Spanish (**Principle 5: importance of L$_1$ proficiency/literacy**), as a way to build understanding of the content and procedures. During whole-class teaching, Mr. S. used scaffolds to assist students' participation in extended discourse. A scaffold is language support that enables students to talk about ideas they would not be able to talk about on their own (Cazden, 1988). For example, when a student gave a one-word response, or offered a simple explanation, Mr. S. would try to pull language out of him or her by rephrasing the question or by adding additional information. On other occasions, Mr. S. even tried using his rudimentary Spanish to get an idea across. Although Mr. S. used some kind of scaffold almost every-time he talked with students, he relied on them less and less over time. Once he felt that a student could handle the discourse on her own, he pulled back and encouraged the student to continue the exchange without his assistance (**Principle 1 and 2: language socially shared, learning socially constructed**).

As in all content areas, students have myriad new vocabulary words and ideas to learn. However, Mr. S. was not overly concerned that students use the technical or formal vocabulary as they formed their ideas about the content. For instance, he encouraged students initially to use *starchy* and *not-starchy* parts, rather than the technical terms. This decision ensured understanding, and more importantly, sustained interaction.

Another noteworthy characteristic of Mr. S.'s way of interacting with students was that he "thinks language" (Enright & McCloskey, 1988) when he exchanged ideas with students. "Thinking language" means that Mr. S. was constantly paying attention to what he feels students need in order to make sense of and participate in the various parts of a lesson. Accordingly, not only did Mr. S. try to anticipate vocabulary that might be difficult for English learners, he also incorporated extralinguistic support to invite and sustain interaction. Some of the ways that he did this were by (1) using graphic organizers for big ideas (e.g., graphs, outlines, pictures); (2) having students make simple drawings of procedures to follow; (3) pointing to specific features as he or students were discussing them; (4) using hand and facial movements; and (5) rephrasing and repeating students' oral and written contributions. Mr. S. also clearly marked the boundaries of the lesson for the students so they could focus their attention on the discourse rather than on where they were in the lesson. Thinking language was part of a larger goal Mr. S. had for the class: He wanted students to feel comfortable using academic talk; namely, the discourse of science. This particular discourse is heavily loaded with hypothetical "if–then" and "what if" statements and logical connectors, *because* and *the reason is.*" As Lemke (1990) has pointed out, learning science is really about learning to talk science in ways that members of the science community would recognize as legitimate (**Principle 2: learning socially constructed**). Learning to talk science enables students to join the science community club.

High School Sheltered Language Arts Class

This final vignette presents a class for ninth and tenth grade students who are nearly ready for all-English classes. There are no native English speakers in the class, which has a total of twenty-four students. Nineteen of the students are Spanish–English bilinguals. Of the remaining students, three are from Taiwan, one is from Central Africa, and one is from Brazil. The five non-Spanish-speaking students are highly literate in their first language(s). All of the Spanish–English bilinguals are of Mexican descent. Six were born in the United States; the rest, in Mexico. The Spanish–English bilinguals have a wide range of literacy abilities in their first language, Spanish. However, all can read and write fairly well in English. There are no native, monolingual

English speakers in the class. The sheltered language arts class is part of the bilingual program at the same high school where Mr. Sinclair teaches biology.

The teacher, Ms. Cunningham–Kelly, volunteered to teach the class. She had had a number of English learners in some of her prior classes, and she enjoyed their enthusiasm for learning. She has no special academic preparation in sheltered content teaching. She considers herself to be a holistic teacher with the conviction that students learn language and literacy through talk and by constantly writing for legitimate purposes.

The class has recently completed a reading of *Sarah, Plain and Tall* (MacLachlan, 1985). This is a story about a family of two children and their father, a widower, who lives on the prairie in the heartland of the United States. After several years of being alone, the father places an ad in the newspaper for a wife to come and live with him and his children. Mr. Witting, the father, receives a reply in the form of a letter from Miss Sarah Wheaton, who lives by the sea in Maine, but "feel[s] a move is necessary" at this point in her life (MacLachlan, 1985, p. 9). Sarah goes to the prairie to meet and stay with the family, but after a short time begins to yearns for the sea and its surroundings. The children, Caleb and Anna, sense this. As time passes, however, Sarah, who is plain and tall, adapts to the new environment, and learns that she can live happily with her memories of Maine and the sea. Ms. C–K. chose this particular story, not only because it is wonderfully written, but also because its message is one that the students in her class all can relate to: yearning for home when you move to a totally new environment, and then learning how to adapt to the new environment.

After reading and responding to the story, Ms. C–K. asks the students to write one or more descriptions of the characters in the story, including the animals. To assist with the description, the students first worked in groups to generate words and phrases that are associated with the various characters. For example, for Caleb, the young boy in the story, students suggested the following: "talks a lot, asks lots of questions, likes to sing, loud and pesky." For Seal, the cat, students listed: "catches mice, lives in the barn, brown like a seal, likes to stretch." When the students have completed their descriptions, Ms. C–K. asks them to volunteer to read what they wrote to the entire class, who then gets to guess the identity of the character. Everyone in the class participates eagerly in this activity. Ms. C–K. openly praises the students for their creativity in describing the characters accurately, but also in ways that make guessing who the characters are interesting. Here is what Li Fong wrote:

> *He is sly. He works on the prairie. His friend is Old Bess. He helps Papa in the field. Papa loves him. Sarah goes to town with him.*

Several students raise their hands immediately. "Is it Matthew, the neighbor?" guesses Carlos. "I know. I know. Is it Jack, the horse?" says Carolina.

The description is indeed of Jack, the horse that Sarah learns to ride and that Papa uses to plow the fields.

Another student, Jesús, reads what he has written:

> *I have long brades. I help my brother and my father. Sarah write the first letter to me. Sarah give me a stone of Maine.*

Many hands go up when Jesús, with a big smile on his face, finishes reading. Several students can be heard saying "¡Qué facil!" [How easy!] Ms. C–K. calls on Marisol, who, after several seconds of suspense, reveals her answer: "It's Anna. I am sure." The class agrees, and then another student takes a stab at trying to stump her classmates.

After all of the students have had an opportunity to read their descriptions, Ms. C–K. refocuses the lesson to move on to the next phase, a writing activity in which students "write off" some aspect of the story they particularly enjoyed. The audience for the writing pieces are, as in the character descriptions, classmates and the teacher as a trusted adult. The "write off" activity is one of a three-part sequence in which students "write on" the story, giving a summary of what they think the story is about. They also have an opportunity to "write back," meaning they can write about parts of the story they would like to know more about. They share these with classmates, who then try to answer the queries, based on their understanding of the story or their personal experiences.

Ms. C–K. spends several minutes at her desk, one-on-one with each student to work on revising and sense of audience. In this manner, she reads each student's draft several times before it is ready to be made available for the entire class. In these writing conferences, Ms. C–K. asks students for clarification of ideas and talks with them about how to expand ideas that are vague. However, she also talks with students about editing for spelling and conventional grammar usage. She does so in a nonthreatening way, by simply reminding students to circle words they think might be misspelled, and by underlining sentences that are giving them trouble or need additional work. Students make their own dictionaries of words they learn in stories and that they use in their writing.

Discussion:

The teacher in this class believes that students should be at the center of learning. In other words, Ms. C–K. sees her role as a sheltered language arts teacher as a facilitator to help students jointly construct their understanding of literature and writing by reading, talking, and writing about topics that matter to them (**Principles 2 and 3: learning socially constructed, centrality of meaningful content**). This is a student-centered classroom in the sense that Ms. C–K. organizes the class so that students do much of the teaching among themselves, and are responsible for generating ideas about the literature they read and write about (**Principle 3: centrality of meaningful content**). This was evident in both the *Sarah, Plain and Tall* and the "write off" activities. Ms. C–K. planned and implemented the lesson, but the students came up with the ideas on their own. The story invited students to think, talk, and write about their experiences living in a new land (**Principle 4: language and literacy intertwined**).

There were a number of times during the class when Ms. C–K. asked the students not to use Spanish, but rather to try to explain their ideas in English. However, she did not discourage students from using Spanish during small group work, nor did she admonish them for calling out in Spanish when classmates presented their ideas (**Principle 5: importance of L₁ proficiency/literacy**). Ms. C–K. believes that students need to try to express their thoughts in English when they are sharing with the whole class. Swain (1985) argues that "pushing" students in this way helps them develop syntactically. That is, it encourages them to use syntax (how words are ordered in a sentence) and extended discourse to express and explain ideas in detail, rather than relying on phrases and isolated words (**Principle 2: learning socially constructed**).

Ms. C–K. also encourages students to expand their written language, explaining to students that the reader needs as much information as possible to follow the ideas. She does this during writer's conferences, when she can interact with students personally, and the two of them can talk about how to improve the writing by keeping the audience in mind (**Principle 1: language socially shared**). For example, when a student wrote, "Sarah was sad. She wanted the sea by her. I think she was equal to me. I am missing my friends in Mexico." Ms. C–K. asked the student to clarify what she meant by "She wanted the sea by her" and "She was equal to me." Ms. C–K. also talked with the student about using different tenses (past and present) to express ideas, asking her to think about why it might be better to say "I miss my friends in Mexico" and then to follow this statement with a reason. This highly personal interaction supports the creation and sharing of meaning between the writer and the reader, and invites the student to see herself as an author (**Principle 4: language and literacy intertwined**).

Concluding Remarks

This chapter shares information about secondary bilingual education in various contexts. The scenes represent some of the middle and high school classrooms we have observed and learned from. After reading this chapter, we hope you notice that much more is known about elementary bilingual school communities than secondary ones. In fact, you would be hard-pressed to find any studies of secondary bilingual education conducted before 1990, and there continues to be a shortage of studies in the various ways that secondary students from various language groups are schooled bilingually. For us, this is what makes the vignettes in this chapter so important—they give a glimpse of what happens in some secondary bilingual classrooms, and in this way, help us understand bilingual school communities.

We hope that you saw that, regardless of the school organization, grade level, content, or the language/ethnicity of the students, teachers and students engaged some or all of the principles for language and learning. In other words, the principles are not grade or level specific. We believe that if you understand about language and learning, you can use these principles as your foundation for teaching literacy and content at any level of schooling. That doesn't mean that there aren't content-specific or culturally relevant ways of teaching in middle and high school. Lemke (1990) has shown that the discourse of science differs from that of other content areas, such as history and mathematics. Moreover, there may be adjustments teachers can make to be more culturally relevant to their students, especially in ethnically homogeneous classrooms (Ladson–Billings, 1995). But having a philosophical stance toward language and learning that respects diversity in language and culture and advocates for students must be at the heart of these adjustments.

Teachers in secondary schools have many variables to consider. The teachers we presented in the above vignettes were doing their best to engage students in learning content that mattered to them and to society as a whole. Each one also valued biliteracy, and showed this by having students read and write to various audiences for real purposes, as well as for practice.

References

Cazden, C. (1988). *Classroom discourse: The language of teaching and learning.* Portsmouth, NH: Heinemann Educational Books.

Constantino, R., & Lavadenz, M. (1993). Newcomer schools: First impressions. *Peabody Journal of Education, 69*(1), 82–101.

Enright, D. S., & McCloskey, M. (1988). *Integrating English: Developing English language and literacy in the multilingual classroom.* Reading, MA: Addison-Wesley.

Faltis, C. (1993). From kindergarten to high school: Teaching and learning English as a second language in the U. S. In S. Silberstein (Ed.), *State of the art TESOL essays: Celebrating 25 years of the discipline,* (pp. 91–114). Alexandria, VA: TESOL.

Faltis, C., & Arias, M.B. (1993). Speakers of languages other than English in the secondary school: Accomplishments and struggles. *Peabody Journal of Education, 69*(1), 6–29.

Friedlander, M. (1991). *The newcomer program: Helping immigrant students succeed in U.S. schools.* Wheaton, MD: National Clearinghouse for Bilingual Education.

García, E. (1993). Project THEME: Collaboration for school improvement at the middle school for language minority students. In *Proceedings of the third national research symposium on limited english proficient student issues: Focus on middle and high school issues,* (pp. 323-350). Washington, DC: U. S. Department of Education, Office of Bilingual Education and Minority Language Affairs.

Krashen, S. (1993). *The power of reading.* Englewood, CO: Libraries Unlimited.

Ladson–Billings, G. (1995). Toward a theory of culturally relevant teaching. *American Education Research Journal, 32*(3), 465–492.

Lemke, J. (1990). *Talking science: Language, learning, and values.* New York: Ablex.

Lucas, T. (1993). Secondary schooling for students becoming bilingual: Issues and practices. In M. B. Arias and U. Casanova (Eds.), *Bilingual education: Politics, research and practice,* (pp. 113–143). Chicago: National Society for the Study of Education.

MacLachlan, P. (1985). *Sarah, plain and tall.* New York: Harper & Row.

Merino, B., & Faltis, C. (1993). Language and culture in the preparation of bilingual teachers. In M. B. Arias and U. Casanova (Eds.), *Bilingual education: Politics, research and practice,* (pp. 171–198). Chicago: National Society for the Study of Education.

Minicucci, C. (1996). *Learning science and English: How school reform advances scientific learning for limited English proficient middle school students. Educational Practice Report: 17.* Santa Cruz, CA: National Center for Research on Cultural Diversity and Second Language Learning.

Minicucci, C., & Olsen, L. (1992). Programs for secondary limited English proficient students: A California study. *Occasional Papers in Bilingual Education, No. 5.* Washington, DC: National Clearinghouse for Bilingual Education.

Padilla, E. (Ed.). (1992). *Sonnets to human beings and other selected works by Carmen Tafolla.* Santa Monica, CA: Lalo Press.

Reyes, M. de la Luz (1991). A process approach to literacy instruction for Spanish-speaking students: In search of the best fit. In E. Hiebert (Ed.), *Literacy for a diverse society: Perspectives, practices, and policies,* (pp. 157–173). NY: Teachers College Press.

Swain, M. (1985). Communicative competence: Some roles of comprehensible input and comprehensible outs in its development. In S. Gass and C. Madden (Eds.), *Input in second language acquisition,* (pp. 235–253). Rowley, MA: Newbury House.

The International High School at La Guardia Community College (1991, March). *Forum, 14*(3), 6.

Valdés–Fallis, G. (1976). Social interaction and code-switching patterns. A case study of Spanish/English alternation. In G. Keller, R. Teschner, and S. Viera (Eds.), *Bilingualism in the bicentennial and beyond.* New York: Bilingual Press.

7

Caring about Bilingual
Education

This is the final chapter of the book, but certainly not the final word on bilingual education in elementary and secondary schools. There will continue to be debates, discussions, and silence about bilingual education at all levels of schooling. This is the time when you can have an influence on what counts as bilingual education. You can influence others about the social and educational value of providing classroom environments that make sense for children and adolescents who are becoming bilingual. You can invite them into discourse in ways that benefit them as well as their teachers, their native English-speaking peers, and society in general.

Caring as Empathy

Being an influence, however, means not only that you understand about bilingual education, but also that you care about what happens within bilingual, ESL, and sheltered content classrooms. For many of us, caring means *empathizing with the needs of others* (Noddings, 1984). Having empathy for others involves projecting ourselves into a situation in order to feel the needs of others, and to base our actions on our projected feelings. This is akin to the familiar saying about "walking a mile in some else's shoes." With respect to bilingual education, this entails caring for the children and adolescents who are becoming bilingual because we have empathy for them. We feel how difficult it must be to make sense of and participate in school for children and adolescents who can't understand or interact with the teacher, the text, and/or classmates because they don't share the language of the classroom.

Moreover, we can feel empathy for the teachers, who even though they may have "teachable hearts" (McLaren, 1994), may experience helplessness because of the language and cultural barriers they face. We may also feel a more general empathy for the children and adolescents because they are being denied an education that other children receive simply because they speak English.

Caring about bilingual education from this perspective may also mean that you feel empathy for non-English-speaking children and adolescents because many of them are from economically poor families who have suffered untold hardships in their home countries. The very reason you decide to become a bilingual, ESL, or sheltered content teacher may be based on the empathy you feel. You act in order to fulfill your need to care for the children and adolescents with whom you empathize. Accordingly, teaching children and adolescents who you perceive to be in need of compassion and caring fulfills a personal desire to care for them.

These are admirable reasons for caring about bilingual education. We can also make a case for caring about bilingual education based on what research tells us. For example, the research evidence we discussed in Chapter 2 points strongly to the conclusion that children and adolescents who enter school as non-English speakers adjust socially and do well academically when they can understand and participate in classroom activities. In addition, the research shows that the more quality time students study and learn in their native language, the better they do later on socially and academically in classes taught entirely in English. Related to this finding is that, in quality bilingual programs, in which students continue to study in their native language even though they are proficient in English, the teachers are more knowledgeable and better prepared than teachers in early exit bilingual programs (Cazden, 1992). Finally, if we believe in the principles of language and learning presented in Chapter 4, we want children and adolescents to be in bilingual, biliterate, ESL, and sheltered content classes that adhere to these principles. Accordingly, we care because, unless students are receiving a quality education, they are likely not to acquire the discourses that we hold in esteem.

Caring as Receiving

While these reasons may convince you to become devoted to bilingual education and the children and adolescents who are becoming bilingual, there is another perspective to consider: caring as receiving. We can make a commitment to care about bilingual education by feeling *with* the children and adolescents, by receiving and sharing what they are feeling (Nodding, 1984). This perspective on caring does not first seek out the source of need and feel for it, but rather brings the source of need inward to feel with it, to work with it, and to do whatever possible to address it concretely. Instead of projecting onto others, we receive others into ourselves. When we project onto others, the question that guides us is: What does it feel like to have or not have quality bilingual education? In the caring-as-receiving perspective, the question becomes: How can I feel with these children and adolescents? The first question goes immediately to an abstraction of a projected need, relying on logic and inference of what it might be like in other people's lives. The second question invites the other into the heart, where feeling the need can be addressed by examining the facts, experiences, and personal histories of the children and adolescents who come into our lives (Noddings, 1984). From the latter perspective, a "teachable heart" becomes a dwelling place for the needs of others; from the former, it projects onto others in order to empathize with their needs. Caring-as-receiving is highly contextual, based on the feelings we bring to ourselves about others whom we perceive as in need of caring. In this manner, children and adolescents in bilingual programs become part of us, and we a part of them.

Receiving children and adolescents in bilingual programs as an act of caring does not mean that we define for them what their experiences in bilingual education should be. But it does require us to be acutely sensitive to the ideals that we hold, and to promote these ideals similar to the ways that parents do with their own children. In this book, we have laid out what for us represent ideals of bilingual education. We have told many stories of teachers who in a variety of ways promote these ideals in their classrooms. While we are making no claim that these teachers viewed caring as receiving, we do believe that each one cared deeply about the children and adolescents they worked and communicated with, not by "walking in their shoes," but rather by feeling their needs and working toward an ideal that took their needs into account.

Caring as Compassion

Caring necessarily involves compassion. Like caring, compassion can be abstract or personal, and stem from different motivations. We can be compassionate for bilingual education because it fulfills a need to help others. Having compassion makes us feel good that we are helping children and adolescents who, because they are poor and from non-English-speaking backgrounds, have been socially and academically neglected in school. This helping-the-needy motivation is based on a psychological motivation for self-fulfillment (Wuthnow, 1991). It is personally gratifying to care for children and adolescents in need.

Having compassion to fulfill a personal need, however, does little to promote the social value of compassion, which promotes compassion because we need to care about one another without expecting a personal gain from it.

Caring as compassion with a social motivation links us with the children and adolescents in our schools. It links us to their future as well. Caring about bilingual education from this perspective means that we have compassion not because we receive something in return (self-fulfillment), but because we value caring in society. When we care in this way, we give something as a member of the group, and hope that the group benefits from the giving, not just any individual. Compassion in this sense is of value for the group because it acknowledges that caring connects people, linking them through compassion (Wuthnow, 1991). As in the caring-as-receiving perspective, compassion for the group is practical in its devotion to caring: It seeks to solve problems because they are there, and there is no expectation of reciprocal caring, only the hope that, in being compassionate, others will become more caring in their relations with others. In other words, compassion begets compassion.

Caring with a Critical Eye

Whatever reason we may have for caring and being compassionate about bilingual education, we also need to consider the role of having a critical eye (Edelsky, 1996; Wink, 1996). Critically caring about children and adolescents in bilingual classrooms means that we must also continue to unlearn and reject practices that unwittingly and, often, subtly diminish the influences we can have on bilingual education. We can unlearn thinking of non-English-speaking children as being deficient; we can unlearn that these children need worksheets, while other children get to read real books and write for real audiences; we can unlearn believing that these children need to learn only English because that is what other immigrants did. We can unlearn the idea that when English-speaking children learn Spanish (even just a few words), that is wonderful, but when Spanish-speaking children learn English and want to keep and develop their Spanish, many consider this a waste of time and energy, even unAmerican. To unlearn these beliefs and thoughts, we need to have a critically vigilant and caring heart.

Having a critically caring eye invites inquiry and reflection about our and others' actions in schools and society. The guiding principles that we presented in Chapter 4 require much reflection to see not only how they work, but why. But reflection and inquiry are only the first steps. You will need to be ready to resist efforts to undermine bilingual education as well as the practices that result from your caring about children and adolescents in bilingual education in the ways that we present above. We hope that the guiding principles and the stories we have told about what happens in some elementary and secondary classrooms not only help you understand bilingual education and care for it with compassion and a critical eye, but also inform the actions you take as a bilingual teacher in school and society.

As you work collaboratively to understand and care for bilingual children, adolescents, and school communities, it is important to become advocates for your own interests as well as the interests of others. The following poem, modeled after one by Martin Niemoeller (1892–1984), may help you see that understanding and caring for bilingual education really matters.

A Poem for Readers

In the United States, they first annhilated the native peoples, taking their languages and cultures,
and I didn't speak up
because I wasn't Indian.

Then they brought in slaves from Africa, taking their languages and cultures,
and I didn't speak up
because I wasn't African.

Then they restricted the use of non-English languages, calling people who used them un American
and I didn't speak up
because I wasn't a dark-skinned immigrant.

Then they forbade the use of Spanish by Mexican children, and immersed them in English-only classrooms
and I didn't speak up
because I wasn't Mexican.

Then they introduced transitional bilingual education to get children as quickly as possible into English
and I didn't speak up
because I wanted to teach.

Then they told me not to use so much of the students' language and cultural ways in class
and I didn't speak up
because I might have lost my job.

Then they told me that I had to use only English with children who come to school speaking a language other than English
and by that time
no one was left to speak up.

References

Cazden, C. (1992). *Language minority education in the United States: Implications of the Ramírez report.* Santa Cruz, CA: National Center for Research on Cultural Diversity and Second Language Teaching.

Edelsky, C. (1996). *With literacy and justice for all: Rethinking the social in language and education,* 2nd Ed. London: Taylor and Francis.

McLaren, P. (1994). Critical pedagogy: Constructing an arch of social dreaming and a doorway of hope. In L. Erwin and D. MacLennan (Eds.), *Sociology of education in Canada: Critical perspectives on theory, research & practice,* (pp. 137–160), Toronto: Copp Clark Longman.

Noddings, N. (1984). *Caring: A feminine approach to ethics and moral education.* Berkeley, CA: University of California Press.

Wink, J. (1996). *Critical pedagogy: Notes from the real world.* New York: Longman.

Wuthnow, R. (1991). *Acts of compassion: Caring for others and helping ourselves.* Princeton, NJ: Princeton University Press.

Name Index

179

Subject Index

182